IMAGES
of America

MORGANZA
PENNSYLVANIA'S REFORM SCHOOL

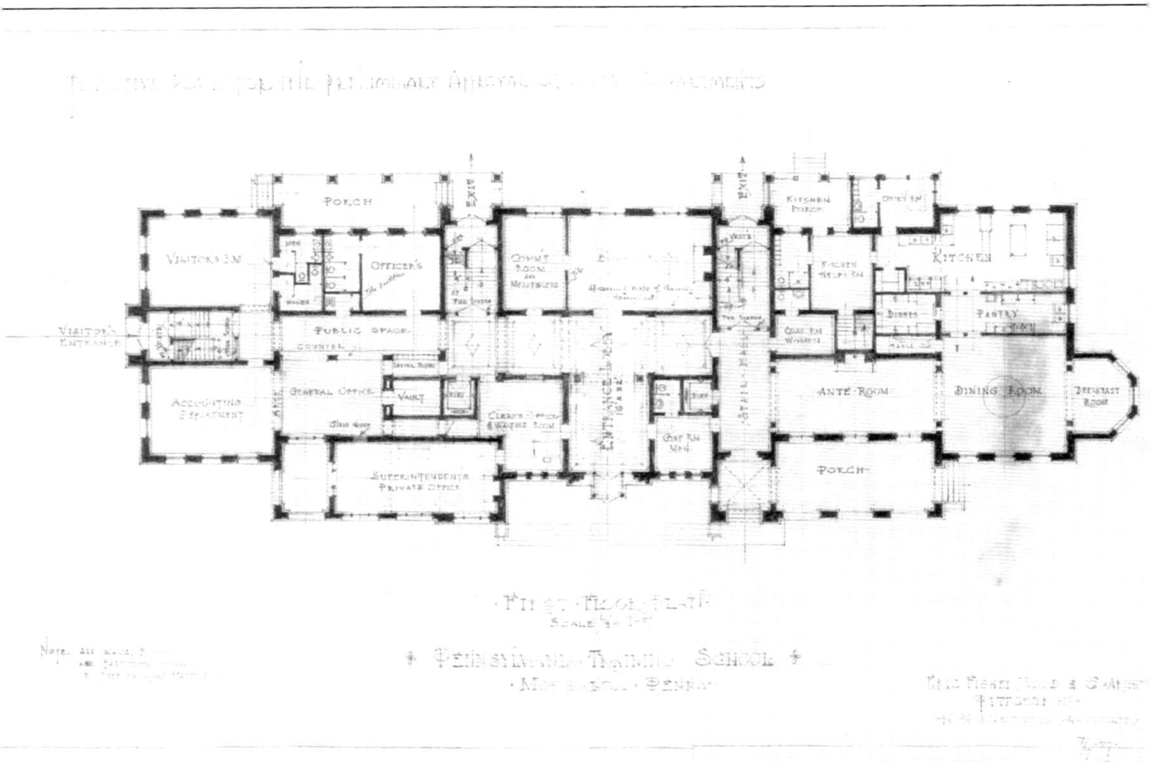

The first floor plan of the Pennsylvania Training School's administration building shows that the south (left) side held the administrative offices and the visitor's entrance. The kitchen and dining room were located on the north side. This administration building was put into operation in 1930. Prior to this, since the founding of the institute in 1854, a total of 11,625 boys and 4,580 girls had been admitted. (Courtesy of Carnegie Mellon University Architecture Archives.)

On the Cover: Diane Hickman dedicated 24 years to helping those less fortunate in their daily lives. Hickman, who served as a nurse to many residents of Western Center between 1975 and 1998, took this photograph of the grand administration building on the hill from the entryway. (Courtesy of Diane Hickman.)

IMAGES
of America

MORGANZA
PENNSYLVANIA'S REFORM SCHOOL

Christopher R. Barraclough

ARCADIA
PUBLISHING

ISBN 978-1-4671-2085-2

Published by Arcadia Publishing
Charleston, South Carolina

Printed in the United States of America

Library of Congress Control Number: 2013943136

For all general information, please contact Arcadia Publishing:
Telephone 843-853-2070
Fax 843-853-0044
E-mail sales@arcadiapublishing.com
For customer service and orders:
Toll-Free 1-888-313-2665

Visit us on the Internet at www.arcadiapublishing.com

*To those who were reformed and treated here,
and to the staff who aided them*

Contents

ACKNOWLEDGMENTS

My most express thanks to James T. Herron of the Jefferson College Historical Society for much of the material used in this book, and to Diane Hickman and Linda Kacvinski for the great knowledge and memories they shared with me.

To the photographers of the past and those who saved historical images, my thanks to James T. Herron Sr., Joseph Solobay, Force Dunlevy, Frank Mirisciotti, Martin Estep, Harry and Gary Mohler, and the photographers of the *Daily Notes*. Thanks to the archived materials of the Pennsylvania State Archives, the Washington County Historical Society, the Pennsylvania Historical and Museum Commission, the Carnegie Mellon University Architecture Archives, and the University of Delaware Library.

A special thanks to others who have helped by providing images of their own: Adam Ryan, Rebecca Brocato, Richard Nowe, Diane Hickman, David Flinchbach, Ed Cononge, and Tracy Tooch.

Unless otherwise noted, all images in this book are courtesy of the Jefferson College Historical Society.

My final thanks are to Citizens Library in Washington and the Frank Sarris Library.

Introduction

At the time of this writing, many historical state schools, hospitals, and correctional facilities continue to close and eventually get demolished. Big cities and small towns reconsider the uses of the land where these historic structures once sat. Historians across the nation struggle to document these amazing structures and the stories kept within them. In this era, the country can look back and see how inside and outside changes influenced this eventual outcome.

The Pennsylvania Reform School at Morganza was one of many of these historical institutes statewide, but it was unique in its own. Established in April 1850 by an act of the Pennsylvania Legislature as the House of Refuge, it became one of the first institutes of its type in the state of Pennsylvania. The House of Refuge opened in 1854 in what was the ninth ward of Allegheny, on the north side of Pittsburgh. In 1876, it was relocated near Canonsburg in Washington County, Pennsylvania. The Pennsylvania Reform School was purposely built in a vast country area surrounded by nature, instead of in the city of Pittsburgh, and introduced the Family System of living. The location was farmland surrounded by sloping hills. Through old photographs, the beautiful rural landscape, located approximately 20 miles south of Pittsburgh and bordering Chartiers Creek, can be seen. Besides the scenic countryside, the land was practical and functional for the Pennsylvania Reform School. The magnificent campus was filled with elegant architectural structures and beautiful landscaping.

Morganza was the name given to the land on which the institution was built. Often, parents would threaten their kids that if they misbehaved, they would be sent to Morganza. The name became the term most used to describe the institution throughout its existence, although it underwent a series of name changes. The school was closed in the 1950s and the remaining inmates were sent to other institutes for juvenile delinquents. The institution then served as a home for the mentally handicapped and emotionally disturbed. The institution maintained the campus until it was closed. It was ultimately demolished in 2012.

Architectural beauty was never the intended purpose of the buildings; they were designed to reform young individuals into becoming proper citizens in society. And, in their later lives, institutions like this were necessary to help people with mental disorders and other emotional handicaps function in society. Throughout its years of operation, concerns such as isolation, confinement, neglect, and abuse arose. Findings and laws prohibiting the use of young adolescents to work in fields and perform other taxing manual labor jobs impacted facilities like this. As conditions deteriorated, whether because of lack of funding or new technological methods, many institutes began to close.

The institution was not flexible enough to face the medical and social challenges of 20th-century reform. With an enormous campus and little to no admittance, a facility of this magnitude could no longer operate. The historical journey of the institution at Morganza came to an end in May 2012 when the final structure was demolished. By turning to books and archives and speaking with historians and others who recalled their experiences, it is now possible to discover what life was like in one of the state's first juvenile correctional institutes.

One

Build and Reform

In December 1876, the inmates at the House of Refuge were transferred to the Pennsylvania Reform School at Morganza. At the time of the move, some of the old buildings at the House of Refuge faced a sudden breakdown of their heating apparatuses and water-supply systems. The removal of the inmates to the new institution went without incident.

Upon the opening, boys were kept busy with grading of the grounds, gardening, and farming. At this time, the laying out of roads and the construction of additional farm buildings and surface drainage were all under way. In June 1876, an application of amendment was placed, putting the institution under the control of the state. The amendment provided for 16 of the 26 managers to be approved by the governor and subject to change by the state senate. Financial difficulties called for the state to take complete control. By 1879, the Pennsylvania Reform School became the first state-owned institute for delinquent children. For the next nearly 90 years, the institute was used exclusively for the care of juvenile delinquents.

The name Pennsylvania Reform School was maintained until 1912, when it was changed to the Pennsylvania Training School in order to eliminate the stigma of the former name. The Pennsylvania Training School had its share of good days, the best of which were in the period soon after the name change. The school also had its share of troubles, including one incident in 1949 when an escapee shot another boy in Pittsburgh. This was followed by a supervised visit from the state secretary of welfare, who stated that there would be a "major shake-up at Morganza" and that it was being run by "remote control." This prompted a visit from the Pennsylvania Bureau of Corrections during which school officers admitted to taking no disciplinary action in letting those who wanted to escape simply leave. At this time, there were an average of 18 escapees per month. A considerable lack of vocational study was also noticed. The school had a total of 19 top administration changes in the 19 years between 1936 and 1955.

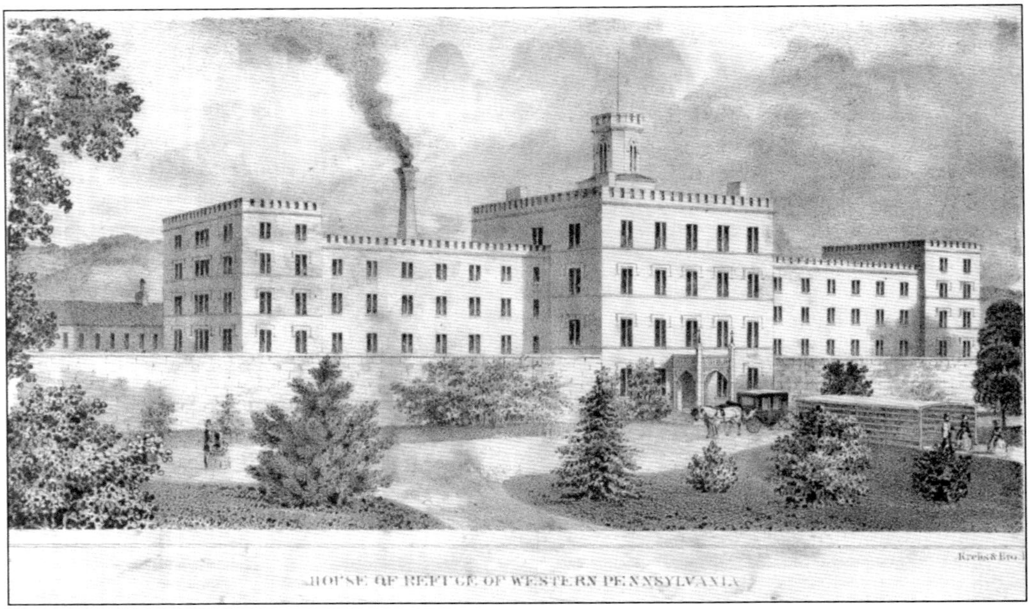

This engraving shows the House of Refuge in Western Pennsylvania in the 1850s. The security at the facility can be recognized through its prison-like walls. These high walls were used to keep the inmates from seeing life outside. The site later became the home of Western Penitentiary.

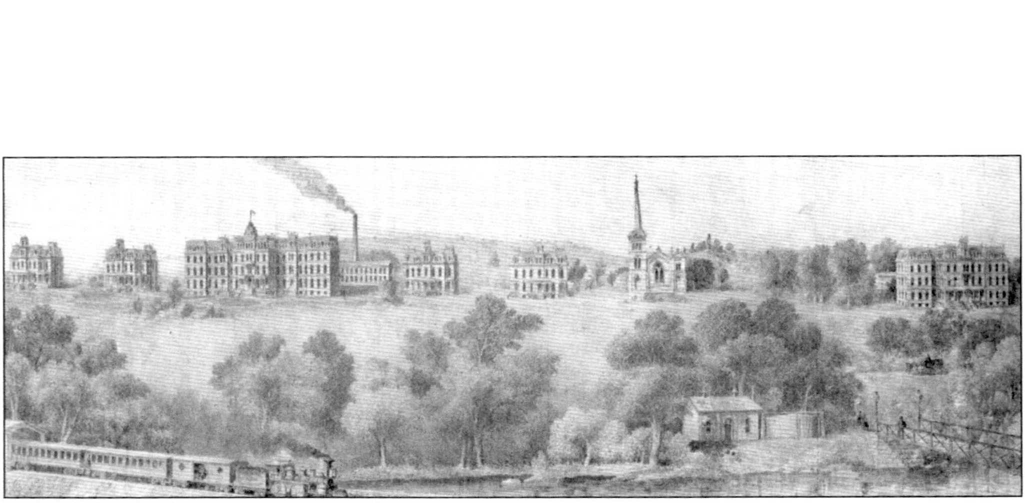

This early drawing shows the Pennsylvania Reform School, with the administration building to the left on the hill. Cottages can be seen on both sides of the administration building. The church shown was never actually built, and the girls' dormitory is on the right. At the bottom of the drawing, a train runs along the railroad line. Chartiers Creek is also shown, along with the bridge to the institution and the pump house.

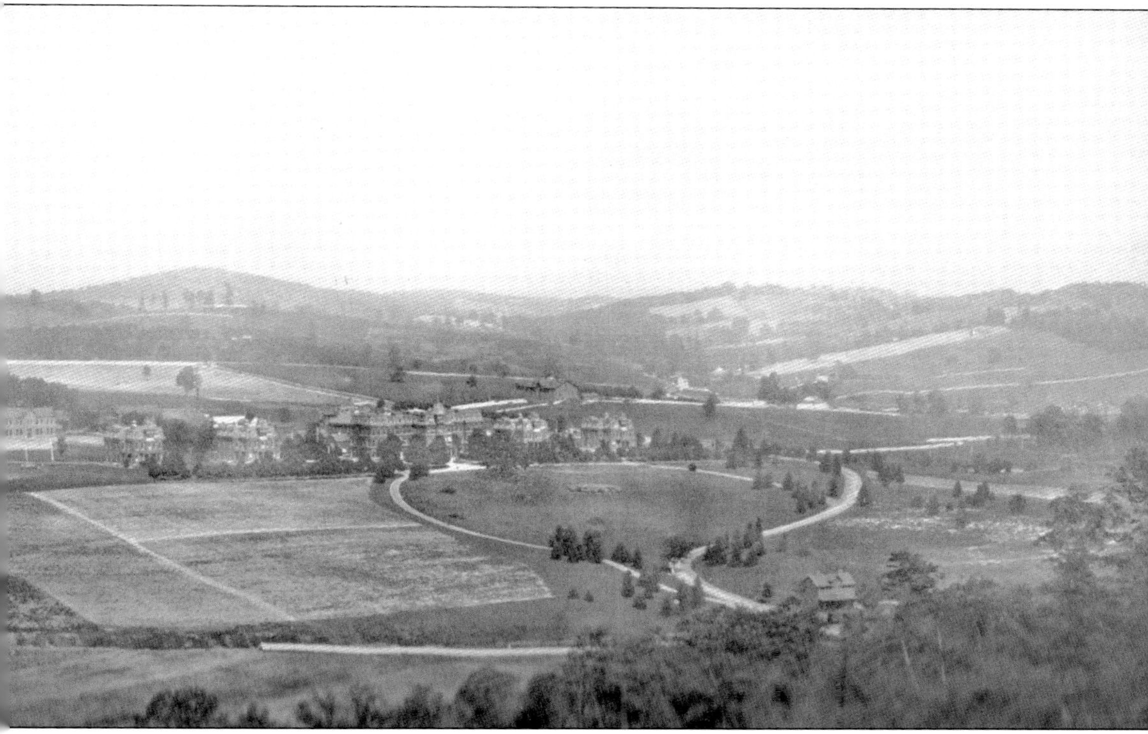

This view was taken of the Pennsylvania Reform School from an adjacent hillside around 1896. The administration building is in the center, with two cottages on each side. The two-story shop building is on the left with open fields in front of it, and a barn is visible on the hill in the back center.

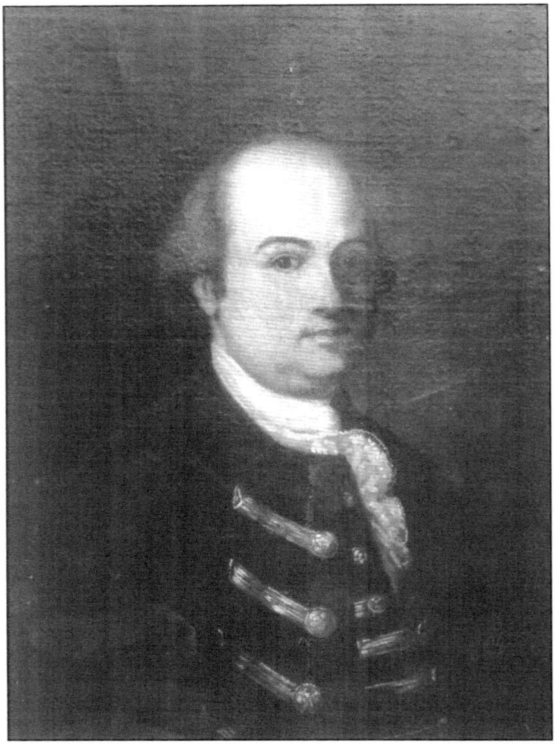

Dr. John Morgan of Philadelphia originally purchased the property in 1769 and 1771. He held ownership of the land until his death in 1789. His brother George inherited the land. George Morgan, a colonel, spent some time at Fort Pitt as a deputy commissary general but lived in New Jersey. He then moved to his property in 1796 and posted an advertisement for tenants in a Pittsburgh newspaper, identifying the property as Morganza. George Morgan lived there until he died in 1810. This portrait of George Morgan hangs in the LeMoyne house in Washington, Pennsylvania. (Courtesy of Washington County Historical Society.)

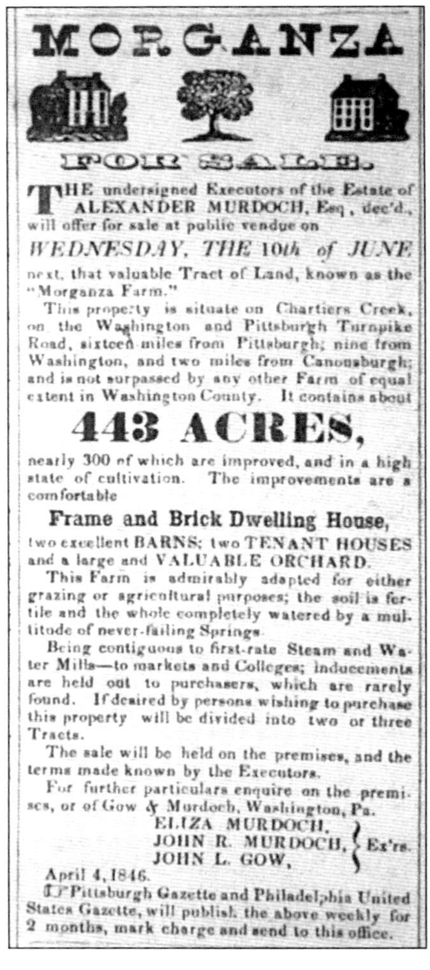

MORGANZA

FOR SALE.

THE undersigned Executors of the Estate of ALEXANDER MURDOCH, Esq., dec'd., will offer for sale at public vendue on

WEDNESDAY, THE 10th of JUNE

next, that valuable Tract of Land, known as the "Morganza Farm."

This property is situate on Chartiers Creek, on the Washington and Pittsburgh Turnpike Road, sixteen miles from Pittsburgh; nine from Washington, and two miles from Canonsburgh; and is not surpassed by any other Farm of equal extent in Washington County. It contains about

443 ACRES,

nearly 300 of which are improved, and in a high state of cultivation. The improvements are a comfortable

Frame and Brick Dwelling House,

two excellent BARNS; two TENANT HOUSES and a large and VALUABLE ORCHARD.

This Farm is admirably adapted for either grazing or agricultural purposes; the soil is fertile and the whole completely watered by a multitude of never-failing Springs.

Being contiguous to first-rate Steam and Water Mills—to markets and Colleges; inducements are held out to purchasers, which are rarely found. If desired by persons wishing to purchase this property will be divided into two or three Tracts.

The sale will be held on the premises, and the terms made known by the Executors.

For further particulars enquire on the premises, or of Gow & Murdoch, Washington, Pa.

ELIZA MURDOCH,
JOHN R. MURDOCH,
JOHN L. GOW, } Ex'rs.

April 4, 1846.

☞ Pittsburgh Gazette and Philadelphia United States Gazette, will publish the above weekly for 2 months, mark charge and send to this office.

This advertisement placed in the *Washington Reporter* in April 1846 listed Morganza for sale. The land was made up of a farm with a house, two barns, two tenant houses, and a large orchard. The advertisement also mentions a series of natural springs throughout the many acres.

In recognition of the career and service of Col. George Morgan during the Revolutionary War and the period following, the Daughters of the American Revolution (DAR) dedicated a monument in his name where his Colonial-era home stood. The marker reads, "On this site and with these stones Col. George Morgan in 1796 built his home, Morganza. Pioneer, trader and explorer 1767–1771. Ardent patriot during the Revolution. Progressive farmer. Friend of Indians. In this house, 1806, he denounced Aaron Burr and immediately notified President Jefferson of the treasonable plot. Erected to his memory, 1928." (Courtesy of Richard Nowe.)

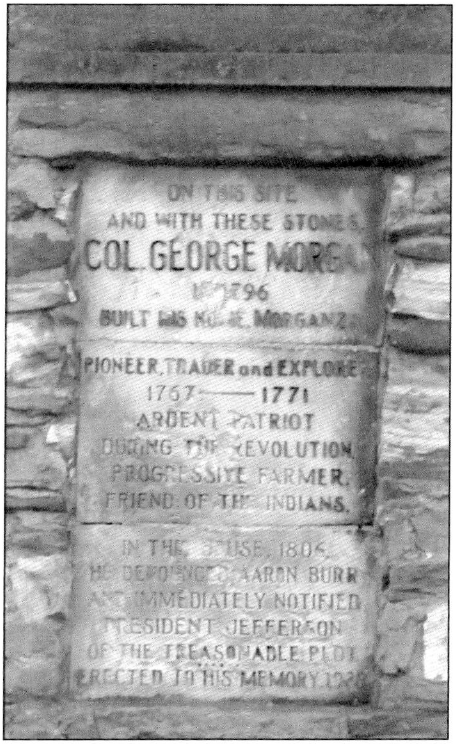

This is a view of Col. George Morgan's house, which stood on the north shore of Chartiers Creek after the railroad line turned right after crossing the creek heading north. The 2.5-story Colonial-style house was likely constructed with logs and weather boarded.

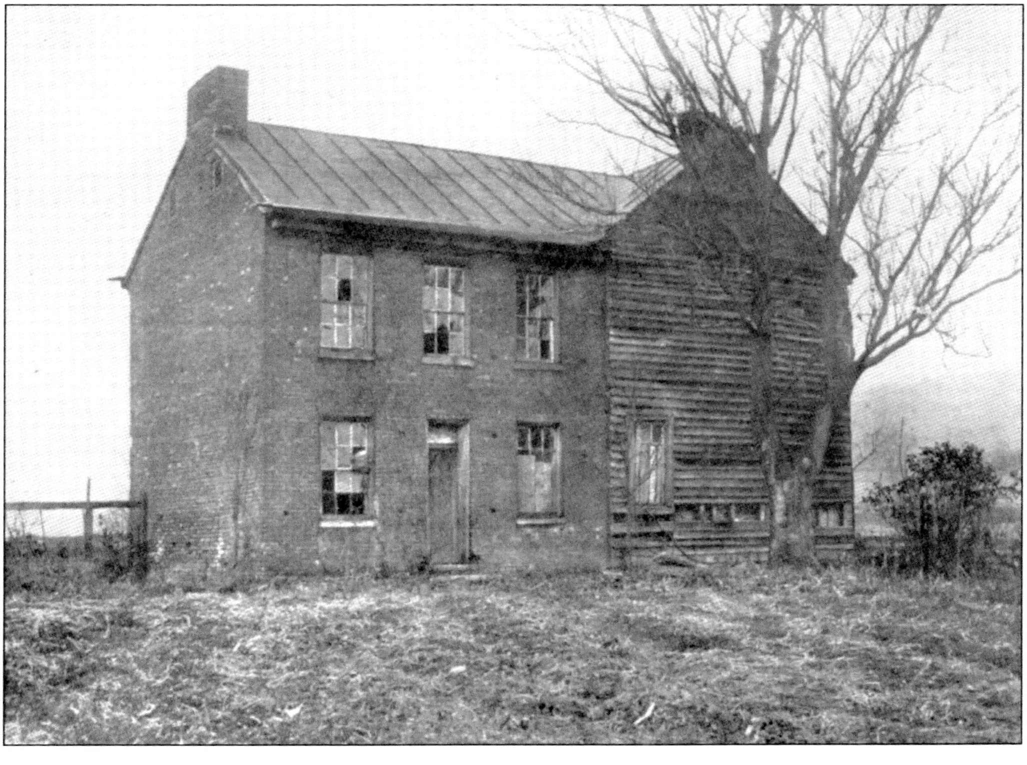

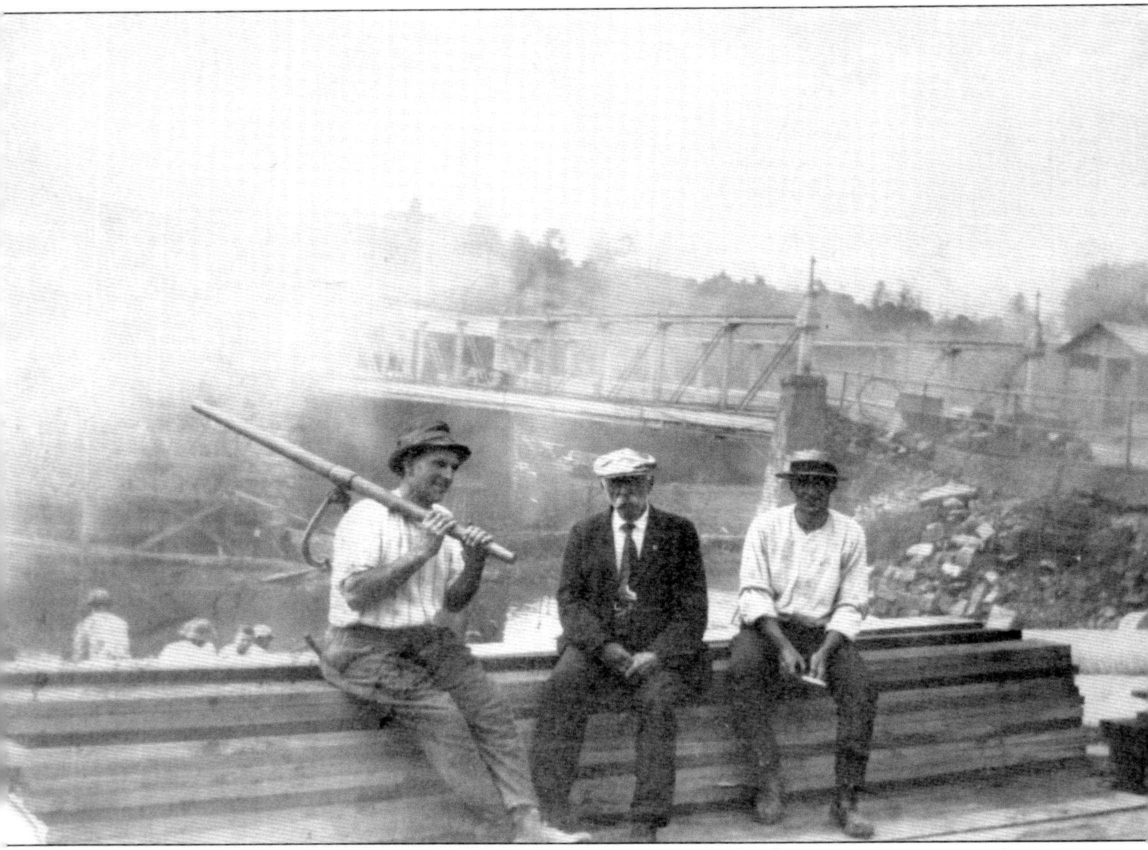

The board of trustees of the House of Refuge purchased the former Morgan farm from Wesley Greer for $180 per acre, as well as a tract from James Craighead for $160 per acre, totaling a tract of 500 acres. This early undated photograph shows three men sitting in front of the bridge to Morganza, which crossed over Chartiers Creek. The photograph was taken looking northeast, facing the front of the institution at the main entrance. Male inmates can be seen down near the banks of the creek.

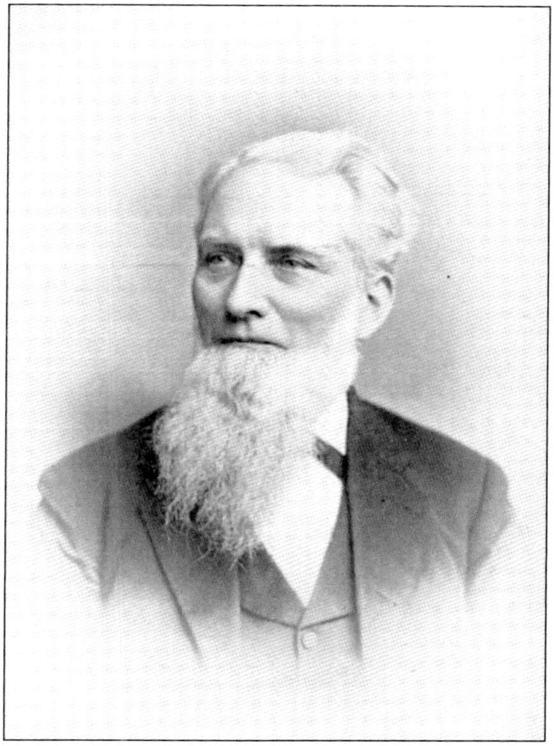

Thomas Wightman, who was president of the board of managers by 1880, served as a member of the board since the organization was established in the late 1870s. The board members were chosen directly by the governor and approved by the senate. Wightman retired from the board in 1904.

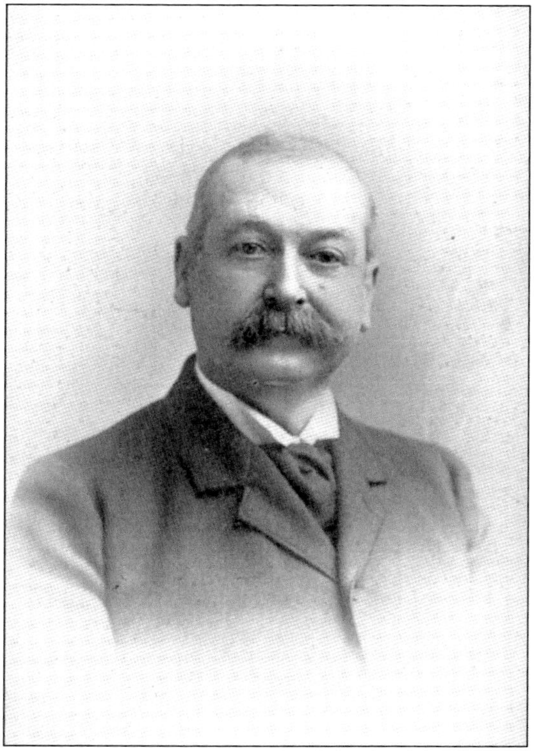

Jerome A. Quay became the second superintendent of the Pennsylvania Reform School in 1880 after the resignation of the first superintendent, Col. George A. Shallenberger. Quay's brother Matthew was the secretary of the commonwealth, which possibly influenced the unanimous election of Jerome Quay as superintendent. He served until 1905.

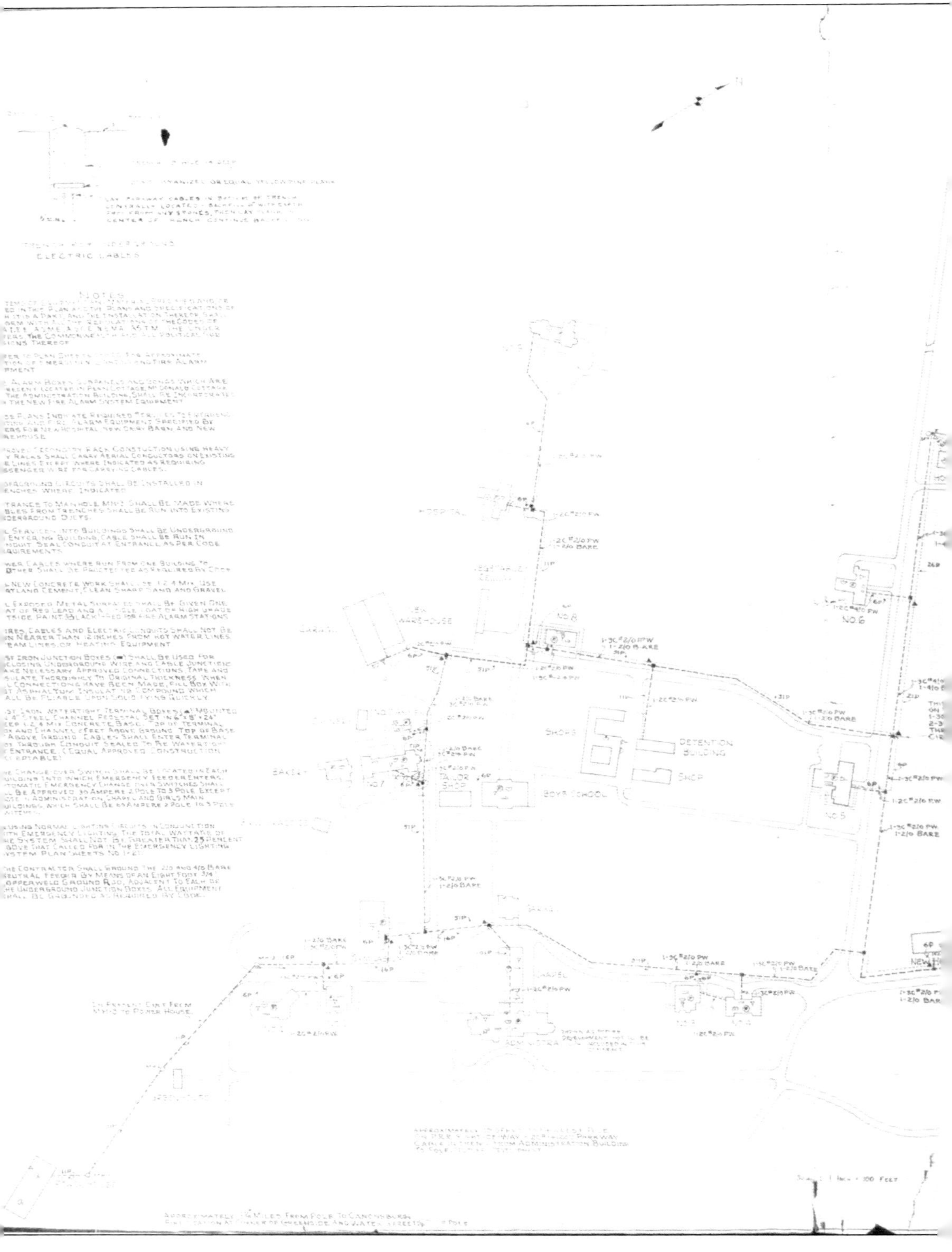

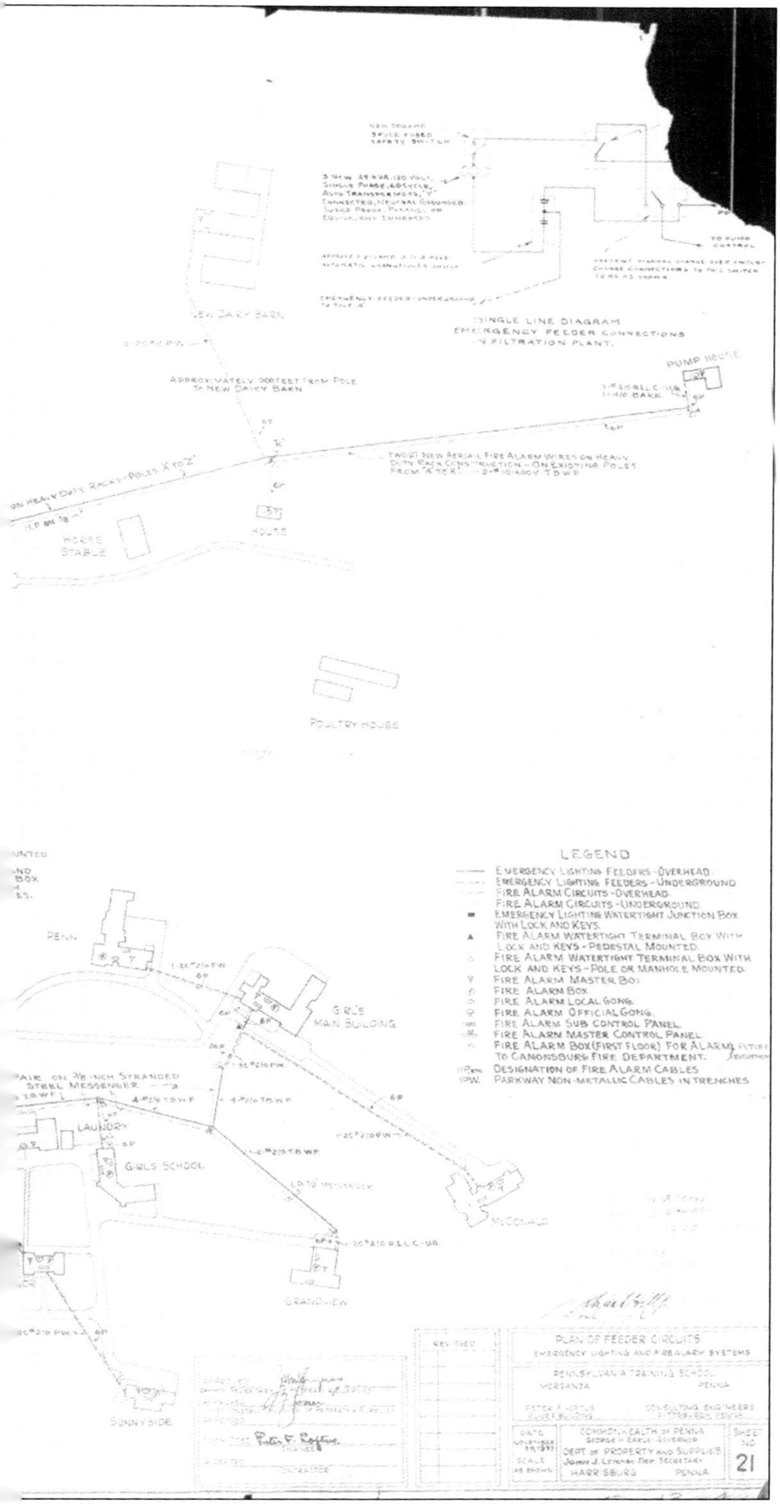

The grounds plan, titled "Plan of Feeder Circuits, Emergency Lighting and Fire Alarm Systems," shows that electrical circuits ran throughout the entire grounds to each structure. This 1937 blue print labels all standing structures at that time, of which there were nearly 50. (Courtesy of Adam Ryan.)

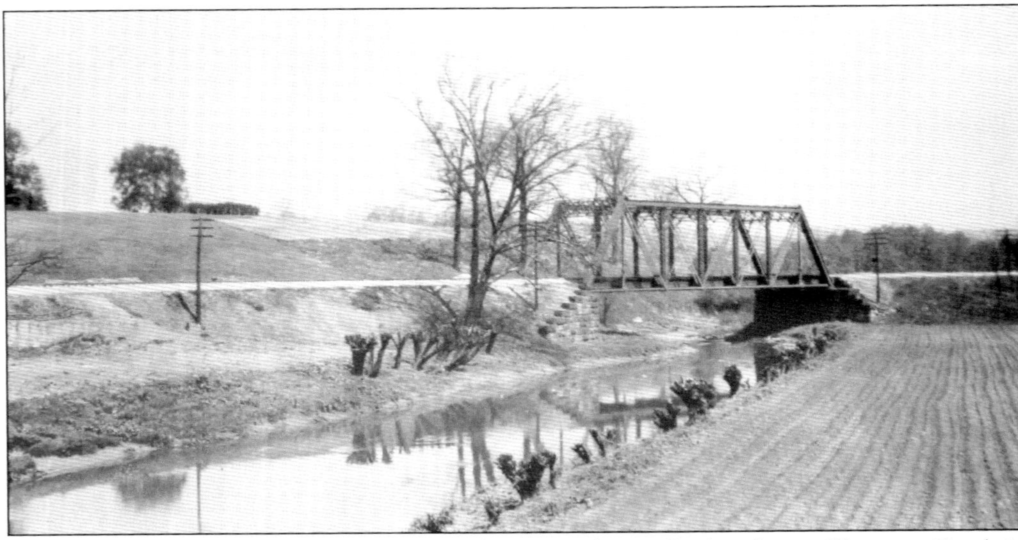

This is a view of the railroad bridge along the Pennsylvania Railroad over Chartiers Creek in 1920. By 1871, the railroad line extended from Pittsburgh to Washington. With vast farmlands and coal mining in the area, heavy manufacturing of coal and farm produce such as milk could now be transported to the city by rail. (Courtesy of Pennsylvania State Archives.)

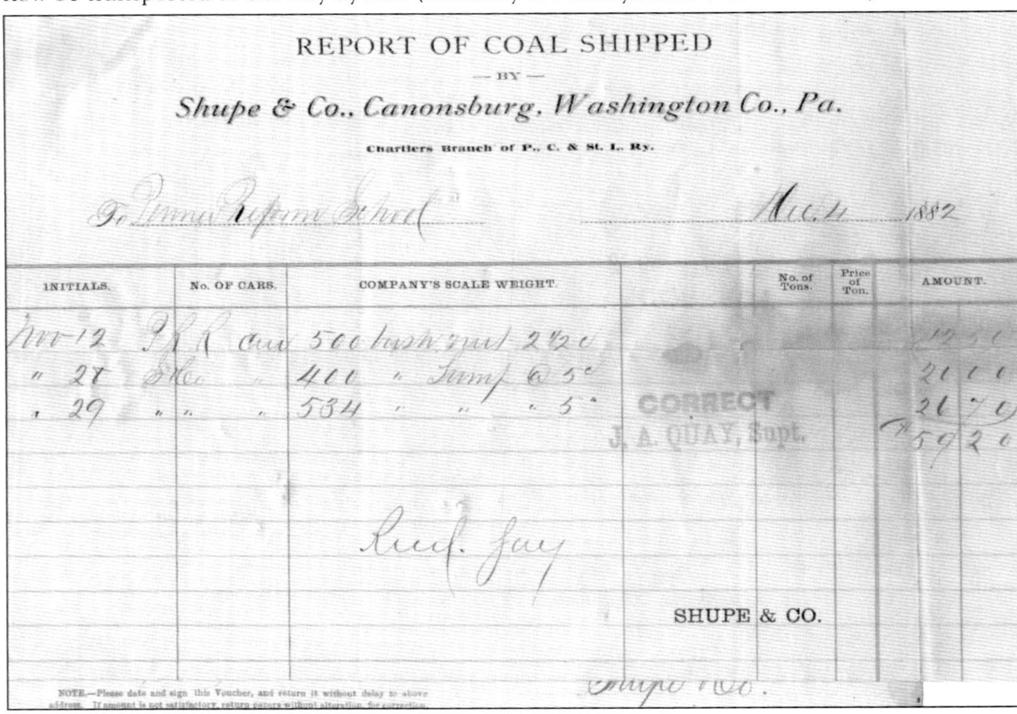

REPORT OF COAL SHIPPED

—BY—

Shupe & Co., Canonsburg, Washington Co., Pa.

Chartiers Branch of P., C. & St. L. Ry.

To Penna Reform School   Dec 4 1882

INITIALS.	No. OF CARS.	COMPANY'S SCALE WEIGHT.		No. of Tons.	Price of Ton.	AMOUNT.
Nov 12	PRR car	500 bush nut 2½c				12 50
" 27		400 " lump @ 5c				20 00
" 29	" " "	534 " " " 5c				26 70
						$59 20

CORRECT
J. A. QUAY, Supt.

Rec'd Pay

SHUPE & CO.

Shupe & Co.

NOTE.—Please date and sign this Voucher, and return it without delay to above address. If amount is not satisfactory, return papers without alteration, for correction.

This document records the sale of coal to the Pennsylvania Reform School from Shupe & Co. of Canonsburg. Dated December 4, 1882, it shows the cost and amount of each purchase from the previous month. Coal was purchased by the ton at the beginning of the month for $12.50. Later that month, coal was purchased for $20 and $26.70. The total cost of coal for the month was $59.20.

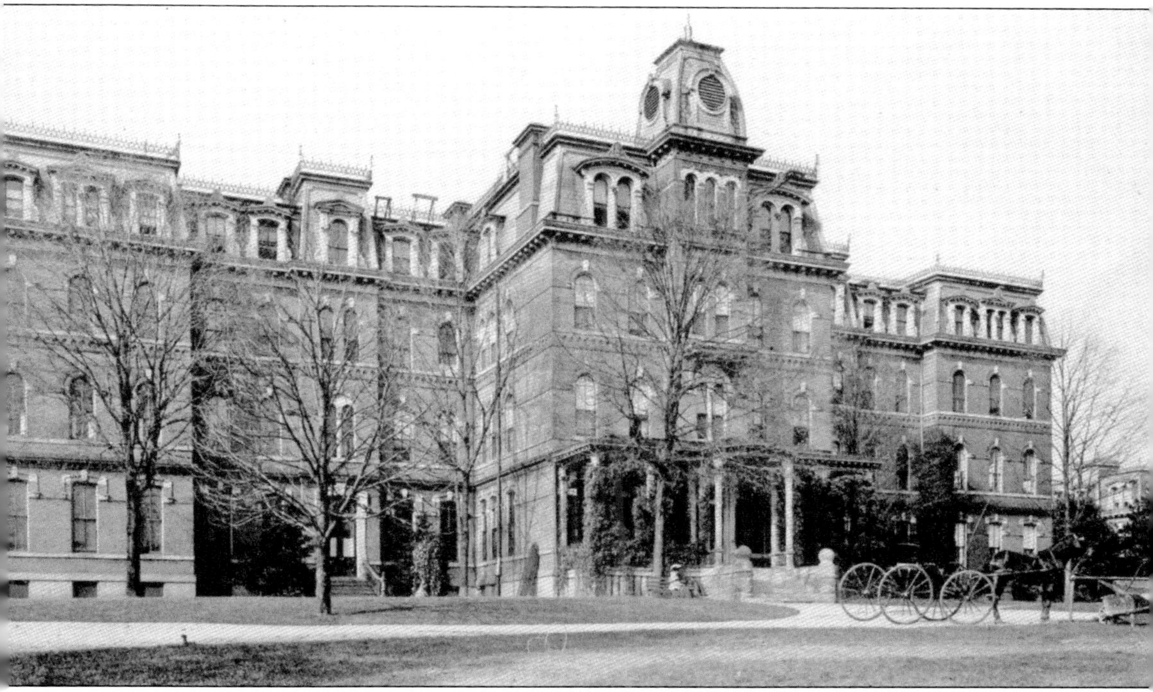

The cornerstone of the administration building was laid in July 1873 by Gov. John F. Hanranft. Construction began in September. The four-story building was primarily made of brick, with a prominent mansard roof. The administration building contained a total of 50 useful rooms, including a kitchen and a chapel.

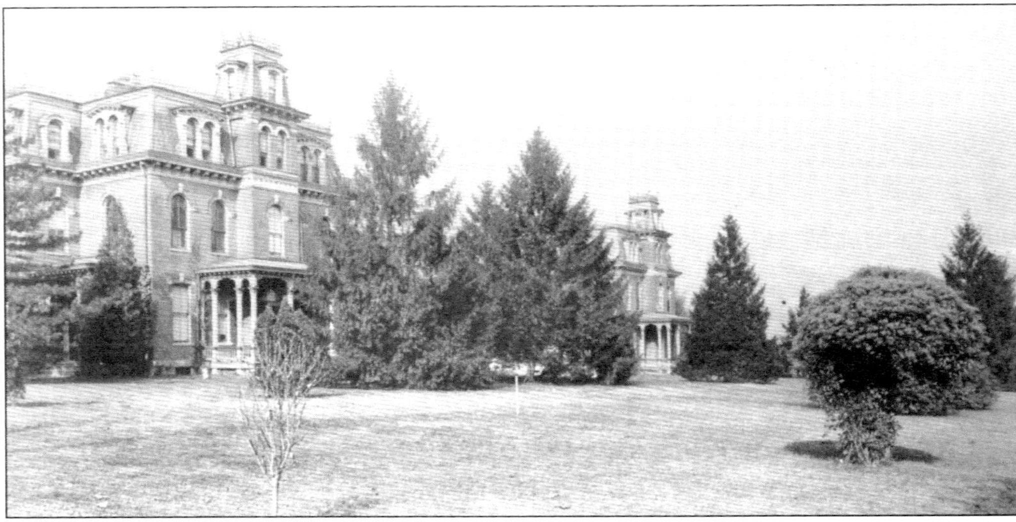

Seen here are two of the first four dormitory buildings that housed the delinquent boys. The four dormitory buildings were similar architecturally to the administration building, all with well-pronounced mansard roofs. The institution established separate cottages based on gender. The girls' dormitory building, also similar in design, was bigger than the boys' dormitory buildings but smaller than the administration building. It was located at the far northern end of the campus.

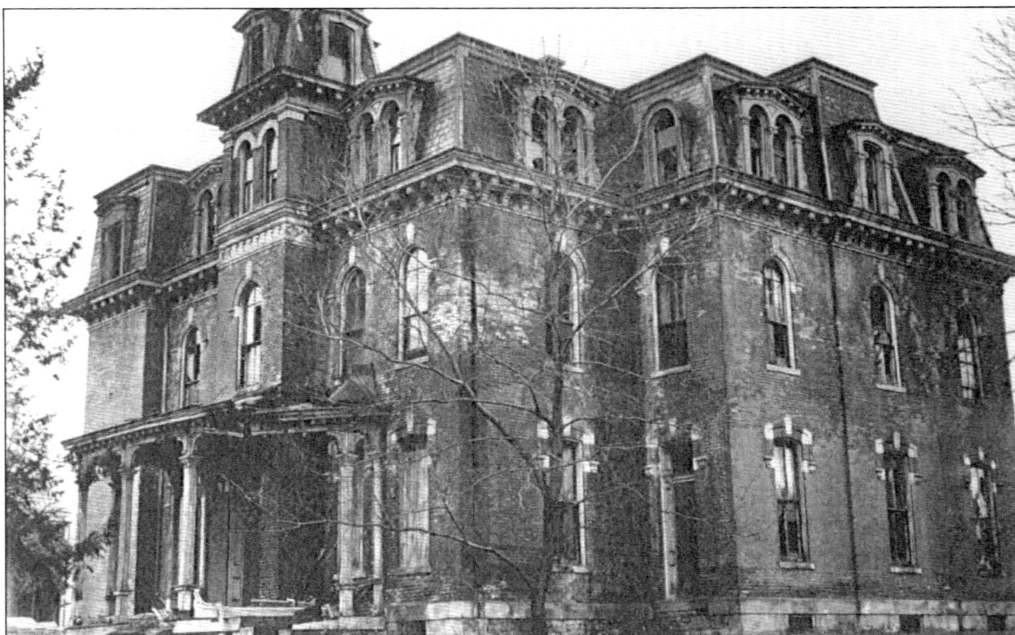

In 1908, a fire occurred in one of the three-story dormitory buildings, known as "A" Division. The cause of the fire was unknown at first but was later suspected to have been caused by a defective flue used for steam heating on the third floor. The building housed the youngest boys, with an average age of 11. Thankfully, none were there when the fire occurred, and no one was hurt. Estimates of damages at the time were $10,000; within the year, it was replaced by a modern cottage. It was the first reported fire since the opening in 1876.

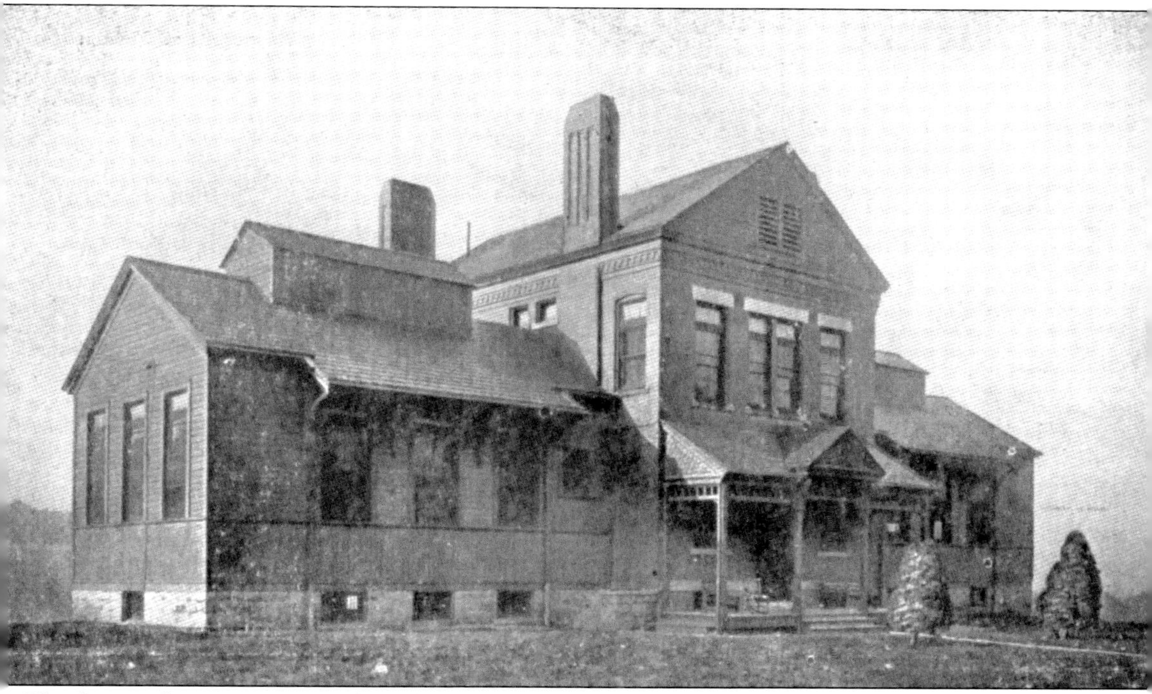

The hospital was constructed by the late 1890s northwest of the administration building, approximately the same distance from the girls' dormitory building as it was from the boys'. The hospital had two single-story wings that served as medical wards for the children of the school, which was connected to a two-story center core. Upon admittance, children were given a thorough physical examination, which often showed physical conditions that were believed to be the cause of their delinquency. Some had bad teeth, were undernourished, or were generally in bad physical condition. (Courtesy of Ed Cononge.)

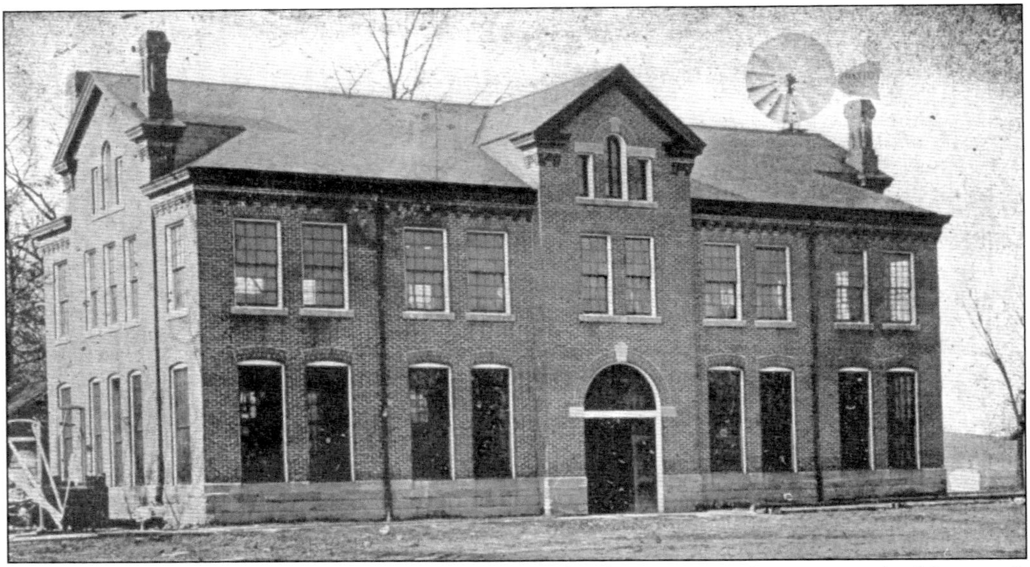

In 1880, a contract was submitted to the legislature for the erection of a two-story building with a basement for the industrial school department. The 36-foot-by-72-foot structure was one of the first industrial buildings constructed. Later, in 1895, this two-story building was constructed for the expansion of industrial schooling.

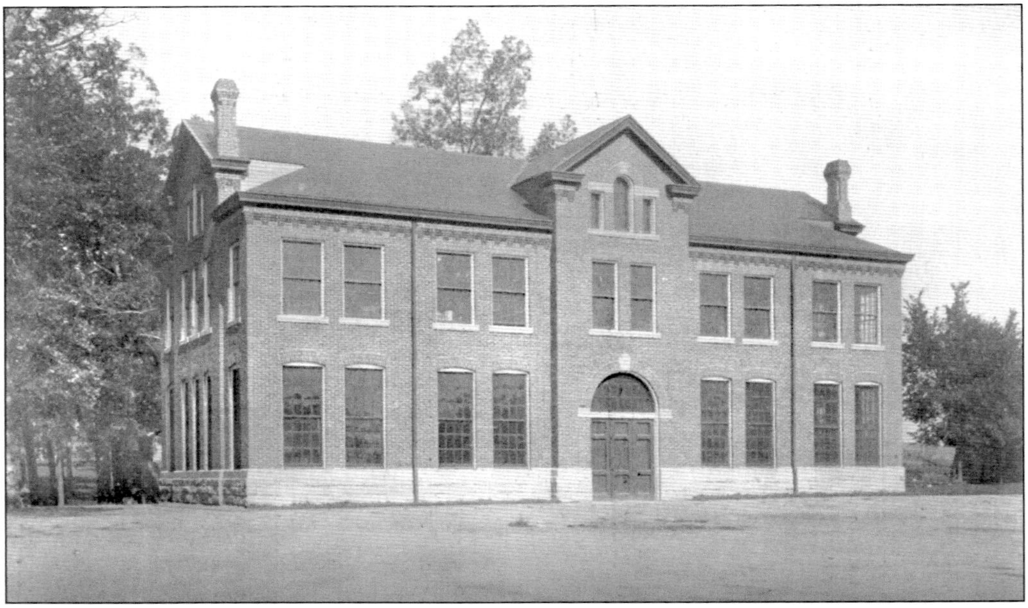

The completed industrial school building contained the blacksmith shop and other shops. Around 1918, the blacksmith shop was moved to another building with newer, more efficient equipment. A 1925 grounds plan shows that this two-story industrial building was razed by that time.

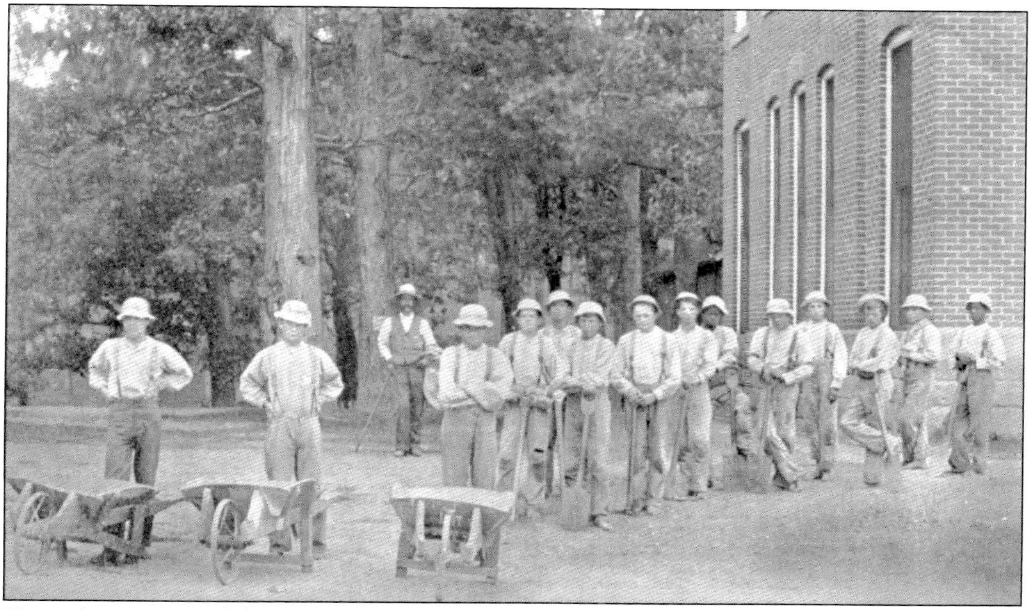

Upon the opening of the Pennsylvania Reform School, much of the work was done by the boys. They are seen here with wheelbarrows and shovels posing for a photograph next to the two-story shop, with their instructor standing behind them.

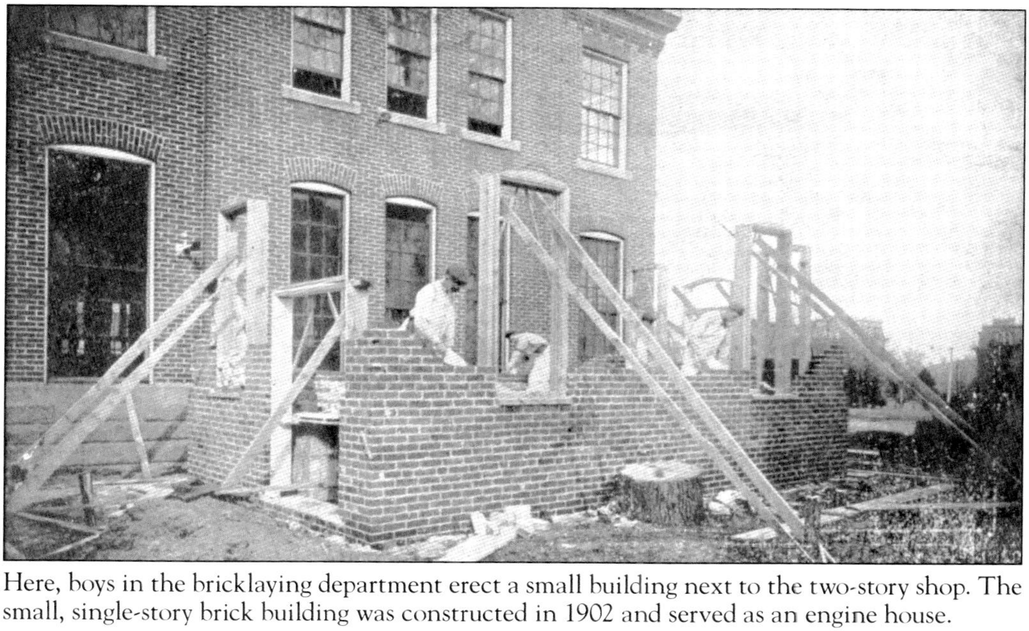

Here, boys in the bricklaying department erect a small building next to the two-story shop. The small, single-story brick building was constructed in 1902 and served as an engine house.

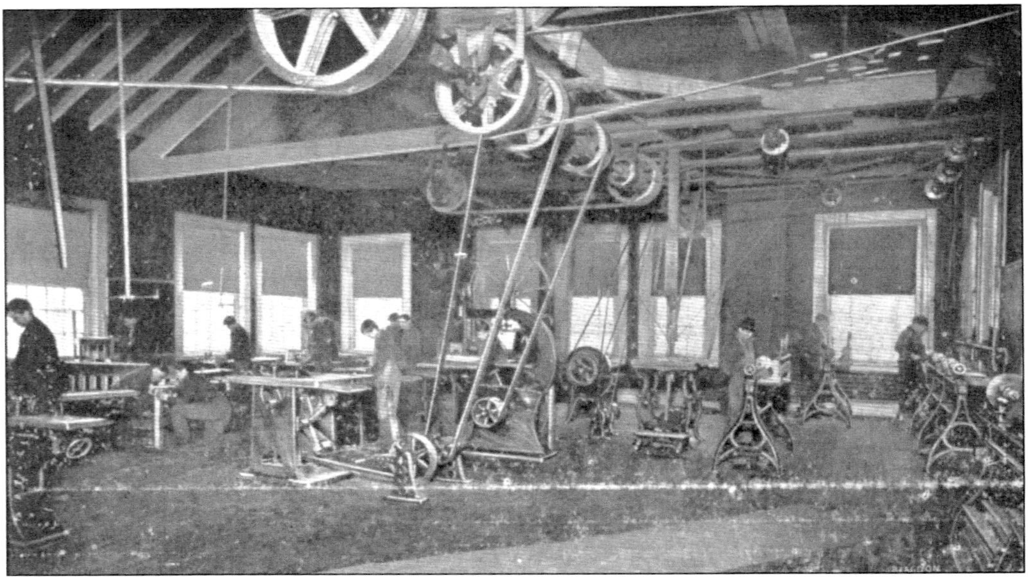

This view of the finished shop building shows the second floor, with the open belts and pulleys used to operate the equipment. The engine house built next to the shop was likely used to run the equipment. The printing department had moved to the second floor of the shop by 1907.

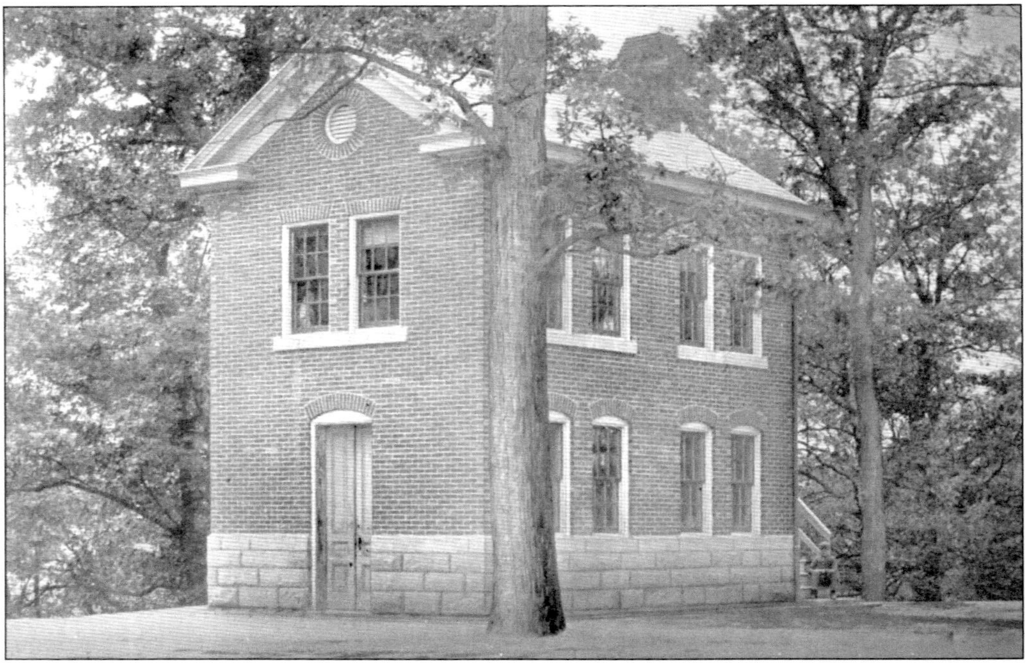

This two-story brick building contained the printing department. It had a single lipped chimney at the rear. Located just south of the two-story blacksmith shop, it was built in the late 1800s and was functioning by the early 1900s. The building had been razed by 1913.

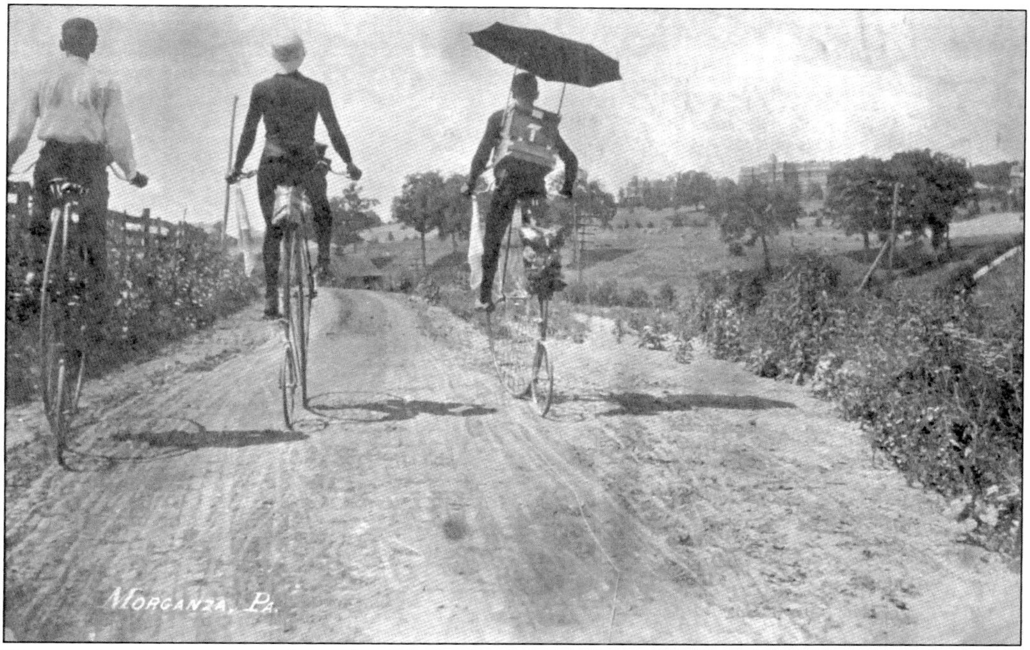

This undated photograph shows bicyclists traveling in front of the Pennsylvania Reform School (right background). These bicycles were imported from France to the United States in 1877 and 1878. They have been identified as penny-farthing bicycles, known for their large front wheel and small rear wheel. These bicycles were considered unsafe because of how high the rider was positioned.

This is an early-1900s view of Curry Hill Road (now Morganza Road) facing north. The interurban trolley line between Canonsburg and Pittsburgh was constructed in 1909 by Pittsburgh Railways. The interurban trolley line was used to transport residents to and from work as well as to shopping areas outside their living community. The trolley line ran until 1953.

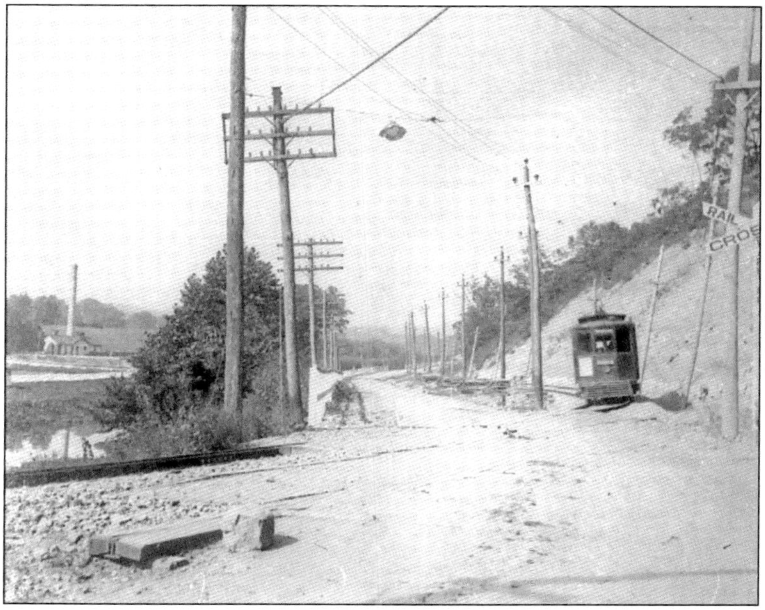

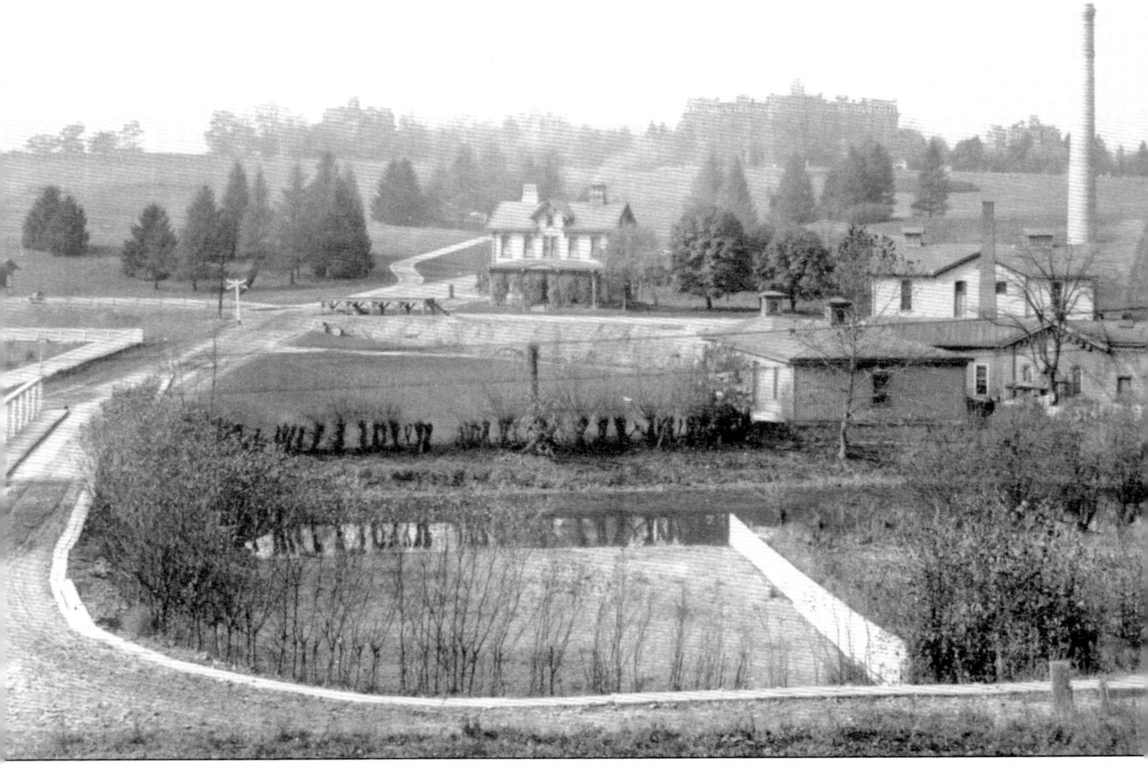

In 1878, a method was developed to filter and pump water from Chartiers Creek, which was badly polluted by sewage, to a stone-lined reservoir constructed with valve inlets along Chartiers Creek. An Eclipse steam engine, run by boilers, operated the pump. H.D. McKnight & Company of Pittsburgh furnished the pump and boilers. The filter house and pump house are seen at closest right with the institution's first coal-fired powerhouse, with its distinctive stack, located behind it. This powerhouse was used until the construction of a new electric powerhouse, put into operation by 1906.

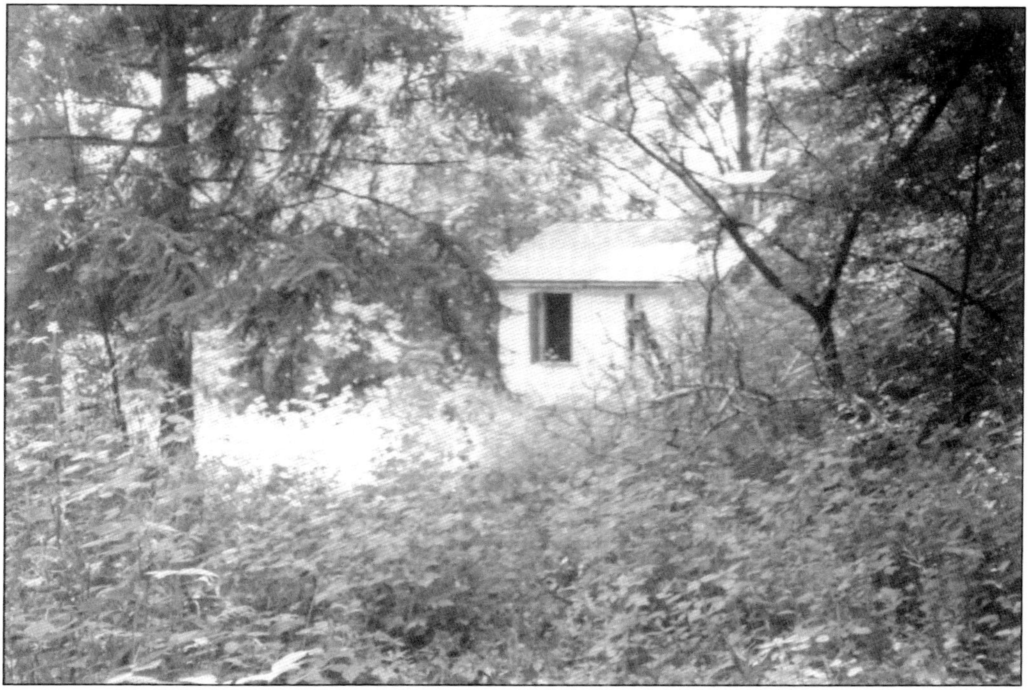

Springhouses, like the one seen here in dense vegetation, were scattered throughout the grounds. Springhouses were built above cold springs and used to keep foods cool. They were used until modern refrigeration was invented, after which they were abandoned. (Courtesy of Pennsylvania Historical and Museum Commission.)

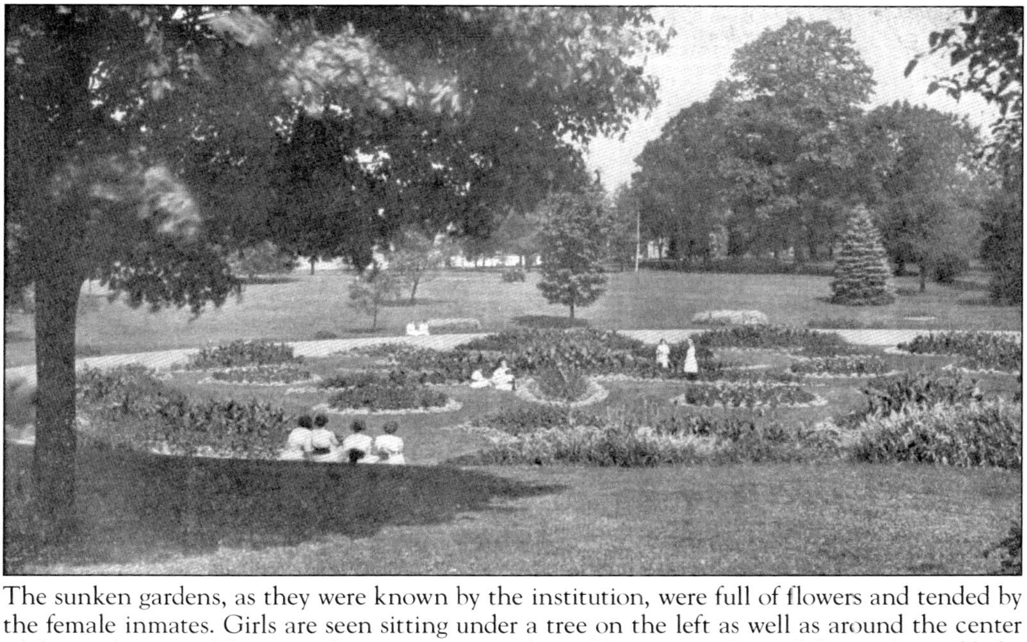

The sunken gardens, as they were known by the institution, were full of flowers and tended by the female inmates. Girls are seen sitting under a tree on the left as well as around the center of the garden area. The grounds were maintained in a Victorian style, and the gardens added a beautiful element to the institution.

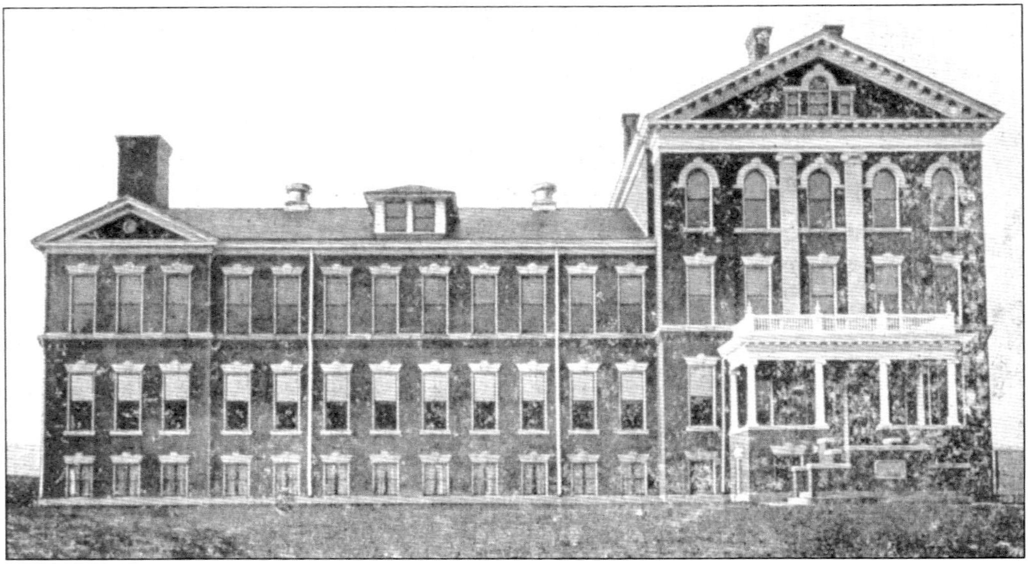

Built in 1904, the girls' main building had a three-story core with two connecting wings. The wings were two stories, one at the rear and the other to the left of the facade. It had many chimneys and a gabled asphalt roof. The building had an enormous amount of lintel windows throughout, including the lintel arch windows above the front porch entrance.

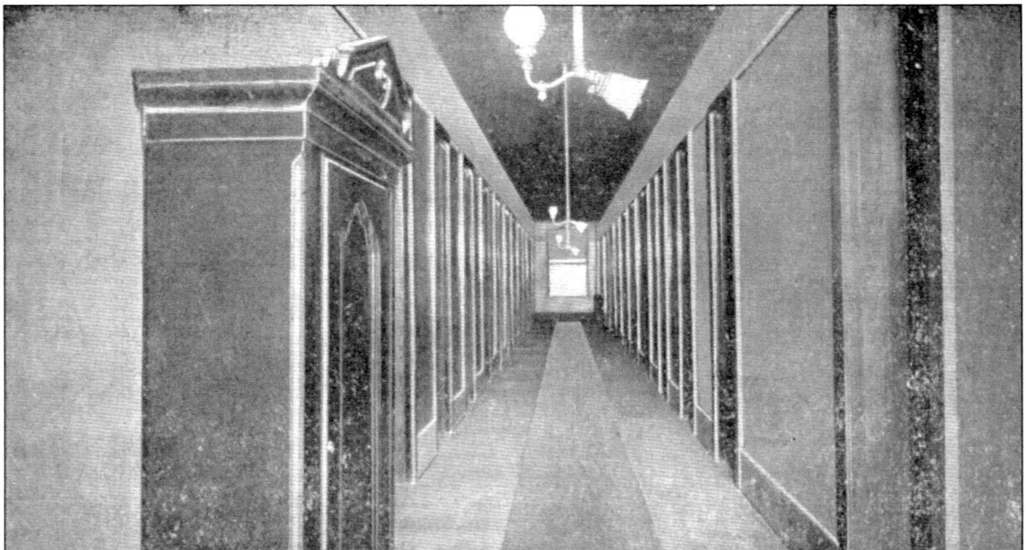

This view of the corridor in the girls' main building shows an abundance of doors leading to individual bedrooms for each girl. The rooms were just big enough for a single bed and another piece of furniture, with a single window centered in it. Both gas lighting and electrical lighting were used in the hall when this photograph was taken in the early 1900s.

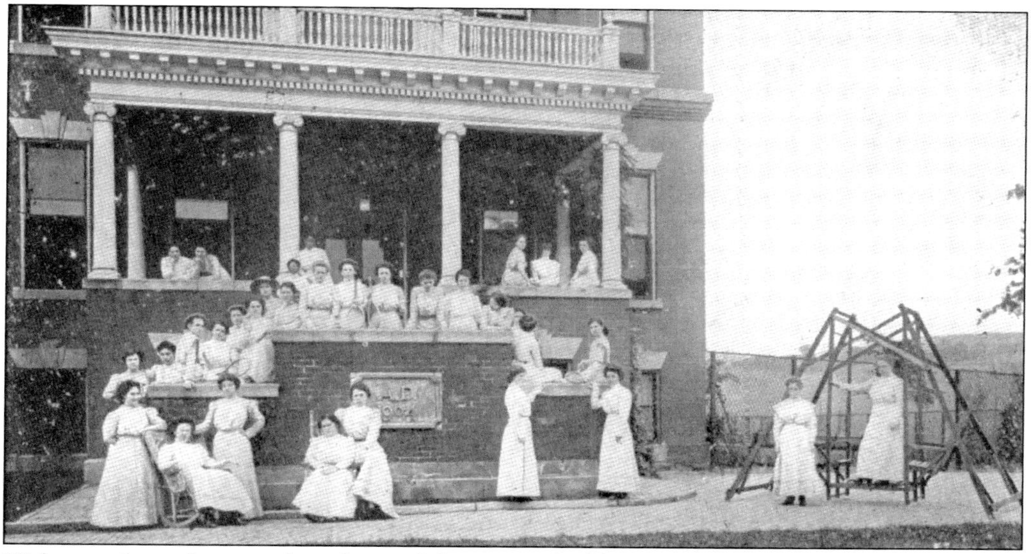

Girls pose for a photograph in front of their main building, at the far northeastern end of the institute. The plaque on the building reads, "A.D. 1904." Some of the girls are holding tennis rackets, while a girl on the right stands on a swing.

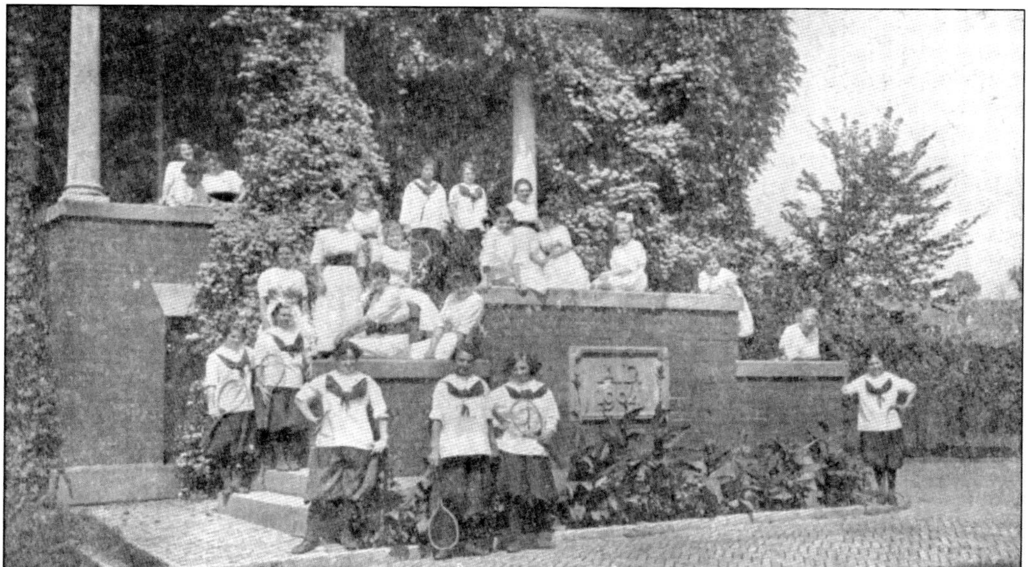

Another view of the front entrance to the girls' main building shows girls dressed in bloomers and midi tops. During the early-1900s era, this was the style of athletic apparel for girls. Many of the girls hold tennis rackets; tennis was one of first athletic sports available to women at the reform school and was one of the most popular for girls.

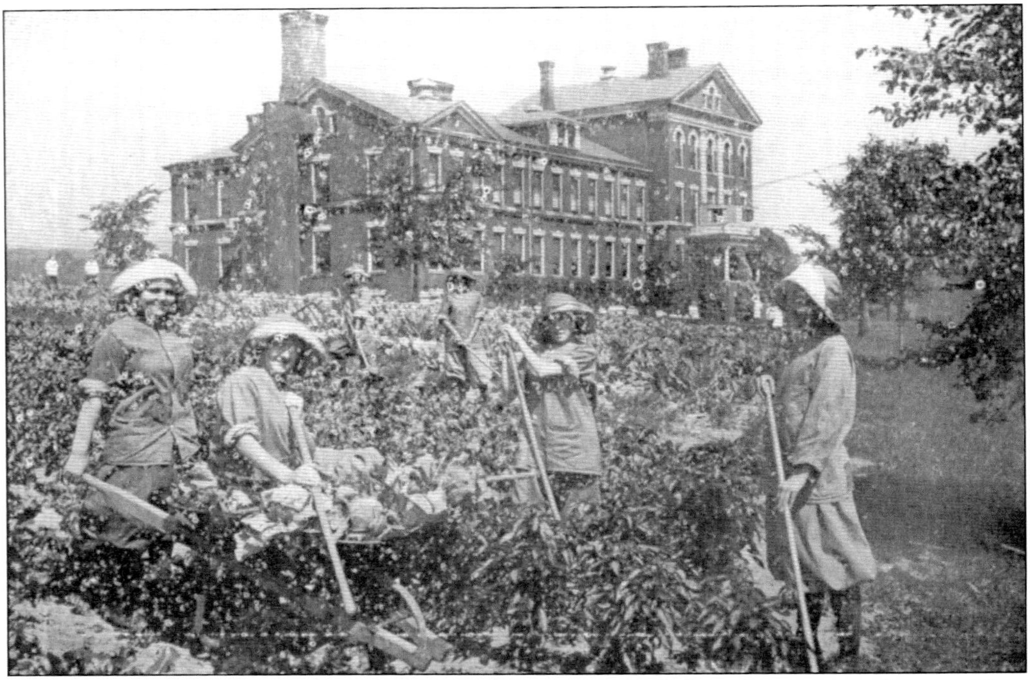

Shortly after the opening of the girls' main building in 1906, all the girls were moved into it. They had originally been housed in a dormitory built around the time the reform school opened, which was in need of major repair. As a result, crowding immediately occurred in the girls' main building, although conditions were still considered sanitary. Here, girls perform gardening work.

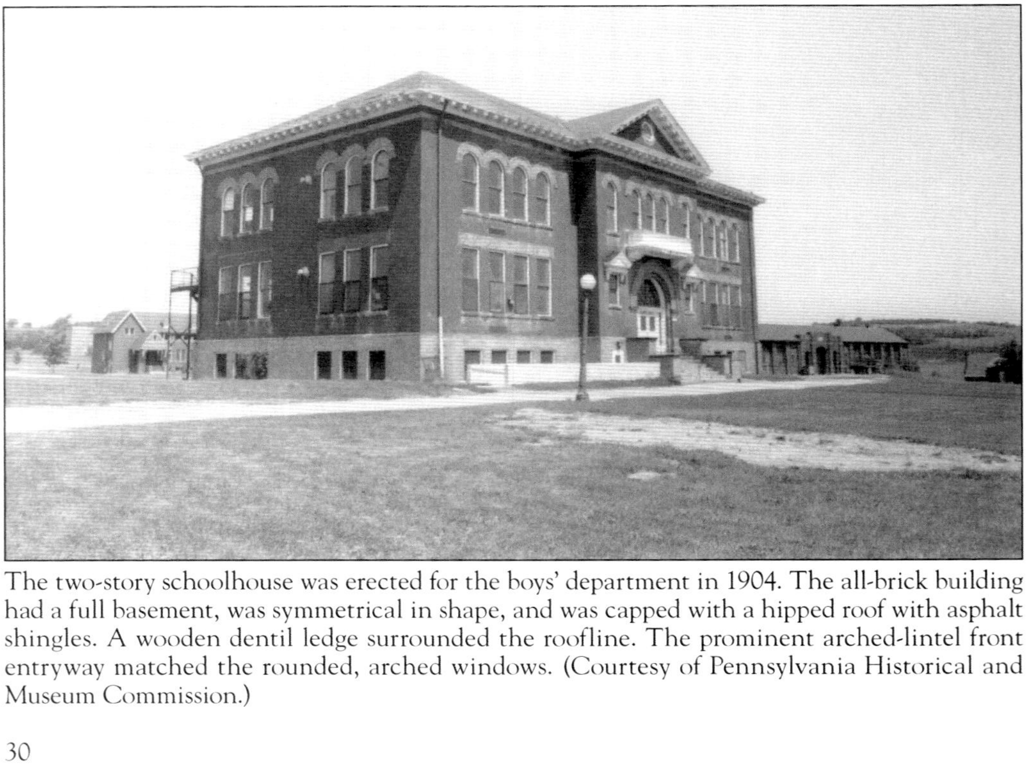

The two-story schoolhouse was erected for the boys' department in 1904. The all-brick building had a full basement, was symmetrical in shape, and was capped with a hipped roof with asphalt shingles. A wooden dentil ledge surrounded the roofline. The prominent arched-lintel front entryway matched the rounded, arched windows. (Courtesy of Pennsylvania Historical and Museum Commission.)

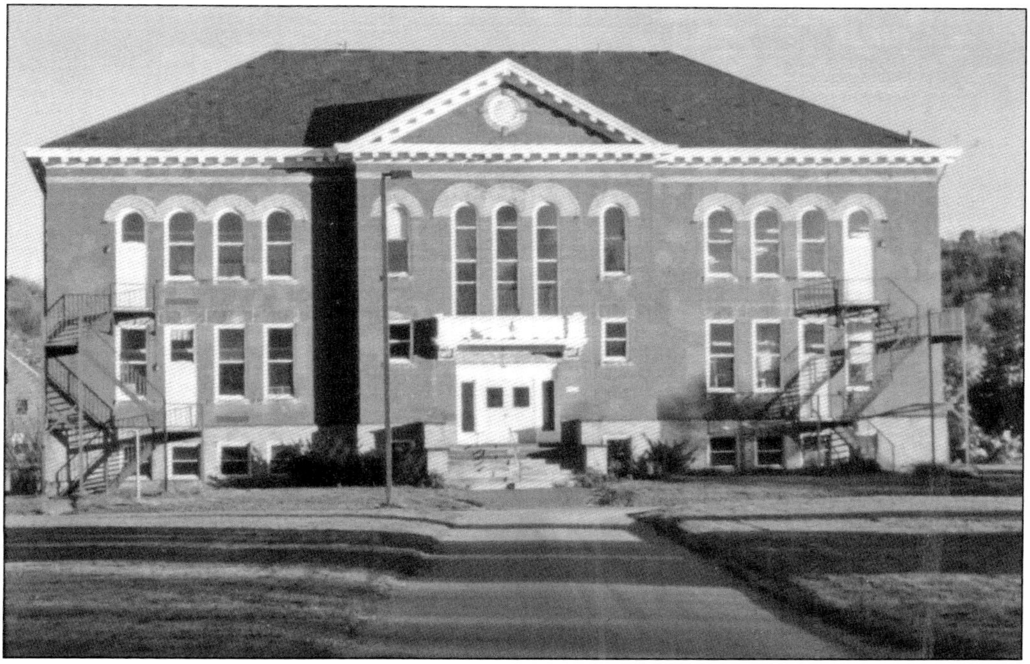

The schoolhouse was opened by 1906. It contained eight spacious classrooms as well as a library room. A grading process was implemented that placed academic schooling on the correct basis. (Courtesy of Diane Hickman.)

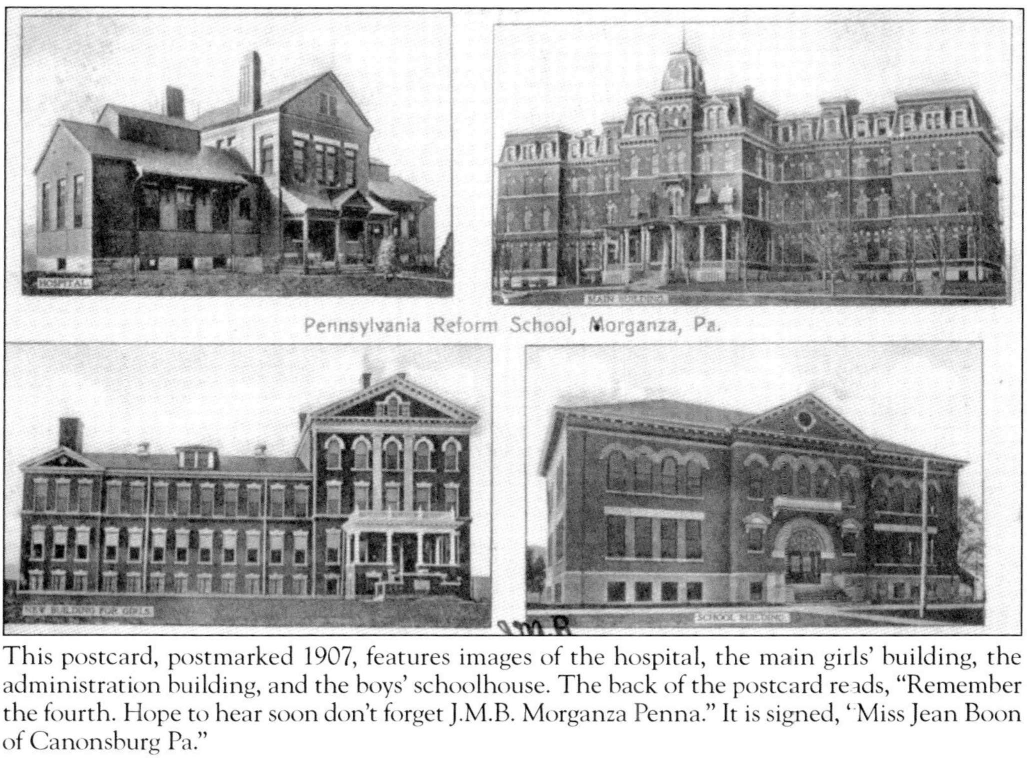

This postcard, postmarked 1907, features images of the hospital, the main girls' building, the administration building, and the boys' schoolhouse. The back of the postcard reads, "Remember the fourth. Hope to hear soon don't forget J.M.B. Morganza Penna." It is signed, "Miss Jean Boon of Canonsburg Pa."

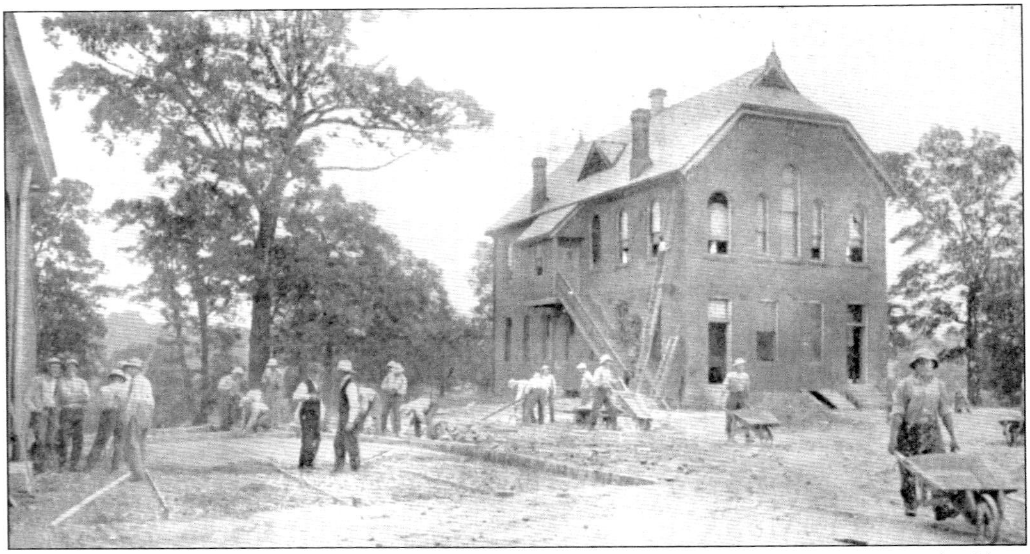

Boys are seen here constructing a roadway in the girls' area of the campus. The two-story building on the right served as a brush shop into the late 1890s. It later served as a school for girls, where domestic science courses were taught. The structure was razed by 1925 and a new schoolhouse for girls was built on the site. (Courtesy of Ed Cononge.)

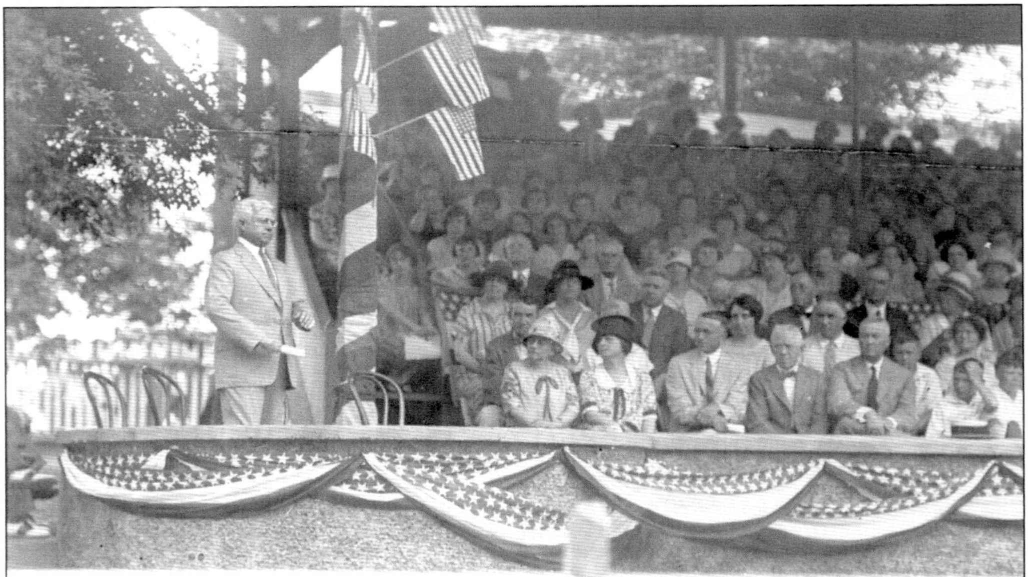

Supt. William Frank Penn stands on the left in the grandstands at a Fourth of July event at the school's track. Penn served as the superintendent from 1905 until he retired in 1936. He was the longest-tenured superintendent in the history of the Pennsylvania Training School.

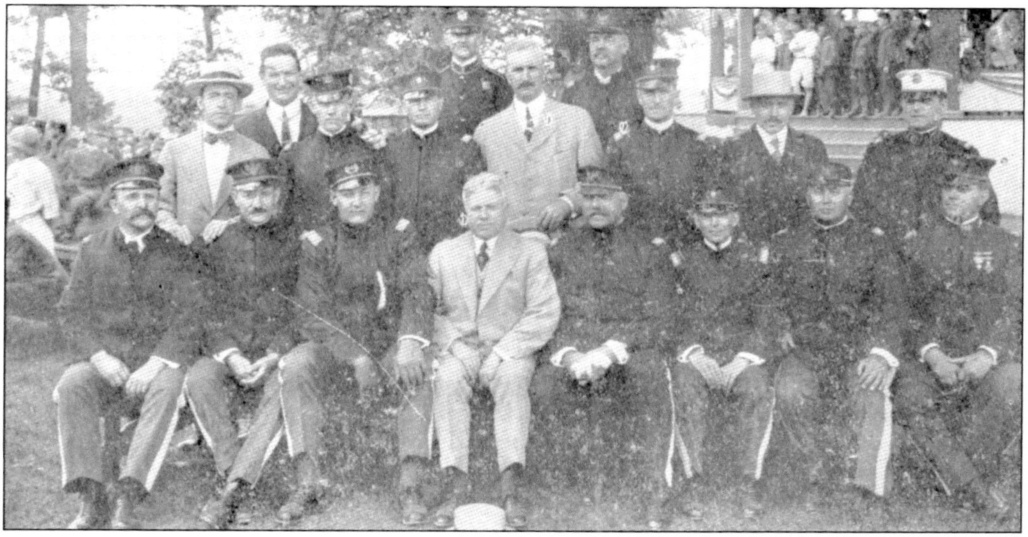

William Penn (sitting, center) poses for a photograph with other officers. Some officers served as parole officers; once an inmate was paroled, it was necessary for the parole supervisor to stay in contact until he or she was 21. The parolee had to stay in contact through monthly letters for at least the first two years, and there also were frequent visits by the parole officer.

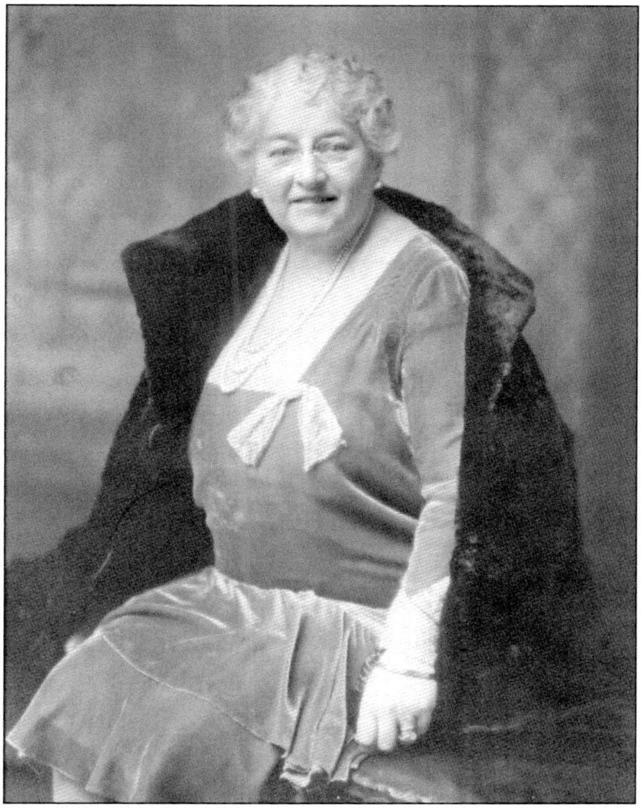

Sara Periette Penn, the wife of William Frank Penn, worked for more than 30 years directing productive and uplifting work for many youths in the institution. She died on February 9, 1933, after a two-year illness. The memorial ceremony held in her honor was attended by all the inmates of the school as well as personal friends of hers from other parts of Western Pennsylvania. Before she married Penn, her interest in the institution was influenced by her uncle James McClelland, a member of the board of managers.

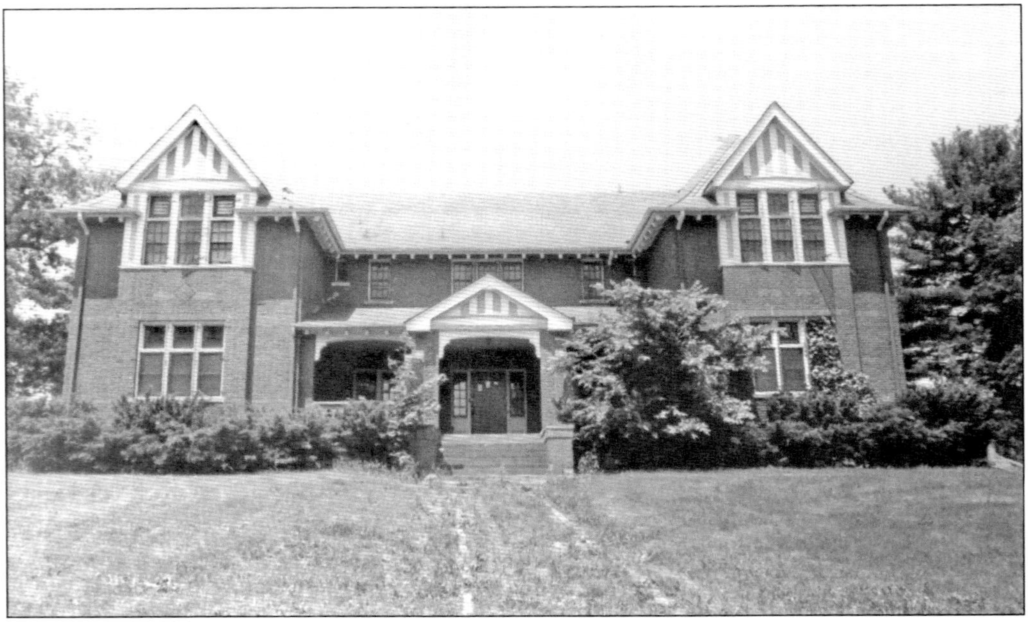

Honor Hall was a Tudor-style cottage located in the girls' department. The two-story brick cottage, built in 1908, had a prominent front porch at the center entrance with a flat archway. It had a gabled slate roof with a noticeable ledger around the roofline. (Courtesy of Pennsylvania Historical and Museum Commission.)

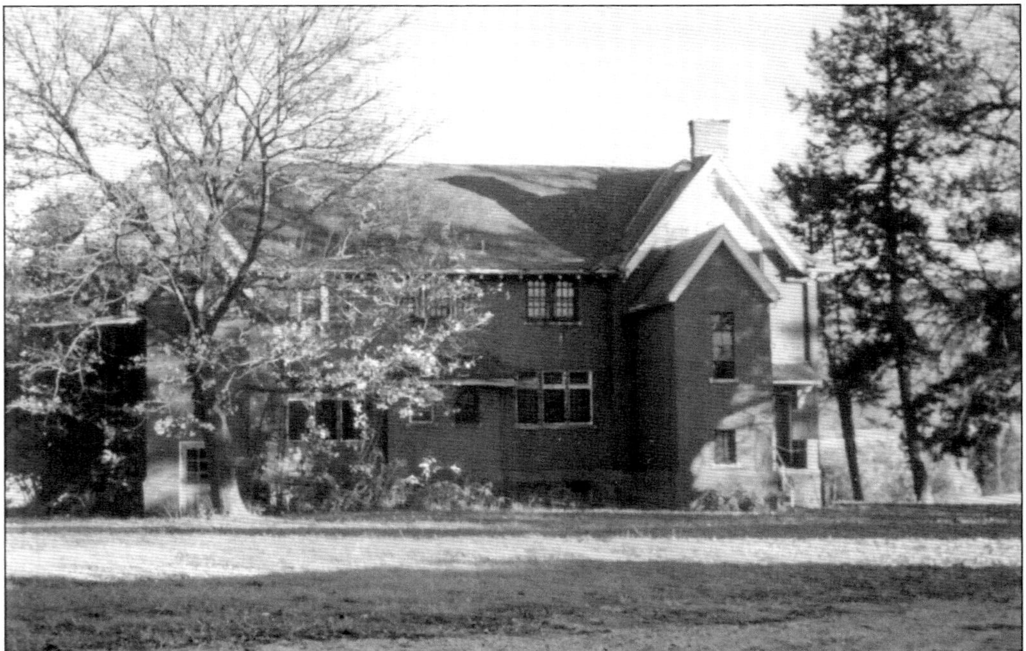

This is a view of the back of Honor Hall. A similar cottage was constructed in the boys' department, on the other side of Cottage No. 3. The new building replaced one of the old three-story dormitories that had stood since the opening of the reform school. (Courtesy of Diane Hickman.)

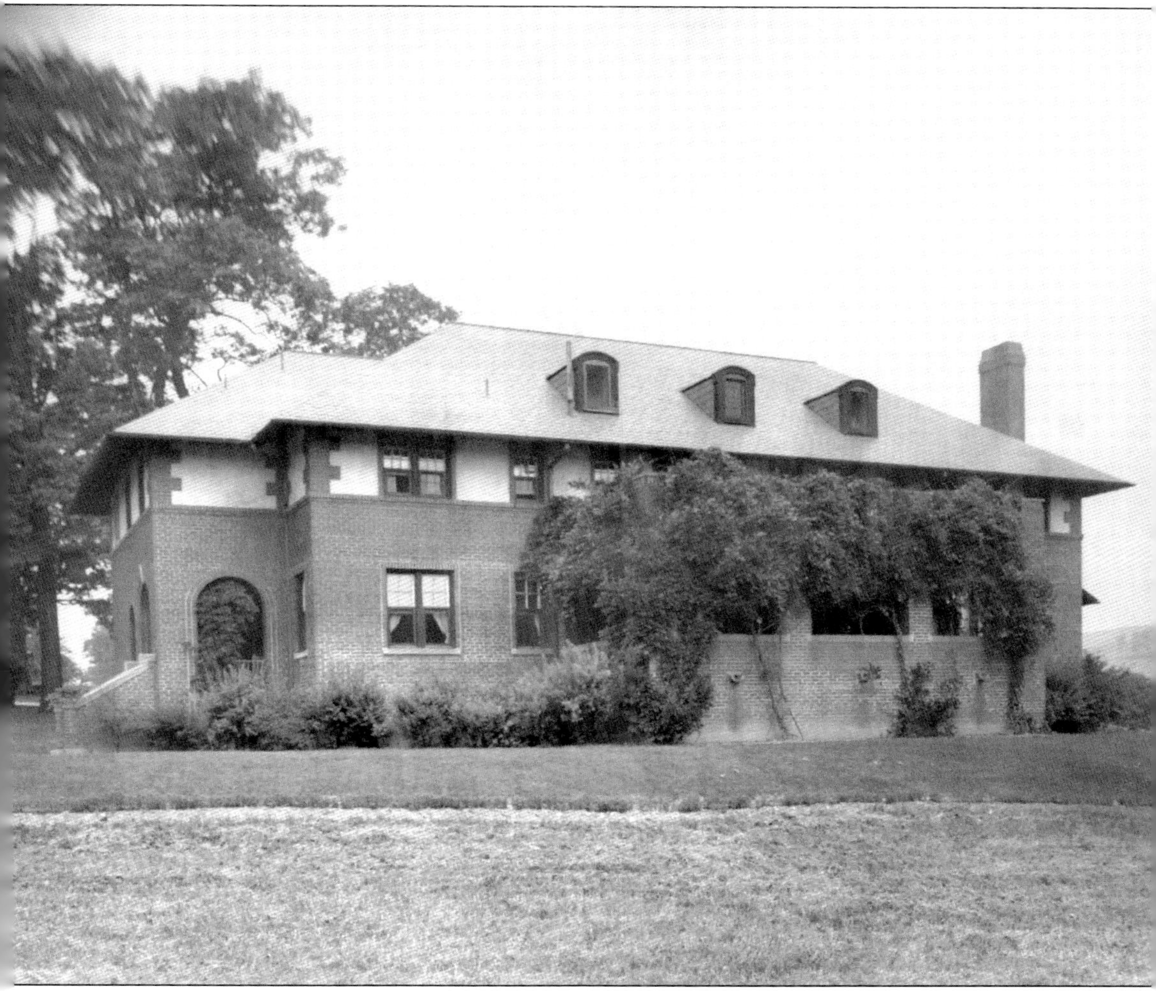

Sunnyside, seen here, was a three-story girls' cottage. In 1955, a female guard was slashed by a piece of glass there while escorting a 14-year-old psychiatric patient to her room after her transfer from Allentown Hospital. Other disturbances occurred during the week the school was under investigation. In the Sunnyside cottage, all the windows on the third floor were busted out. Workers at the school then installed plywood doors and iron grillwork over the basement windows in the cottage.

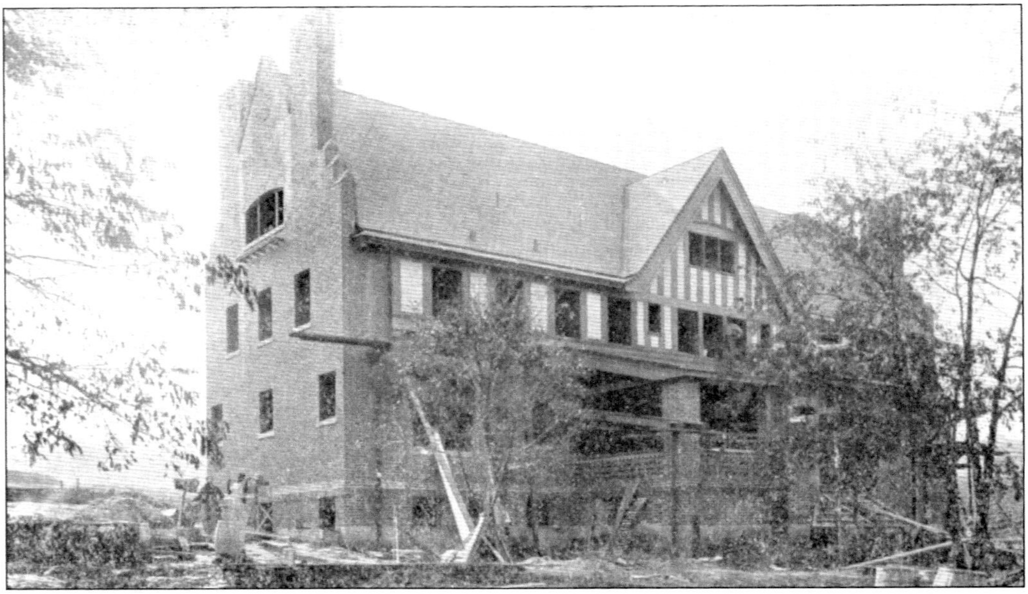

The brick, Tudor-style Cottage No. 5 was built in 1912 in the boys' department. A dominant gabled roof capped the two-story cottage, which also featured two distinctive flush end–mounted chimneys. A porch was located at the entrance. The boy inmates under the Family System were divided into families, or divisions, which were designated by a letter assigned to each cottage group. By 1914, all designations were referred to by the cottage number in the boys' department rather than by family letter. The girls' department was always mentioned separately as one whole group, and the girls' cottages were always given a unique name.

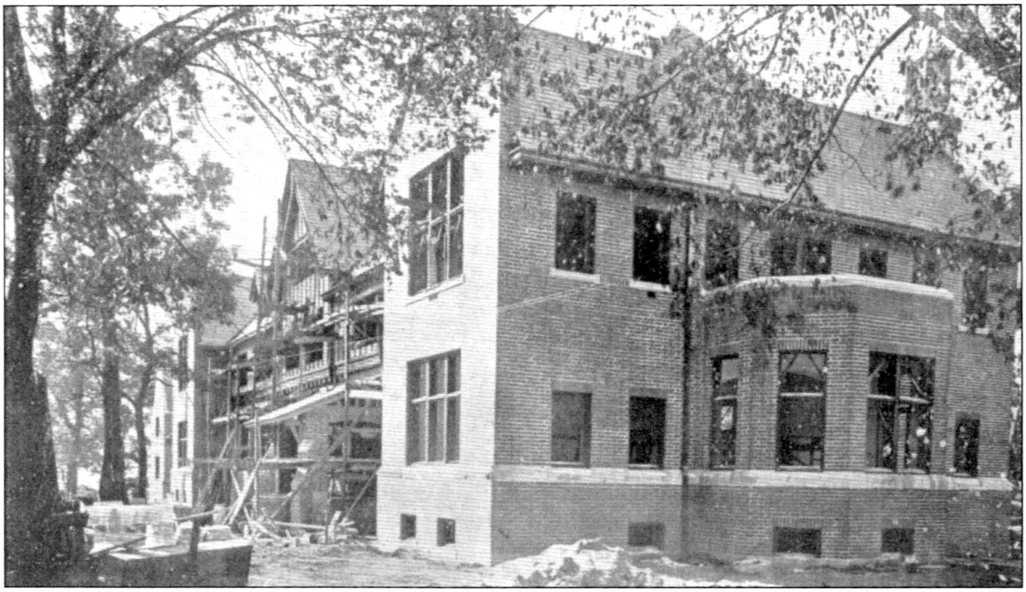

Known as Cottage No. 7 or the dietary building, this structure was erected in 1912. The two-story Tudor styling included two main chimneys, one in front and one in the rear. Another distinctive feature was a well-pronounced bay window on the first floor.

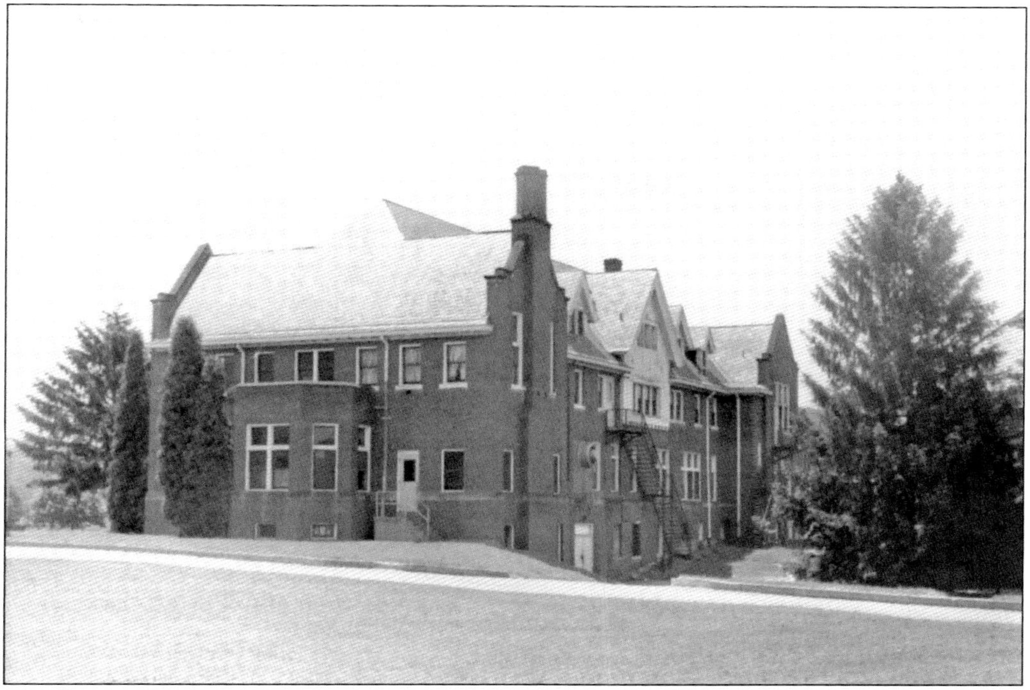

The dietary building was behind the administration building, making it central to the other cottages when it was constructed. Meals were readied in the kitchen of the dietary building and then transported to the other cottages. The building also contained an area for staff members to eat. (Courtesy of Pennsylvania Historical and Museum Commission.)

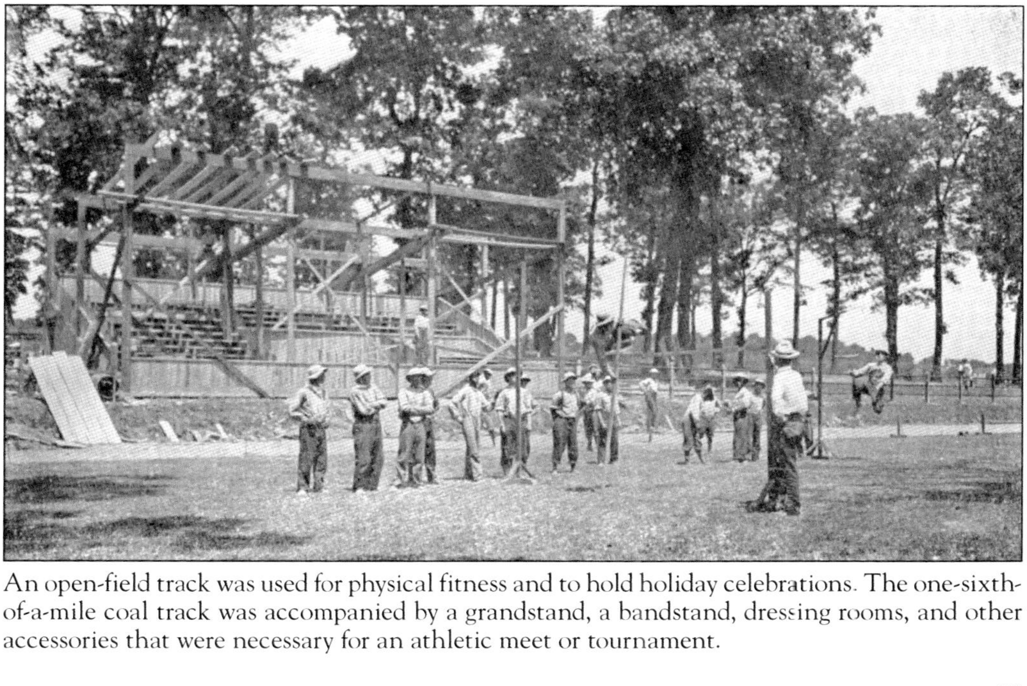

An open-field track was used for physical fitness and to hold holiday celebrations. The one-sixth-of-a-mile coal track was accompanied by a grandstand, a bandstand, dressing rooms, and other accessories that were necessary for an athletic meet or tournament.

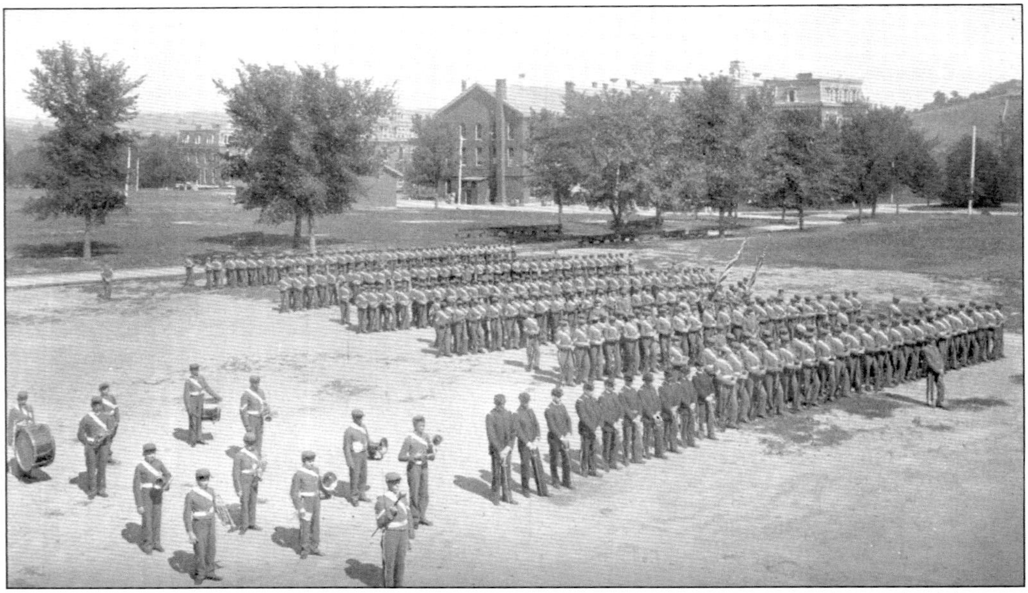

All male students were required to take part in military training if they were physically able. The military unit was on the drill grounds located behind the administration building for 30 minutes every morning except Sundays or during inclement weather. By training boys, it was hoped they would develop into patriotic, physically sound, upright, and disciplined citizens. Boys who had stooped shoulders and slouching gaits upon admittance would often show improvements in appearance, posture, and health in a short time.

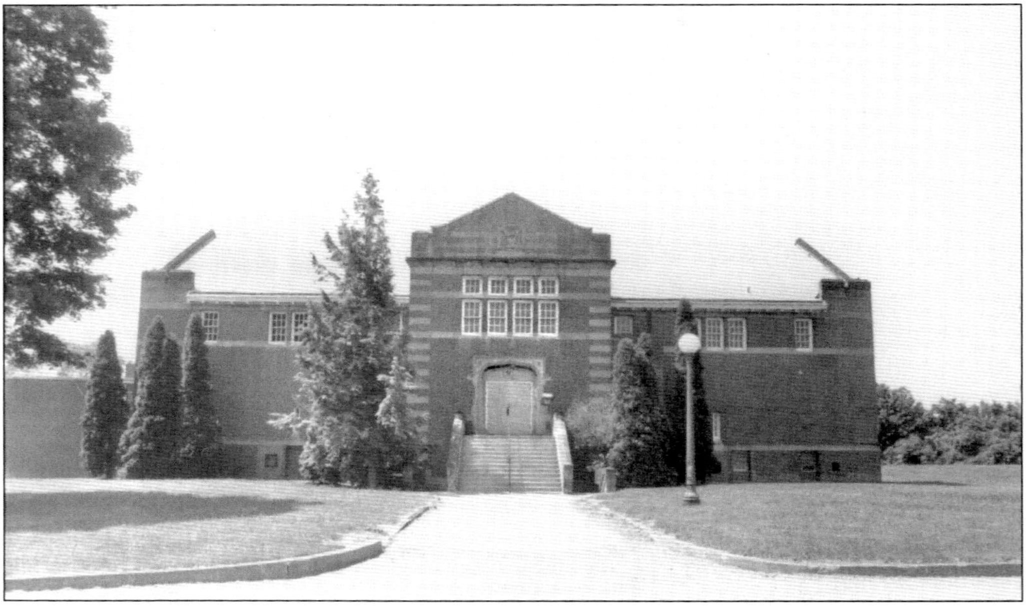

Built in 1911, the gymnasium was designed by architect T.F. Billquist. The Tudor building featured decorative exterior brick walls, four dominant windows in the central facade, and an asphalt-shingled roof. (Courtesy of Pennsylvania Historical and Museum Commission.)

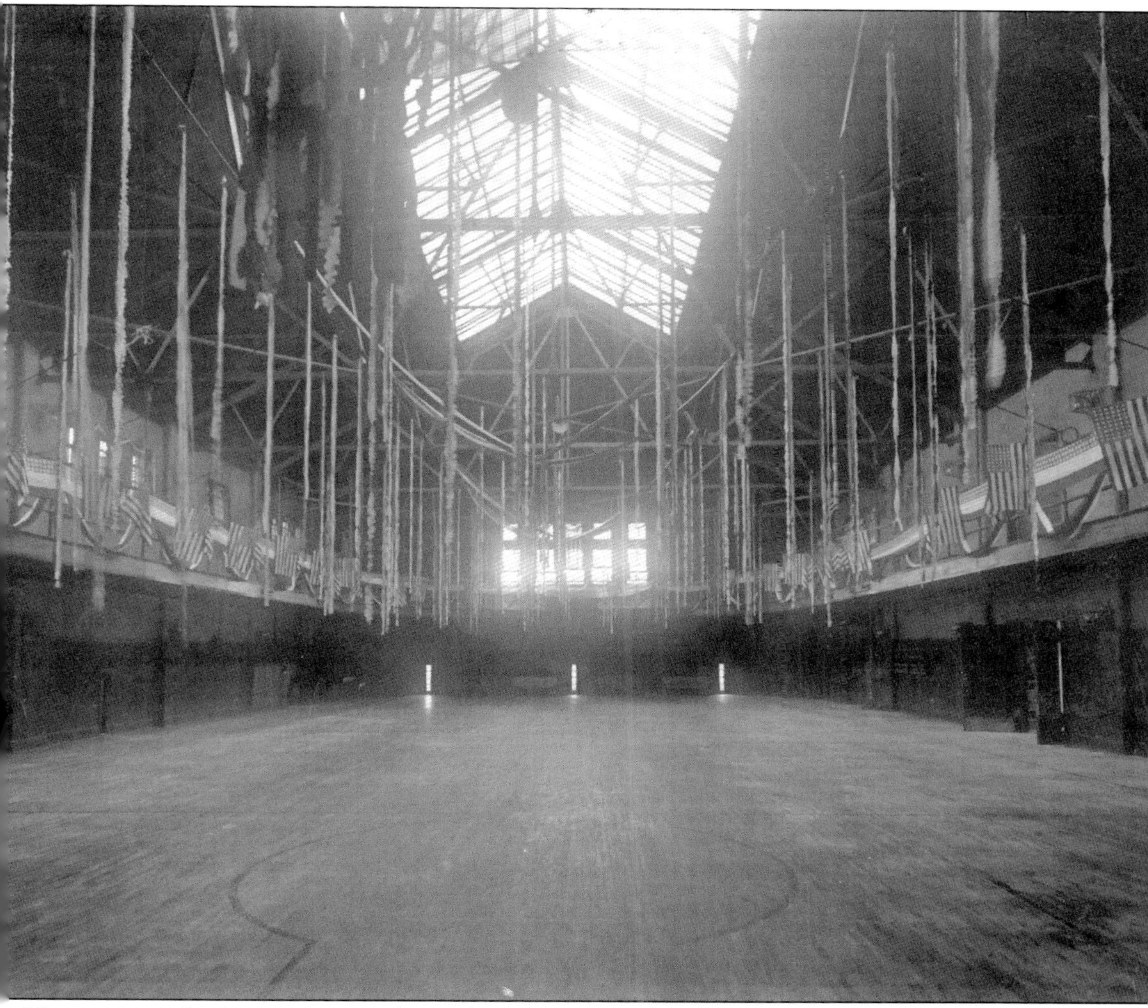

This view inside the gymnasium shows the rather large basketball court. Streamers, banners, and flags hang from the gymnasium ceiling. The skylights in the roof allowed natural light to enter during the day. The gymnasium was 113 feet long and 58 feet wide and had a well-equipped ventilation system. The court was the home of the Morganza Trojans basketball team.

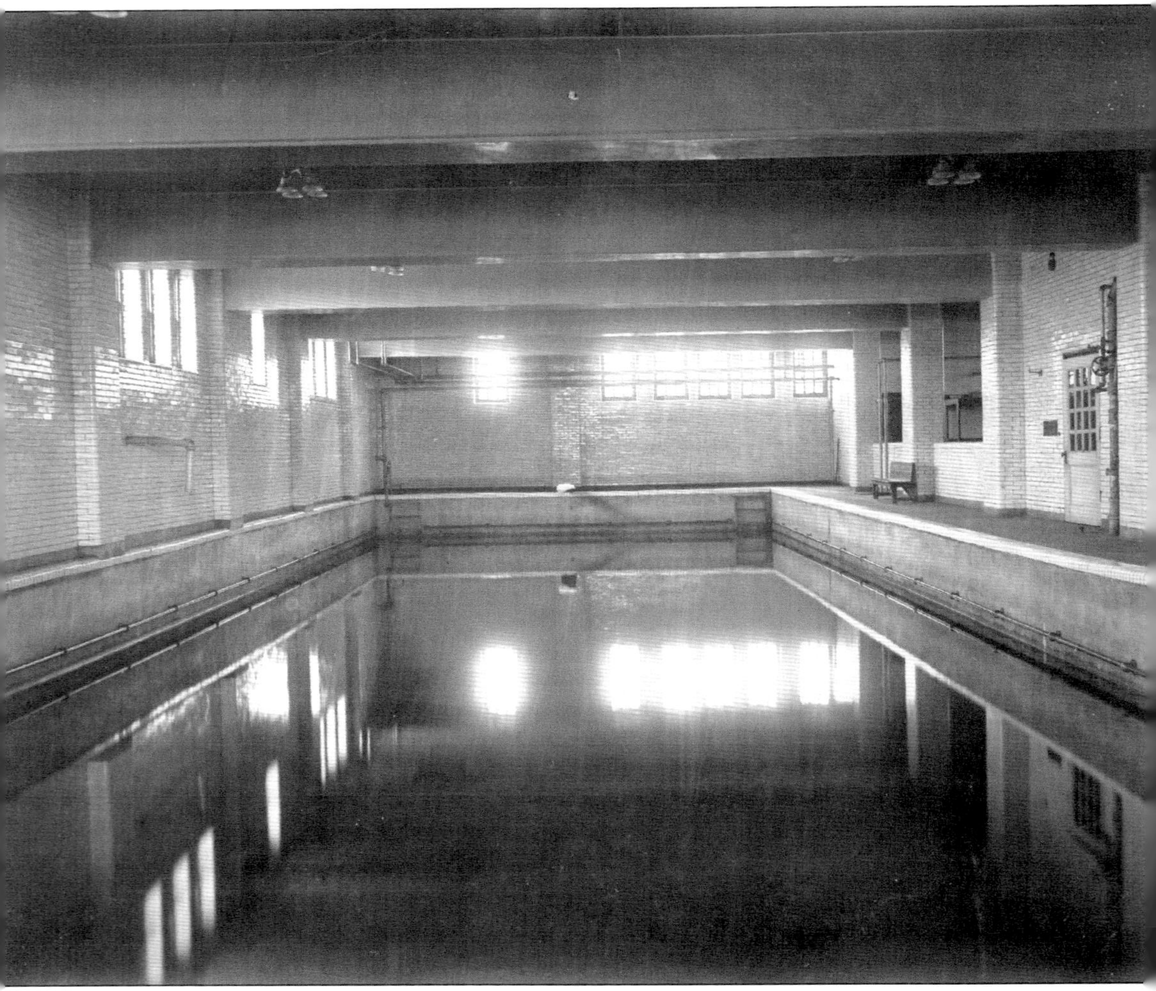

Recreation played an important role at the institution as it helped to promote morality and improved physical and mental health for the boys and girls who lived there. Seen here is the institution's swimming pool, located under the gymnasium. It was large enough to accommodate 100 people, measuring 95 feet long and 31 feet wide with a deepest point of 12 feet.

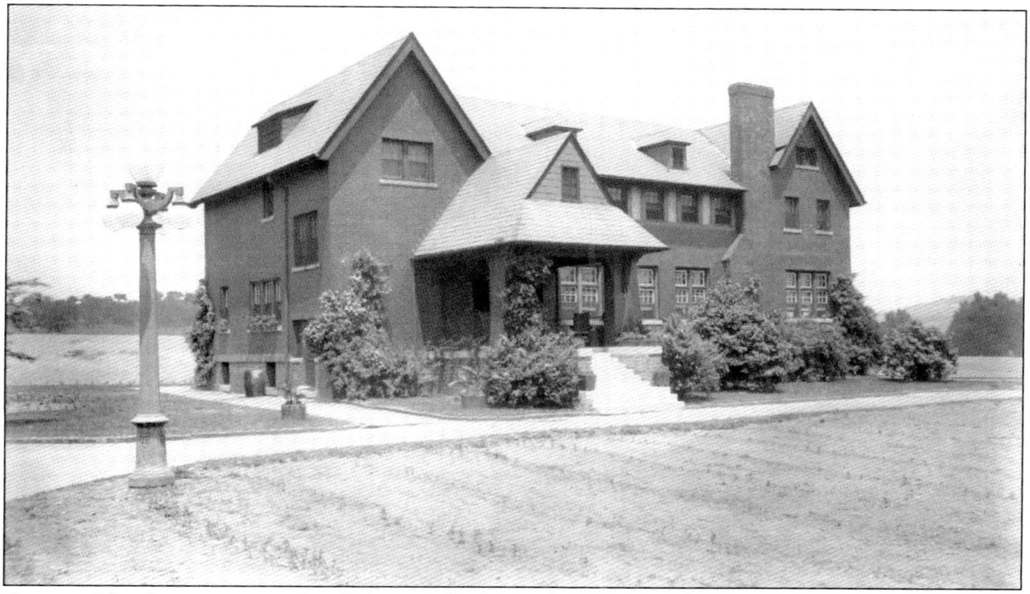

Cottage No. 8, a two-story brick cottage built in the boys' department, was erected in 1913. It had at least four gabled roofs. Other dominant features included a lipped chimney and a well-pronounced porch with an offset front entrance.

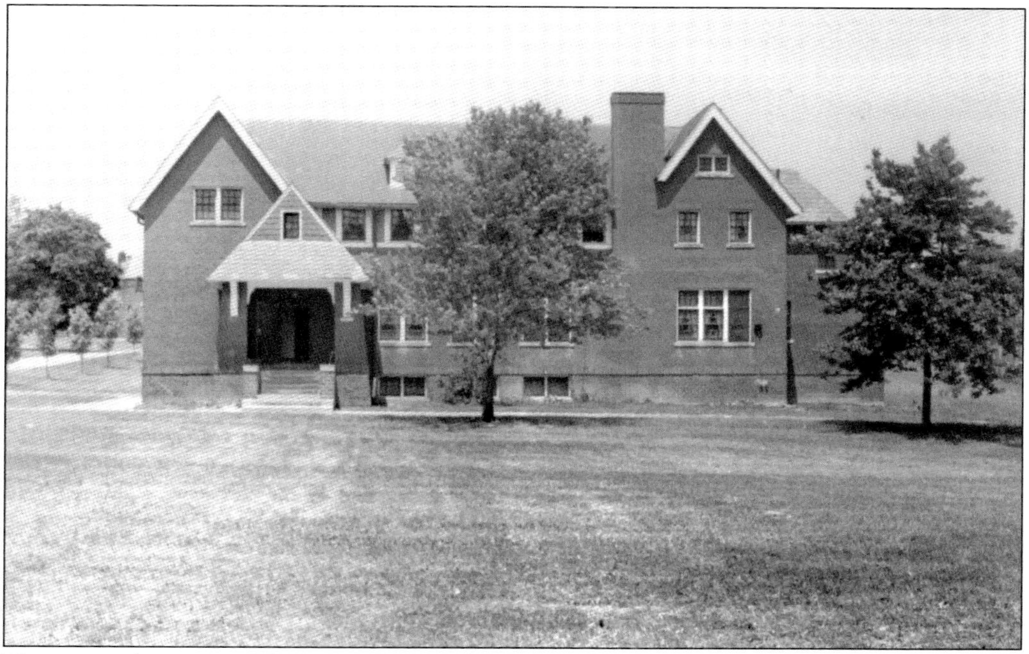

This is another view of Cottage No. 8. Each week, Sunday school was conducted separately in each cottage, including No. 8. Depending on the religious denomination, a minister was secured to teach that religious service. As a rule, each cottage also conducted a prayer meeting on Sunday evenings. Semireligious meetings were held in the cottages once or twice a week in the evenings as well. The meetings were conducted by the boys or girls of that cottage but were supervised by cottage officers. (Courtesy of Pennsylvania Historical and Museum Commission.)

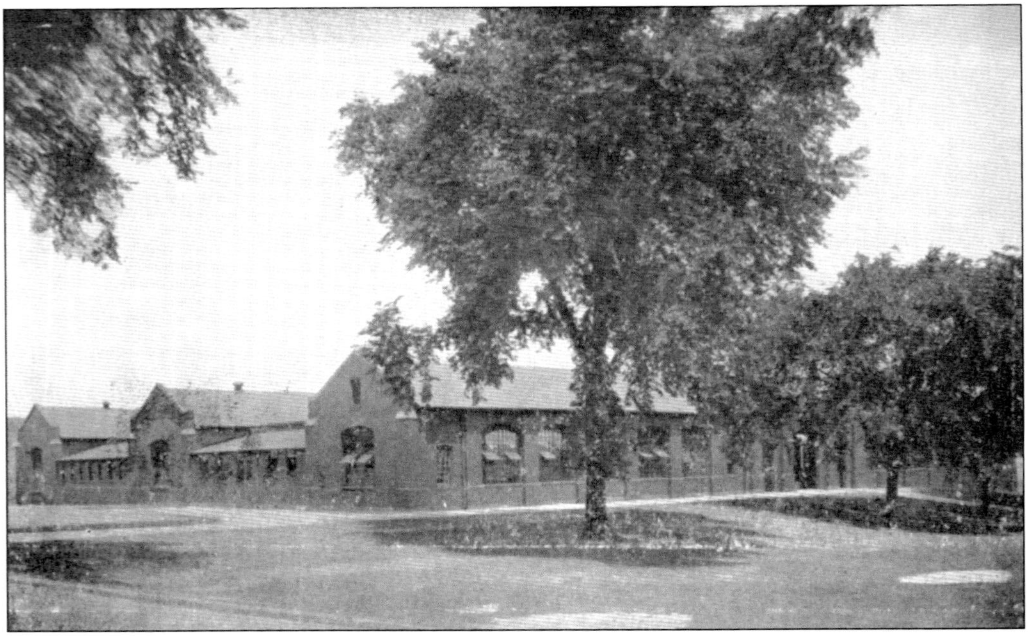

This industrial group of five similar-shaped structures is made up of three single-story buildings connected by smaller segments. Between the trees, an arched opening connected another industrial building. The closest building, completed and opened in 1913, was the home of the carpentry department. The five industrial shops were all completed and in use by 1918.

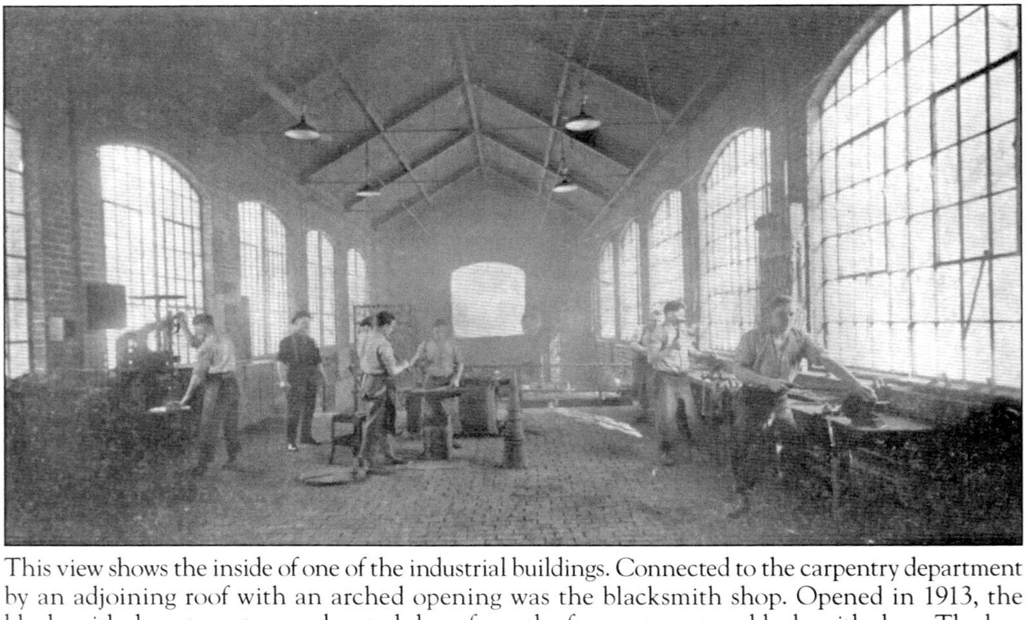

This view shows the inside of one of the industrial buildings. Connected to the carpentry department by an adjoining roof with an arched opening was the blacksmith shop. Opened in 1913, the blacksmith department was relocated there from the former two-story blacksmith shop. The boy at far left operates a drill press, and the boy in the foreground on the right is using a vice.

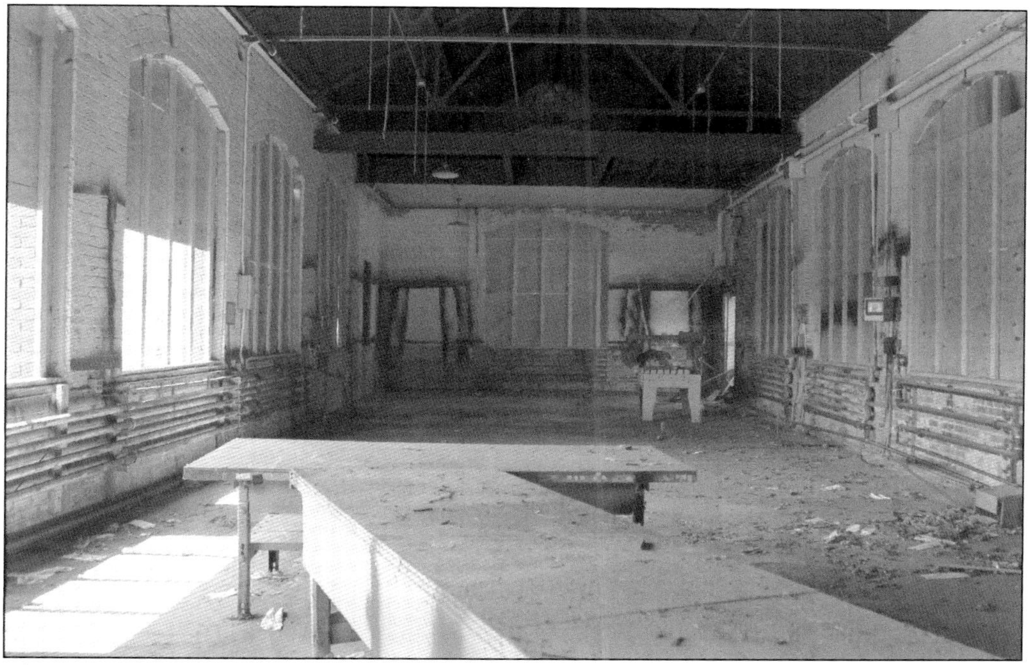

This view inside the carpentry shop was taken shortly before it was razed. Steam pipes are seen running across the wall, wooden tables are in the foreground, and the table in the back right contains a circular saw. (Courtesy of Tracy Tooch.)

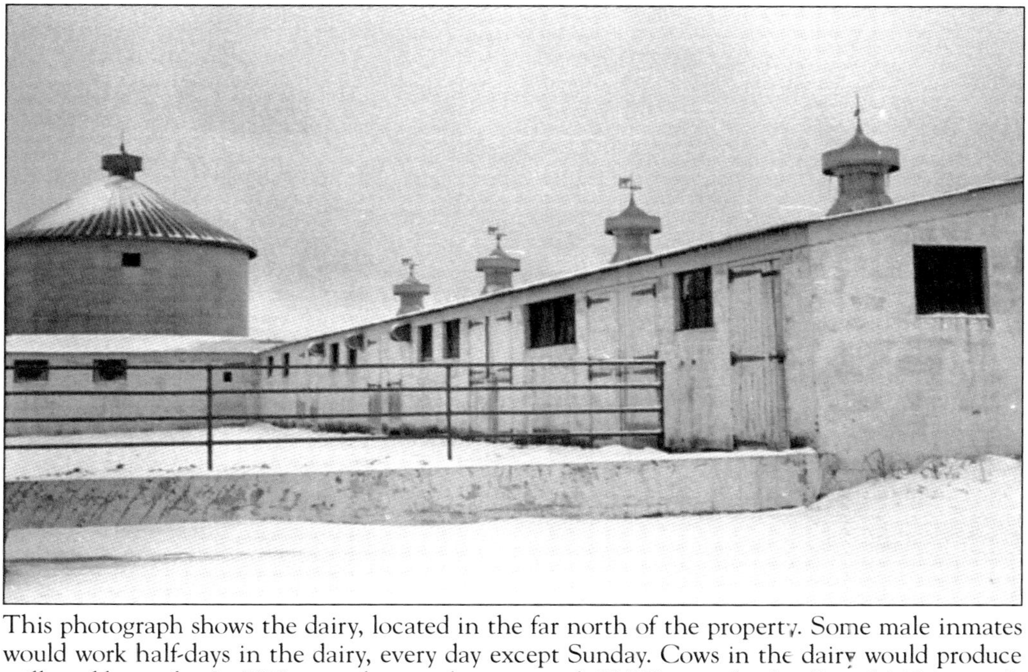

This photograph shows the dairy, located in the far north of the property. Some male inmates would work half-days in the dairy, every day except Sunday. Cows in the dairy would produce milk and butterfat. In 1929, a yearly record was set with 29,725 pounds of milk and 1,184 pounds of butterfat were produced.

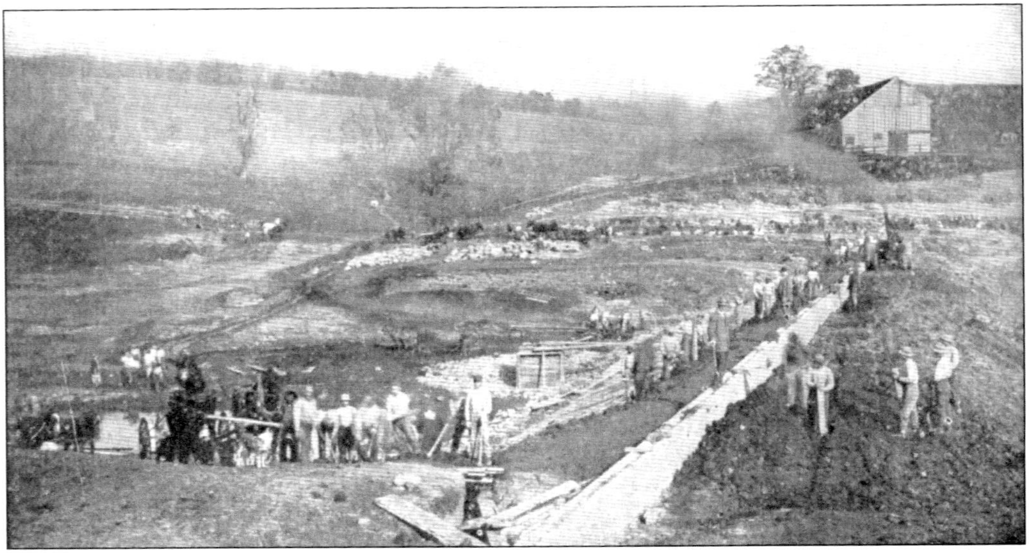

In 1907, the legislature granted $2,500 for improving the water supply. That year, the state department of health also approved plans for the building of a large dam, which took an extensive period of time to construct. After two years of work, about half of the core wall was completed as well as an earthen embankment on either side of the wall. More funds were to be granted in 1909 to complete the dam; however, the appropriation for more funds was not approved until 1911, and most of the money was used to fix existing reservoirs that were built 25–30 years prior. The remaining money was used to complete the dam.

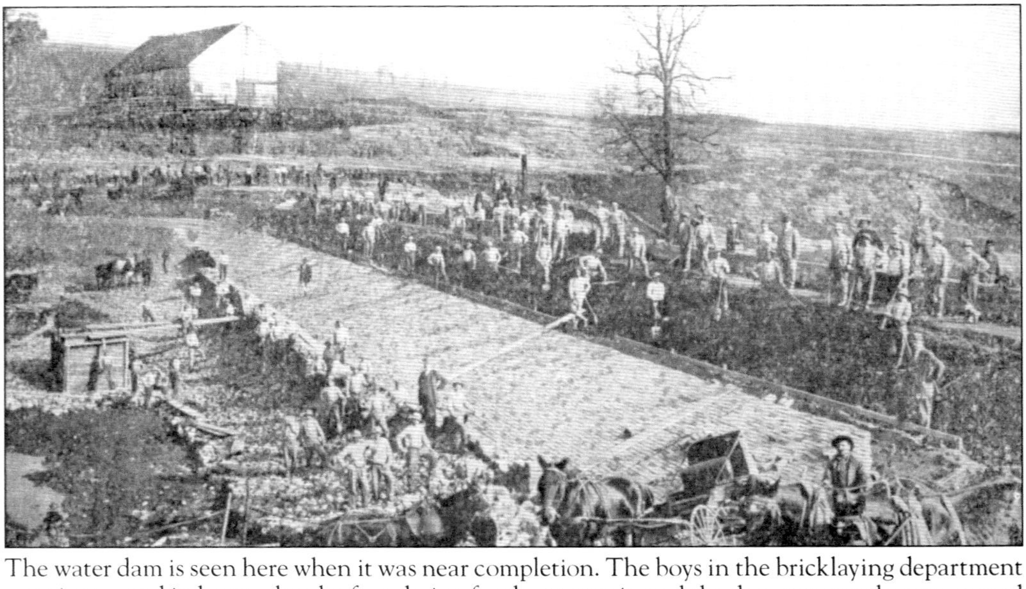

The water dam is seen here when it was near completion. The boys in the bricklaying department were instructed in how to lay the foundation for the reservoir, and the dam was mostly constructed by inmates at the school. The dam's purpose was to collect water for the institution's use.

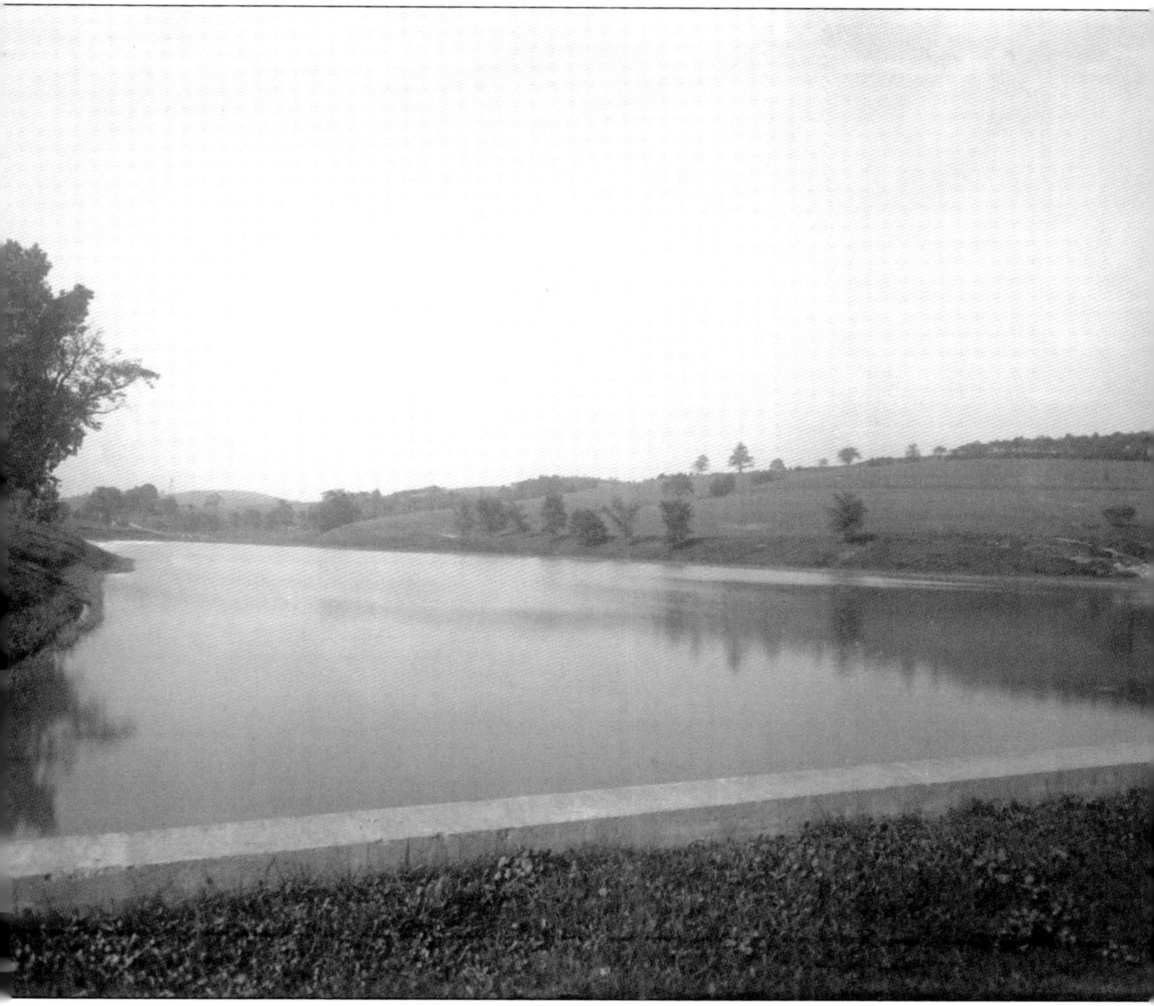

The Morganza water supply seen here was used as an adequate supply of pure drinking water, as it was free of contamination. The school guarded it to make sure that neither pollution nor any other contaminants would affect the water supply. The water supply was tested at frequent intervals and in different places to assure its purity.

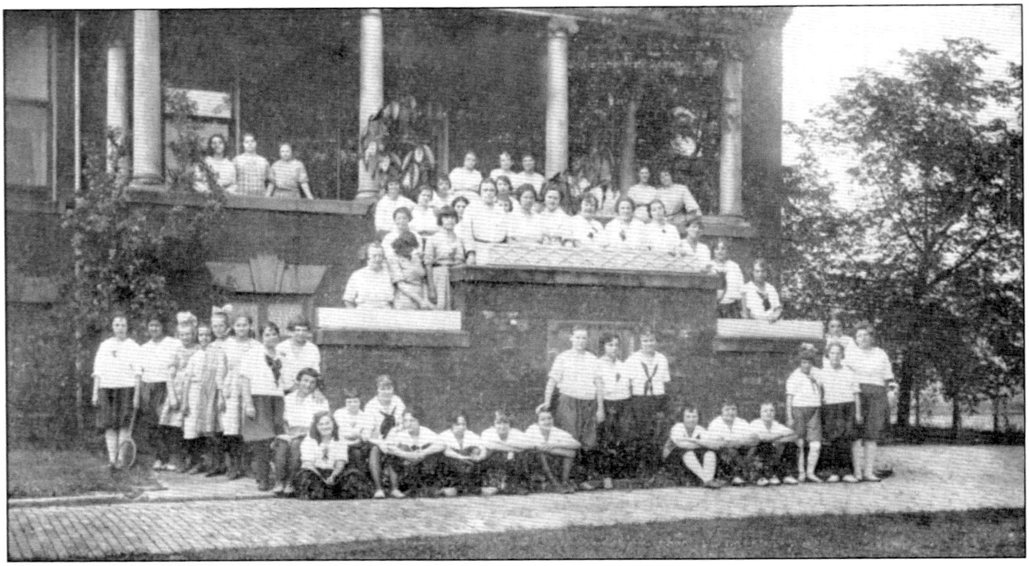

Under Superintendent Penn, girls were permitted to bring their own clothes from home. Also, clothes could be sent to them or they could be made at the institution. An effort was made to make them in a variety of styles and with varied material.

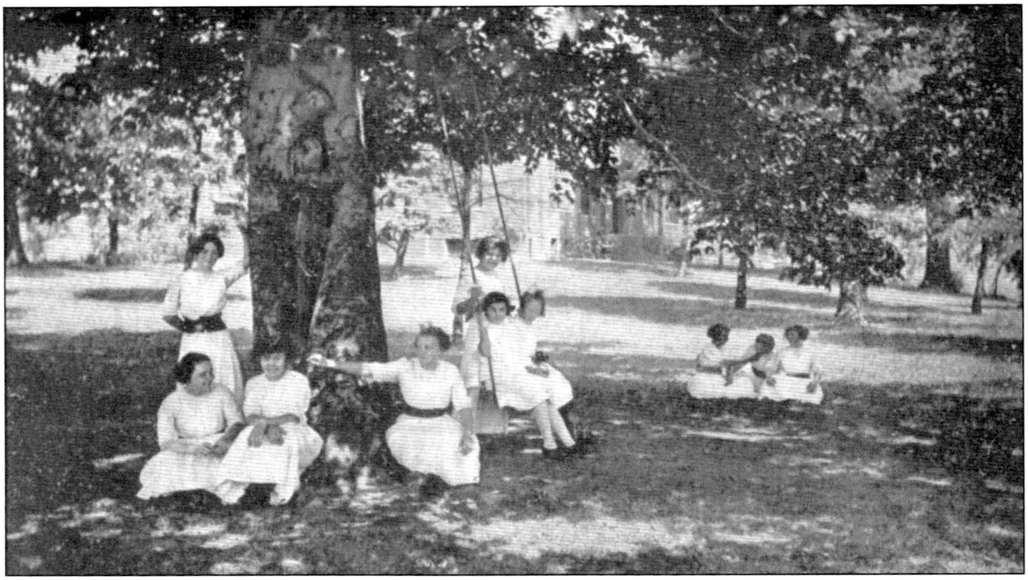

Girls are seen here gathered under a tree on a summer afternoon. Under Superintendent Penn, girls no longer had to wear uniform dresses, which had bonnets and hats of the same exact patterns. One particular hat, which was known as "Noah's Ark," was abolished because it was not modern in design.

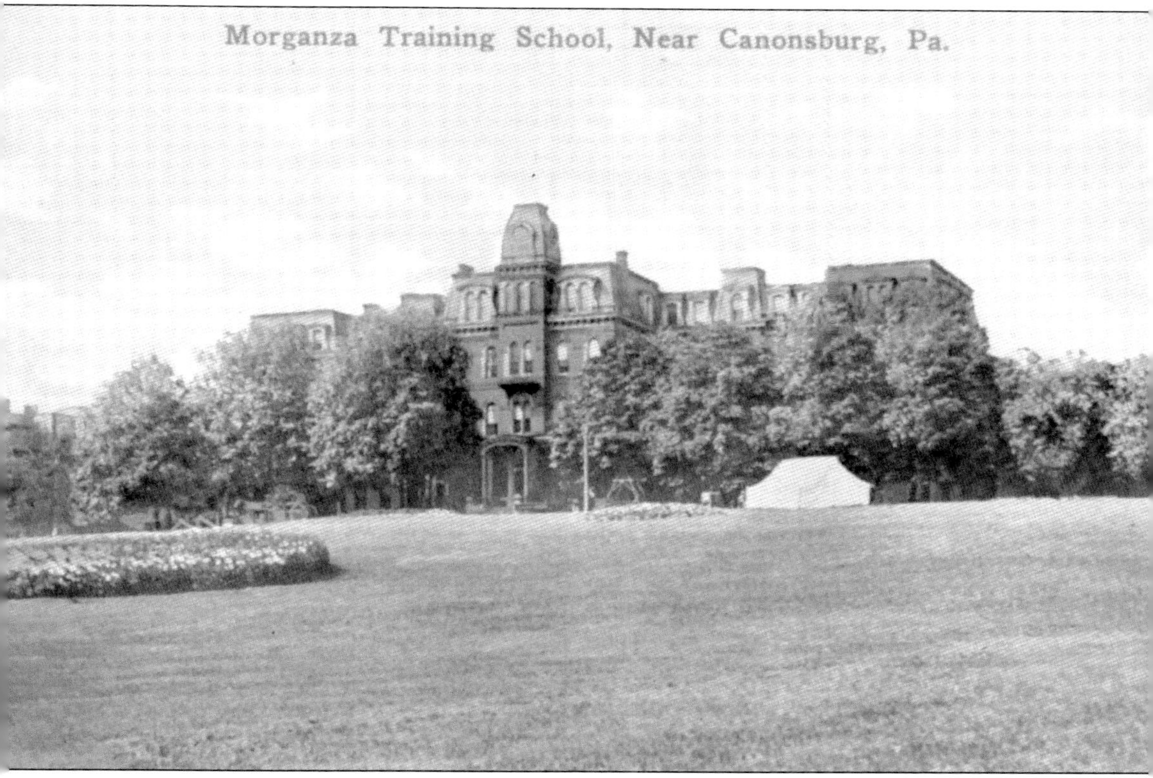

This non-postmarked postcard showcases the first administration building. In 1912, the name of the institute changed to the Pennsylvania Training School, and this postcard represents the change, as it is titled "Morganza Training School." The shrubs seen at left in the postcard are arranged in a circle, as they remained for the entire lifespan of the institution.

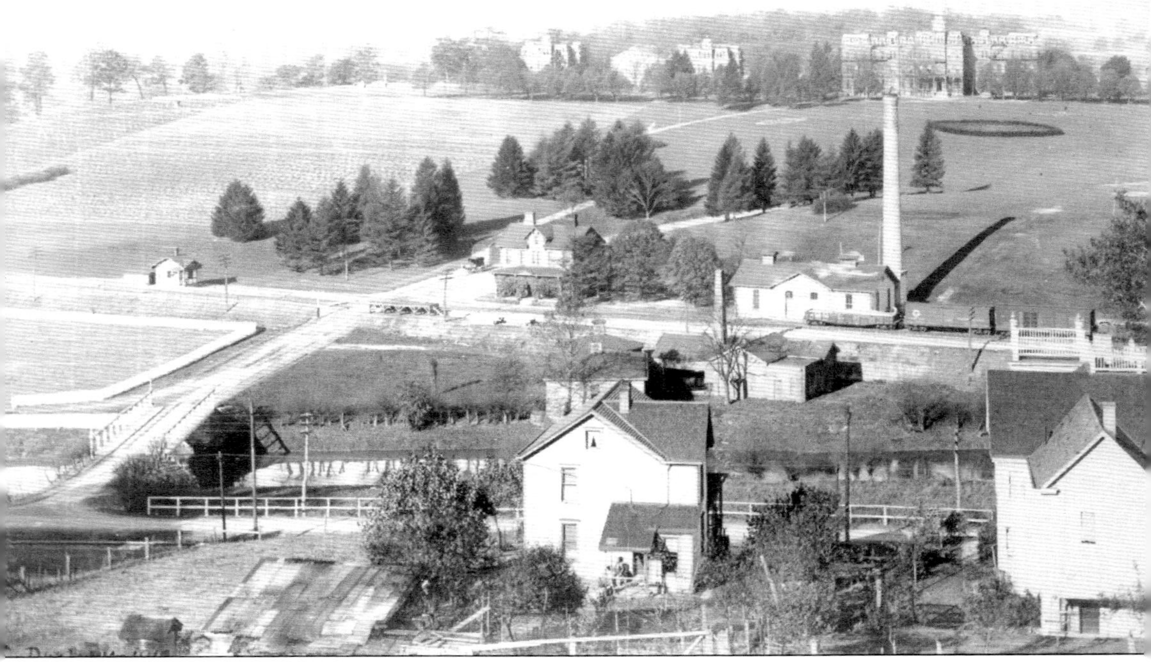

This photograph was taken in 1912 by photographer Force C. Dunlevy. The back of the photograph reads, "Pennsylvania Training School at Morganza Pa a mile east of Canonsburg Pa showing main building other building R.R. Station pump house on Chartiers Creek, electric station for school Pittsburg, Pike and Trolley Road in front of houses in foreground looking north taken in 1912.—F. C. Dunlevy."

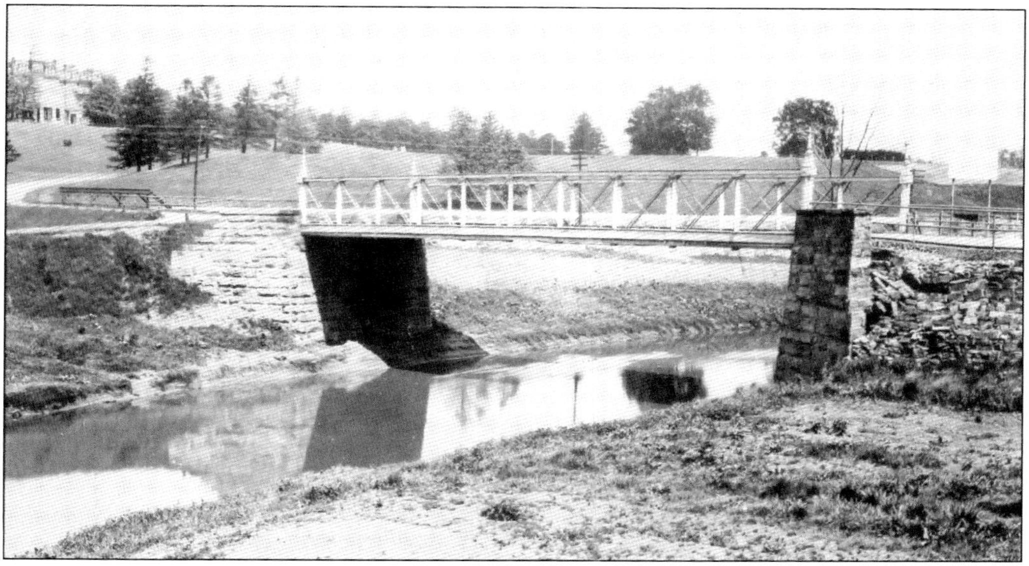

In 1920, Johns Robb Jr., the president of the board of managers, referred to the buildings at the entryway along the bank of Chartiers Creek as "unsightly." As a result, all the structures along the creek were razed, including the old powerhouse, pump house, and filter house. This photograph, taken in 1920, shows where the removed structures had been, on the other side of the creek. (Courtesy of Pennsylvania State Archives.)

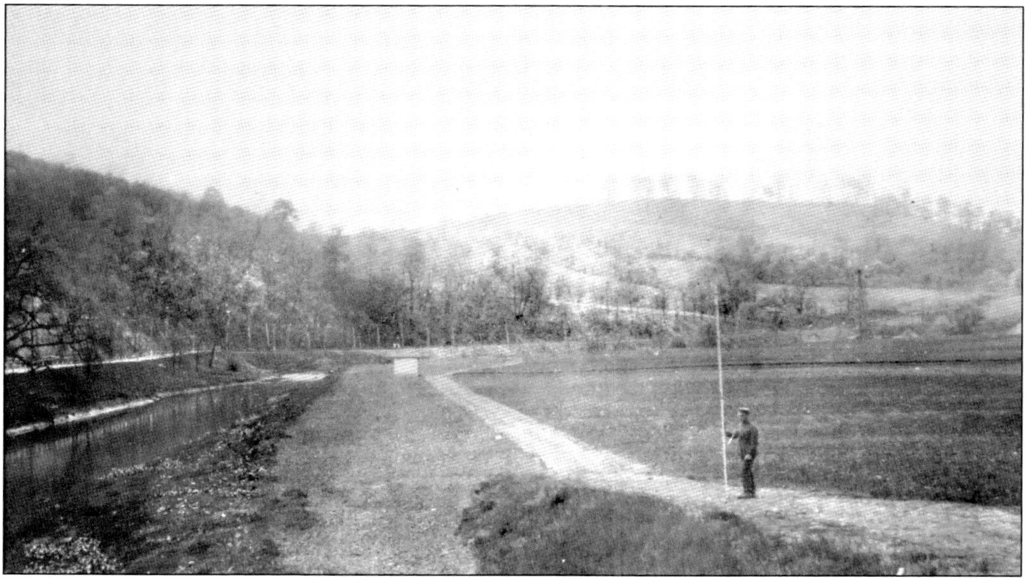

This south-facing 1920 photograph shows a man holding a surveying rod on the roadway along the edge of the facility. Chartiers Creek is on the left, and an open field once used for gardening is on the right. In 1950, approval was given by the board of trustees for the erection of a joint sewage disposal plant that would serve Canonsburg, Houston, and Morganza. The plant was built in 1961 at the end of this field. (Courtesy of Pennsylvania State Archives.)

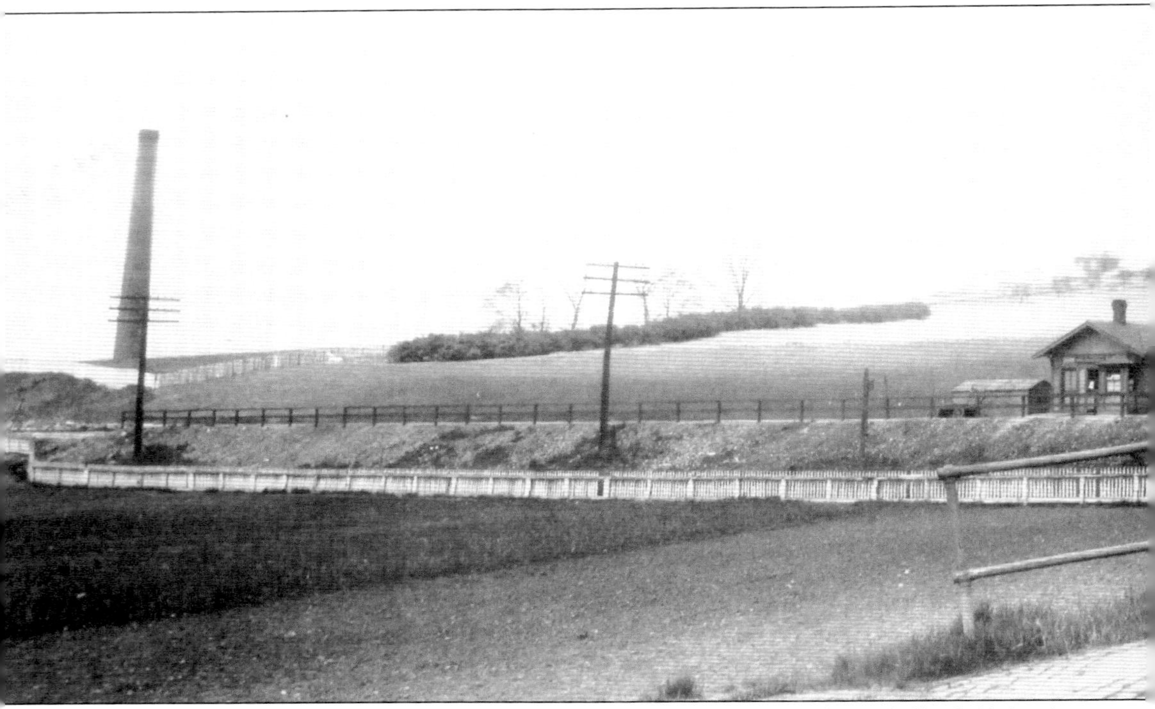

This panoramic view of the front entryway in 1920 shows the smokestack (far left) for the new electric powerhouse. When installed in 1906, the powerhouse provided electricity to just the girls' main building and the administration building. In 1910, two direct-connected dynamos were installed to provide power to the entire institution through underground cables. In the center of the two-page spread is the Morganza train station and post office. The train station was a single-

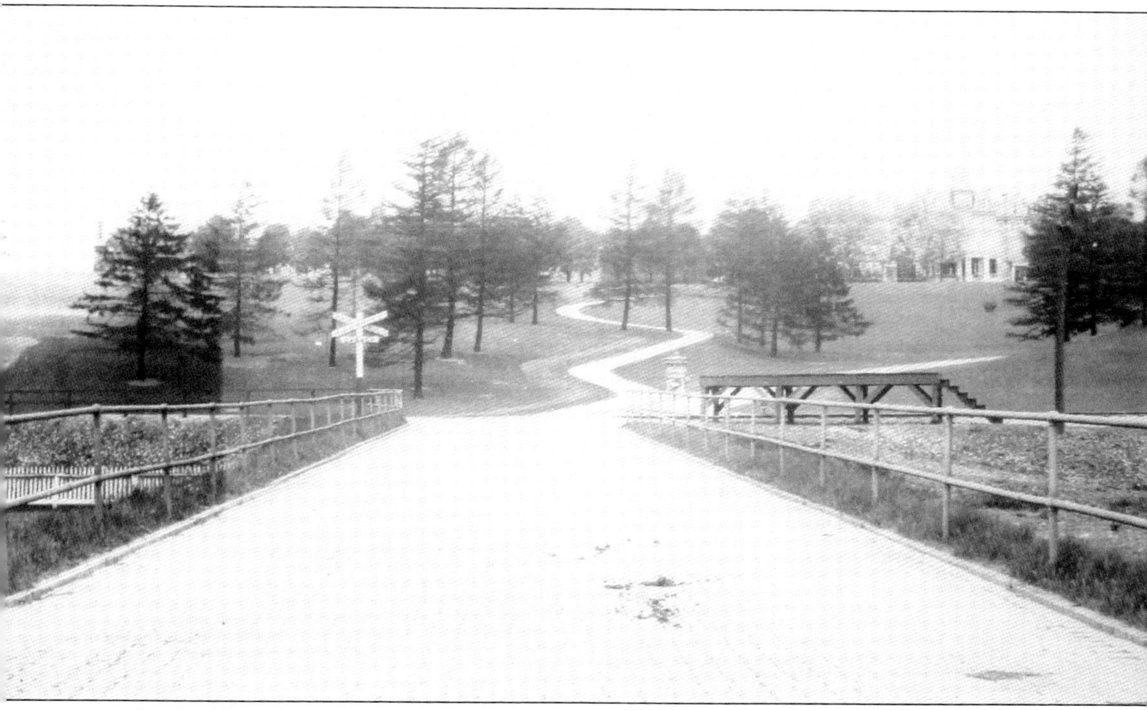

room wooden building that was also used as the post office for the roughly 1,500 residents. In July 1943, an attempt was made to change the name of the post office from Morganza to Chartiers to disassociate the Morgan name from the school. However, residents of Chartiers township and the school board spoke out against it. In 1946, the one-roomed station caught fire and burned down. (Courtesy of Pennsylvania State Archives.)

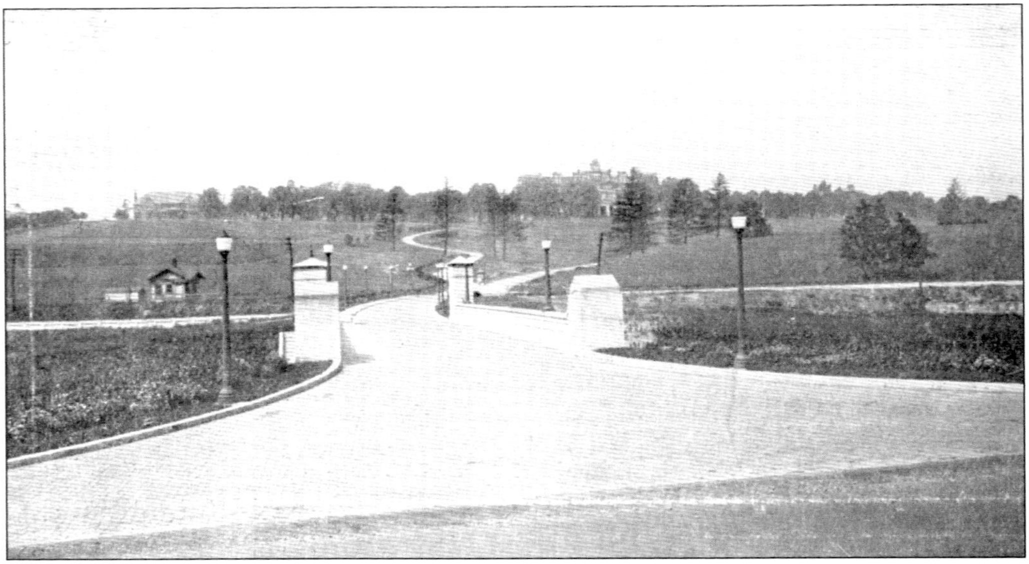

A concrete bridge was built across Chartiers Creek in 1921; it replaced the existing bridge with a much sturdier one capable of supporting heavy motor vehicles. The boys from the institution were instructed to help excavate the abutments that supported the bridge. The cost of the bridge was estimated at $20,000.

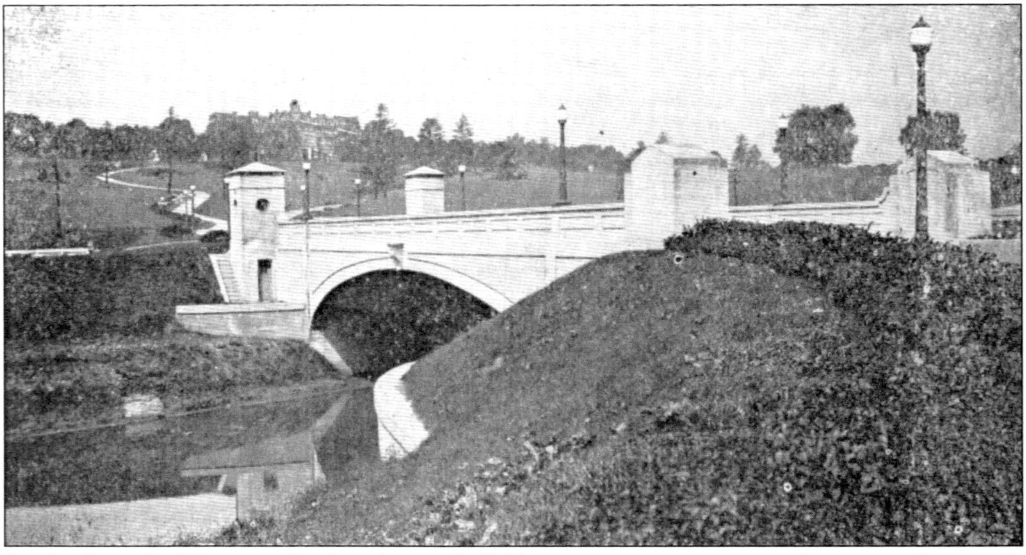

At the far end of the entry bridge, the south (left) concrete post was a guard post, seen here with a staircase leading down to a concrete platform. A door at the base and at the entry side of the bridge leads to a small room at the top with a single window in it. The guard post was eventually closed and bricked in.

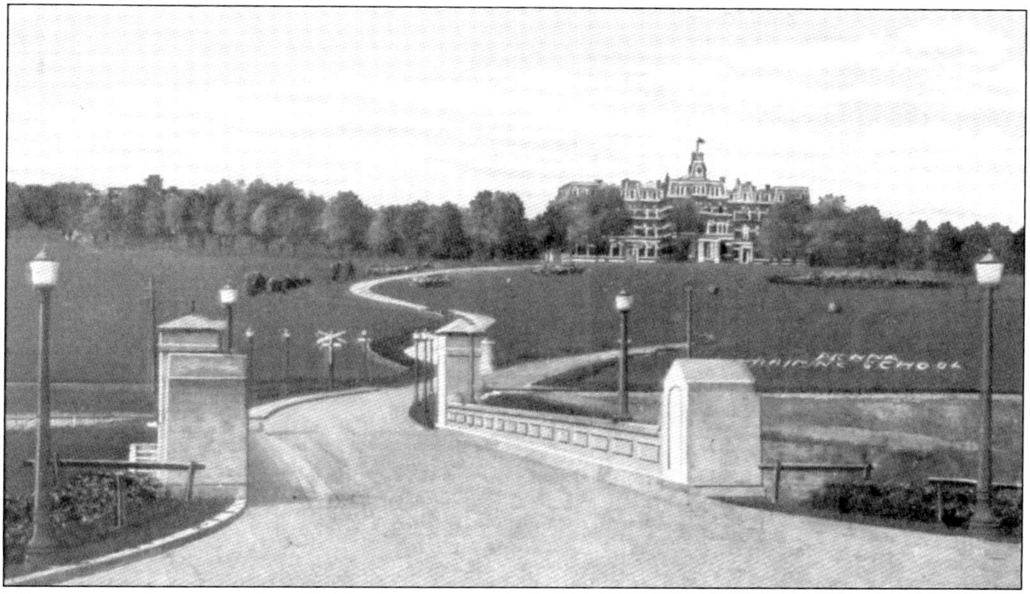

This postcard, postmarked 1945, showcases the original administration building. During this time, the institution's name was the Pennsylvania Training School. The original administration building burned to the ground 18 years prior to the card's postmark.

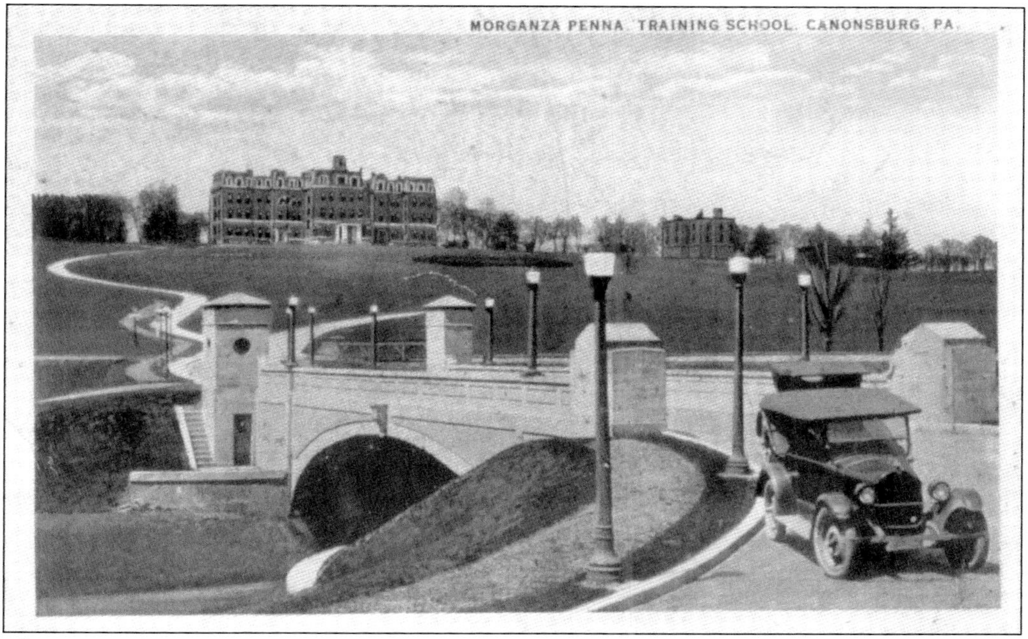

This postcard, produced in the 1920s, shows two cars of that era in front of the bridge. The message on the back reads, "This doesn't look like it does here now as the lawn is all flowers shrubs and trees. This only shows two of the 3-some odd buildings. That front lawn, is a dream now." The card message references the mansard-roofed administration building and the dormitories around it. At this time, two of the four original dormitories had been replaced by two modern cottages.

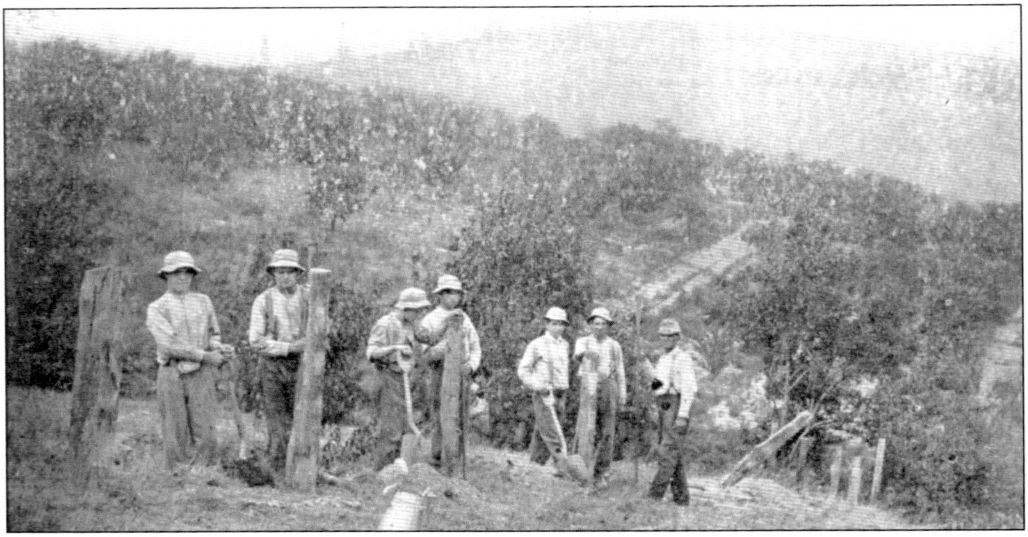

Boys are seen here building a fence along a hillside. In 1920, an extensive amount of fencing was done on former farmlands, separating them from "waste lands." Much of the fencing was completed by 1922, according to the school's biennial report.

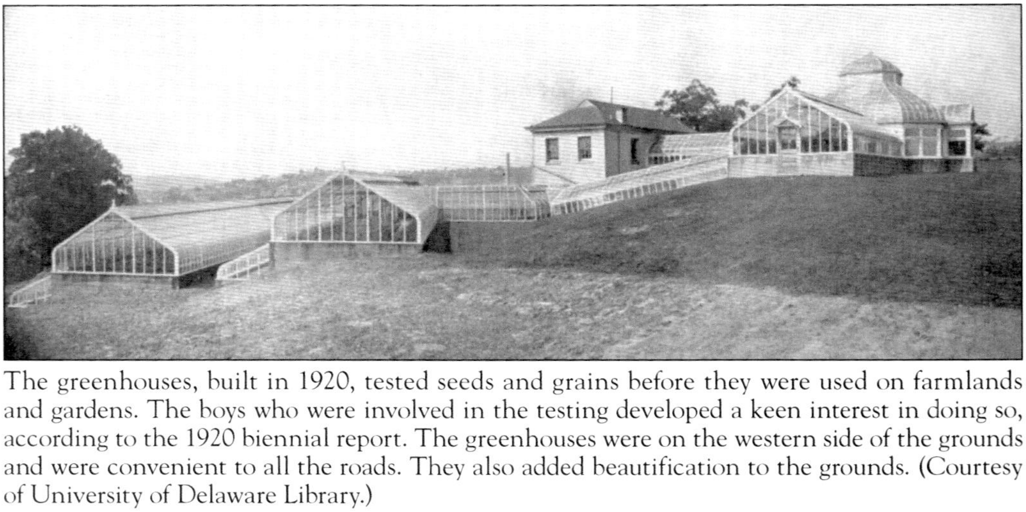

The greenhouses, built in 1920, tested seeds and grains before they were used on farmlands and gardens. The boys who were involved in the testing developed a keen interest in doing so, according to the 1920 biennial report. The greenhouses were on the western side of the grounds and were convenient to all the roads. They also added beautification to the grounds. (Courtesy of University of Delaware Library.)

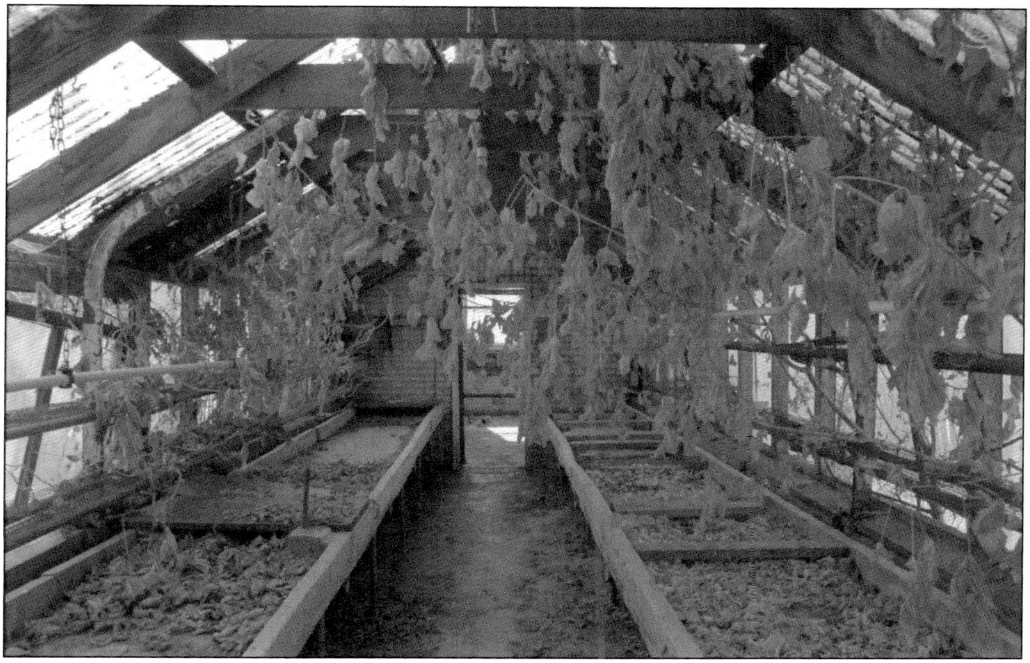

This interior view of a greenhouse shows the arrangement of plant tables on each side. Prior to the building of the greenhouses in 1920, a group of greenhouses was located behind the administration building to the north of the boys' schoolhouse and industrial shops. Those greenhouses, built around the time the school opened, were razed by 1925. (Courtesy of Adam Ryan.)

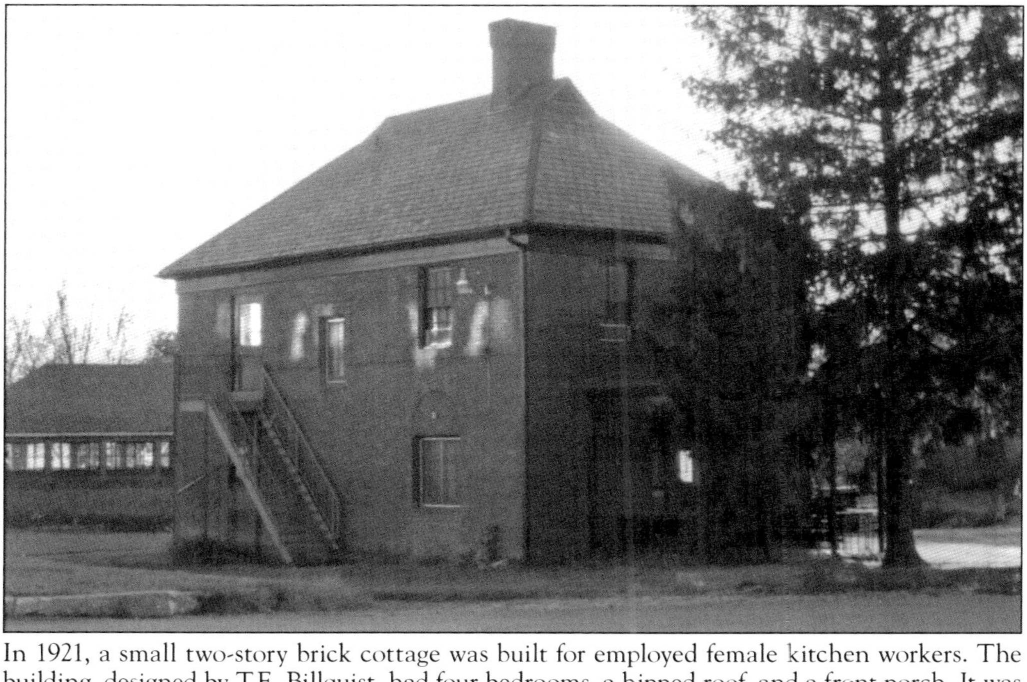

In 1921, a small two-story brick cottage was built for employed female kitchen workers. The building, designed by T.E. Billquist, had four bedrooms, a hipped roof, and a front porch. It was designated as an annex building for Cottage No. 7. (Courtesy of Diane Hickman.)

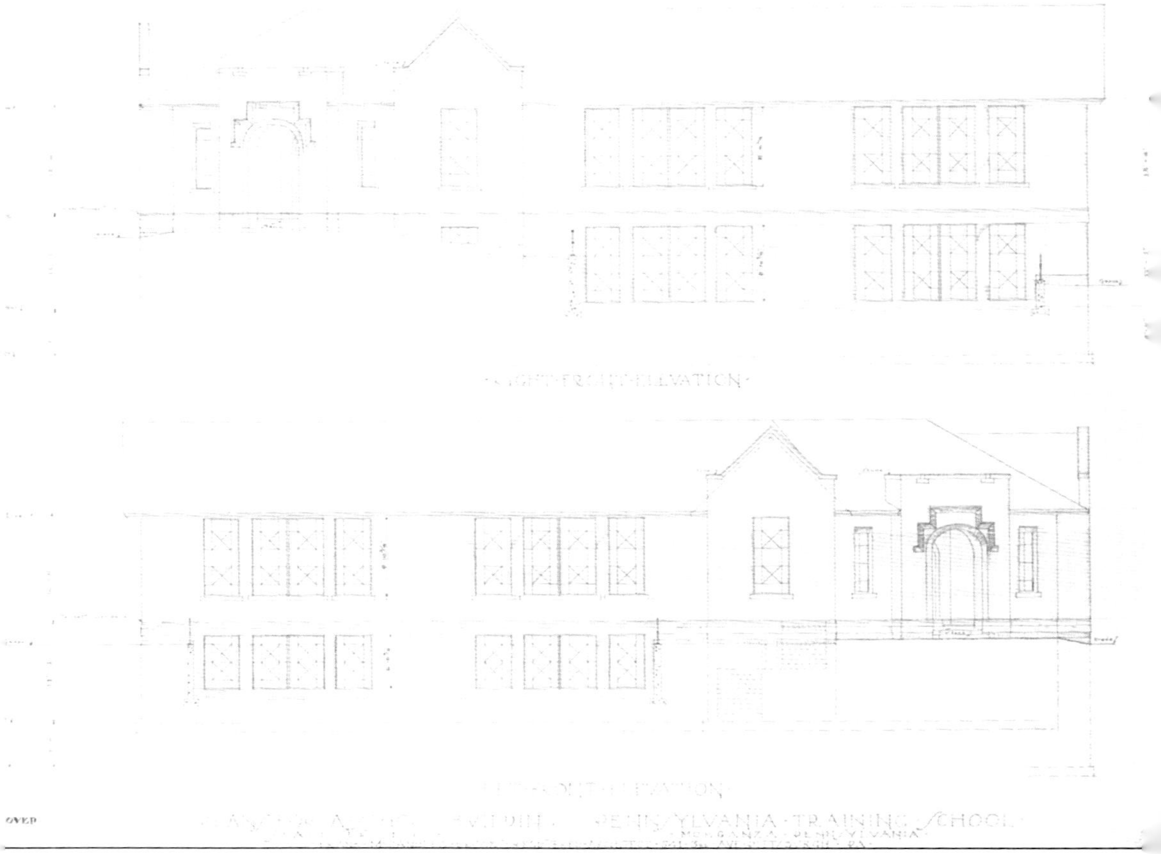

A new schoolhouse for girls was erected in 1926. It, and the laundry building constructed at the same time, was both modern in design and equipment. The schoolhouse contained four classrooms, a gymnasium in the basement, and other rooms for activities on the girls' side of the campus. (Courtesy of Carnegie Mellon University Architecture Archives.)

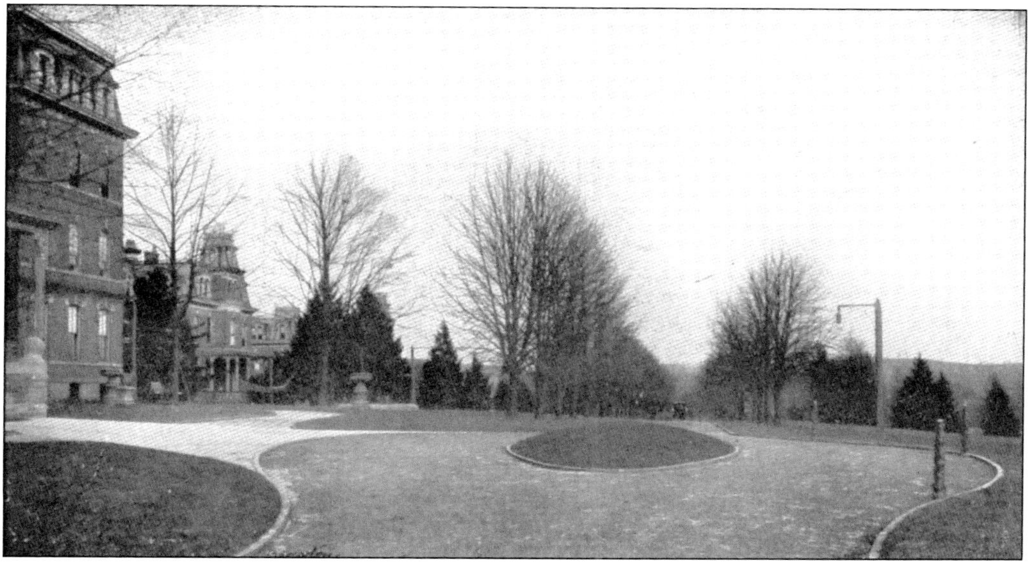

This photograph was taken in front of the administration building facing a tree-lined road. The road led to the girls' department, which was separate from the boys' department. The road connecting the two departments was laid with brick in 1906.

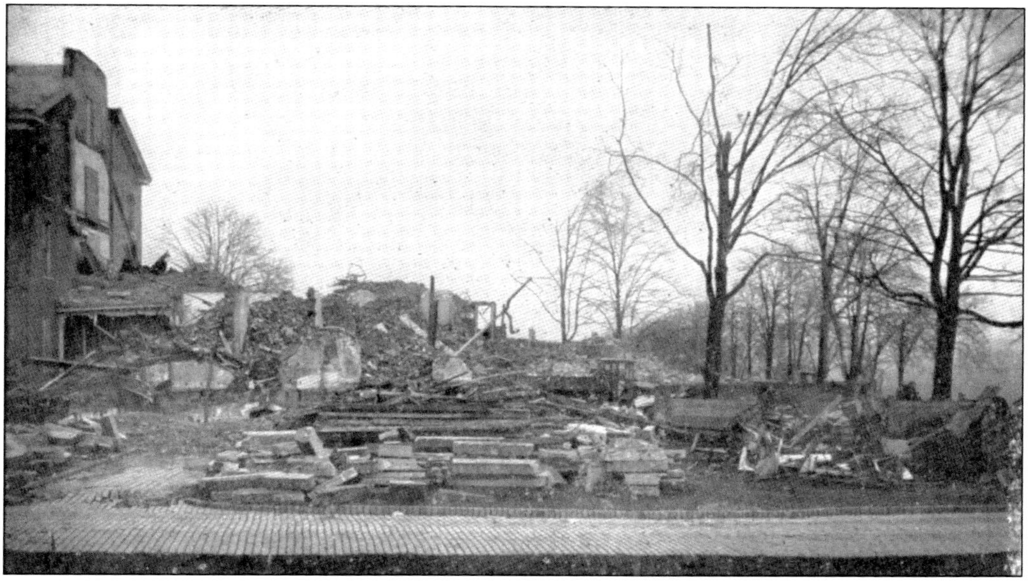

On February 11, 1927, an enormous fire destroyed the administration building. More than 10 fire departments responded to the blaze. Only one of the 750 inmates was injured. The boy was treated for a gash to his left foot.

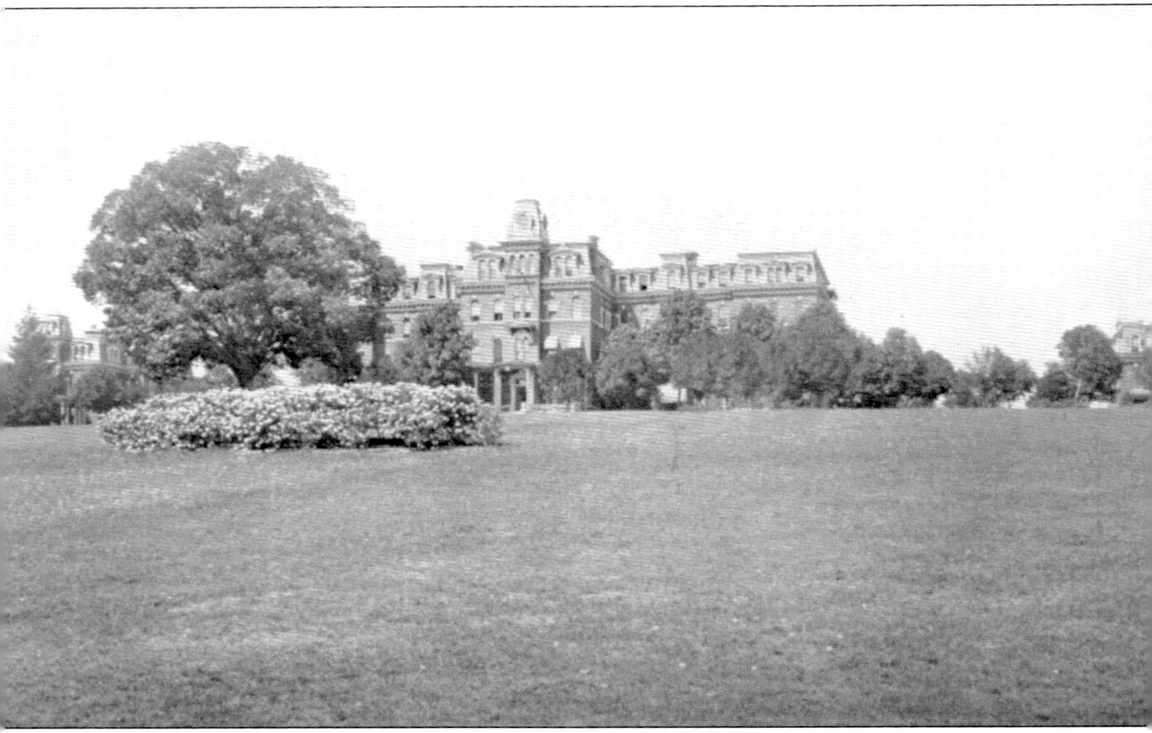

The cornerstone in the administration building contained copies of newspapers, including the July 16, 1873, issue of the *Presbyterian Banner*, of Pittsburgh, and the July 10, 1873, edition of the *Genius of Liberty*, of Uniontown. The paper contained a notification of Horace Greely's nomination for president on the Democratic ticket. Issues of the *Allegheny Evening Mail*, the *Pittsburgh Post*, the *Pittsburgh Leader*, the *Canonsburg Herald*, the *Pittsburgh Evening Chronicle*, the *Pittsburgh Post Gazette*, the *United Presbyterian*, and a German newspaper printed in Pittsburgh were also found. The cornerstone also contained legislative books, state reports, financial and personal statements of the House of Refuge, controllers' reports of Allegheny County from 1872, the city directories of Pittsburgh and Allegheny, many old coins, and newspaper clippings.

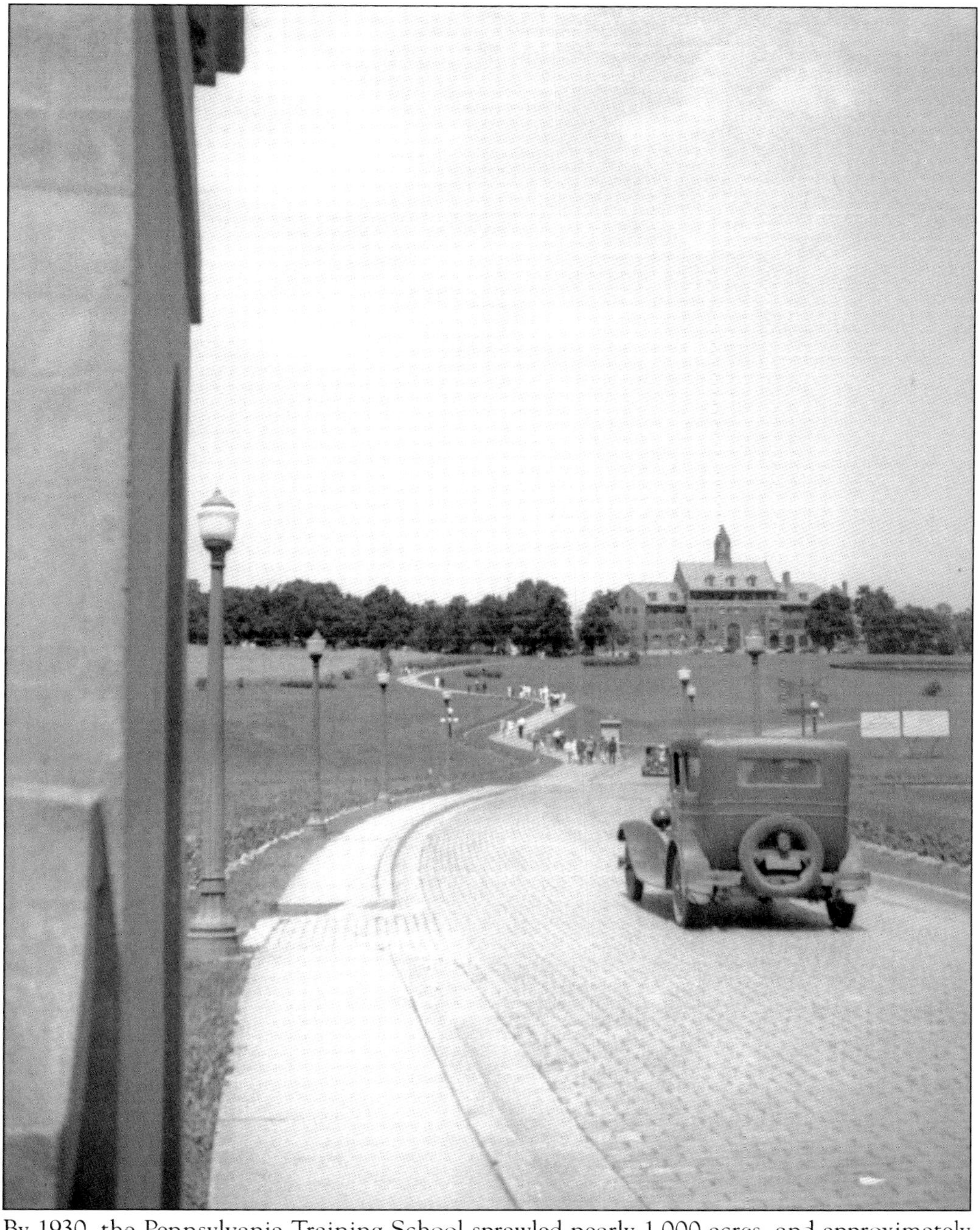

By 1930, the Pennsylvania Training School sprawled nearly 1,000 acres, and approximately 800 boys and girls lived there. The school had reached its highest population. In addition, a new administration building was opened. The estimated value of the property at this time was $3,534,598. (Courtesy of Gary Mohler.)

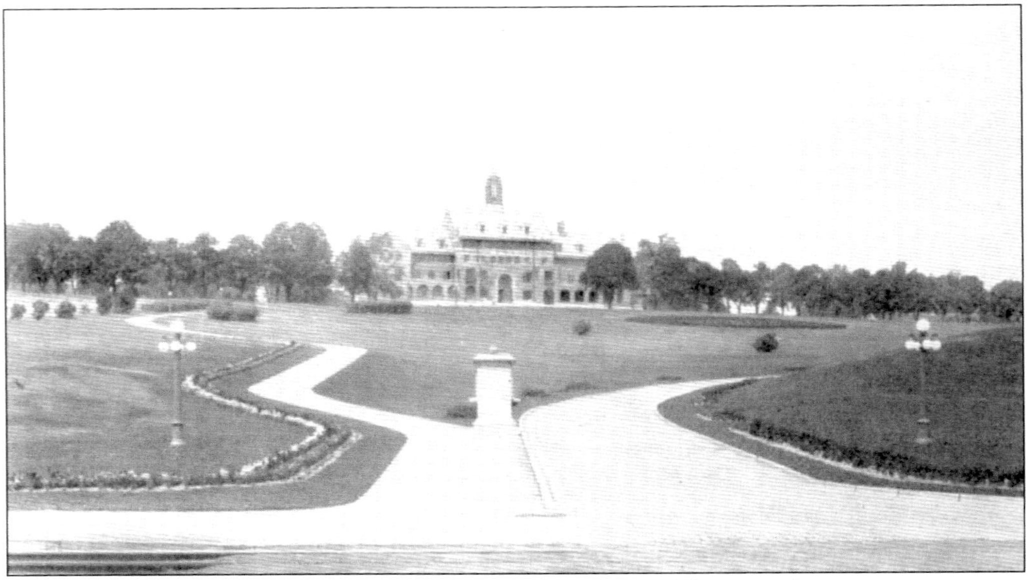

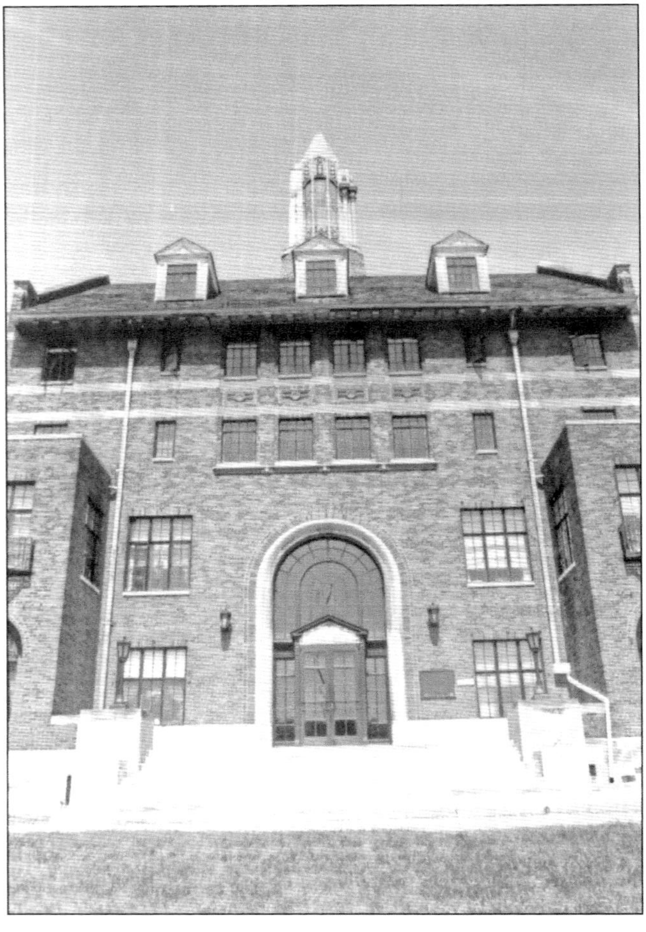

The new administration building was erected in 1929 at a cost of $325,000 on the same site as the first administration building, which was destroyed by the 1927 fire. The new building, which was fireproof, was divided into three main sections: the extreme north wing, the first three floors of which contained the superintendent's living quarters; the central portion and the south wing, which were mostly used for administrative offices; and the remainder of the building, including the entire fourth floor, which were executive apartments.

The imposing main entrance pediment was constructed of glass surrounded by a decorative iron frame. Limestone steps protruded from the entrance. Between the eight grouped windows above the door were concrete Art Deco blocks. Three distinctive pediment dormers protruded from the gable roof. (Courtesy of Pennsylvania Historical and Museum Commission.)

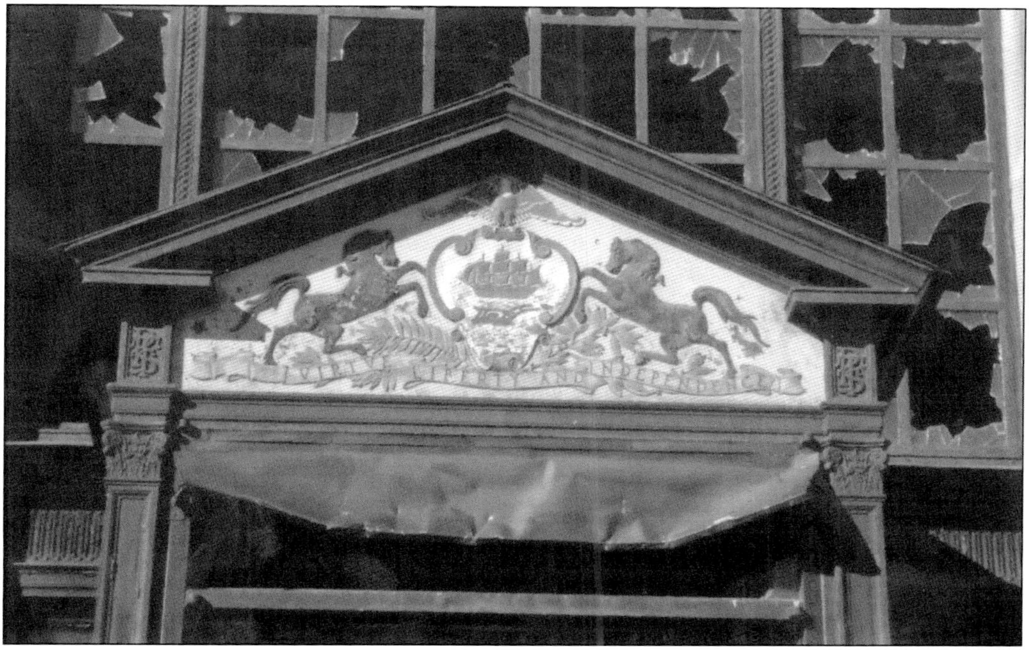

This cast-iron depiction of the Pennsylvania coat of arms was centered directly above the front entrance. The distinctive shield features two rearing horses facing each other and is topped by an eagle with spread wings. The state motto, "Virtue Liberty and Independence," is scrolled at the bottom. The crest was painted periodically through the years. (Courtesy of Diane Hickman.)

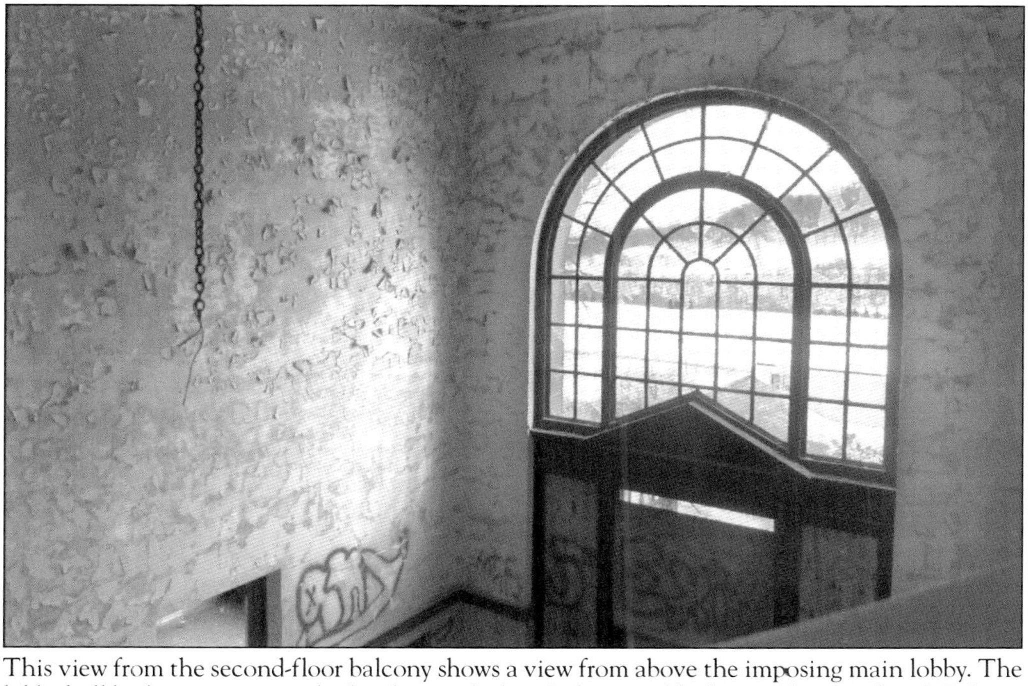

This view from the second-floor balcony shows a view from above the imposing main lobby. The lobby hall had a two-story vaulted ceiling and white Italian marble flooring bordered with Belgian black. A chandelier once hung in the center of the open hall. (Courtesy of David Flinchbach.)

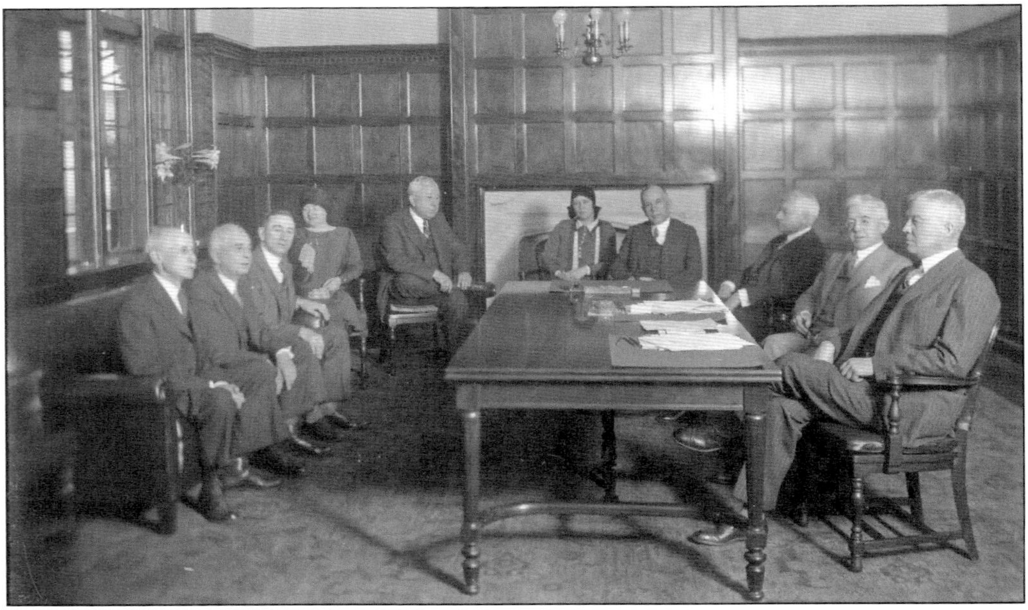

The board of trustees is seen here in the boardroom of the administration building in 1930. They are, from left to right, Judge James I. Brownson of Washington, Theodore A. Straub of Canonsburg, David B. Johns of Crafton, Lucy W. Bigger of Morganza, John S. Robb Jr. of Carnegie, Virginia Waltz of Washington, board president W.D. Cotterrel of Pittsburgh, Supt. William F. Penn, secretary-treasurer Charles Wilson Houston of Pittsburgh, and Richard G. Miller of Washington. Edward McDonald of McDonald was also a board member that year but was not present.

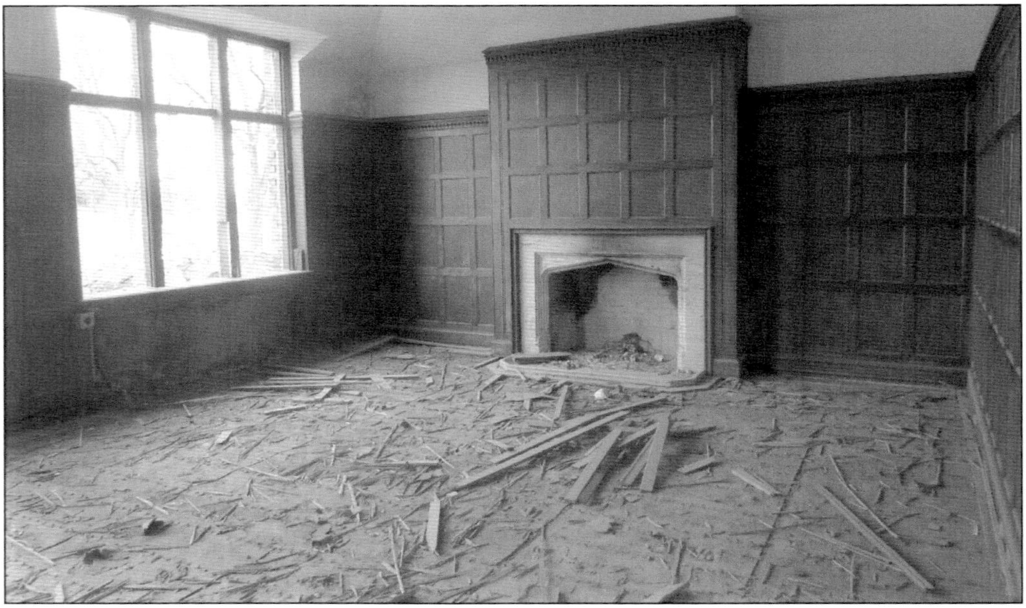

The former boardroom is seen here in its final days before demolition. The room was transformed into the superintendent's office during the operation years of Western State School and Hospital. It featured paneled wood, a travertine fireplace, and oak floors that once covered the entire room. (Courtesy of David Flinchbach.)

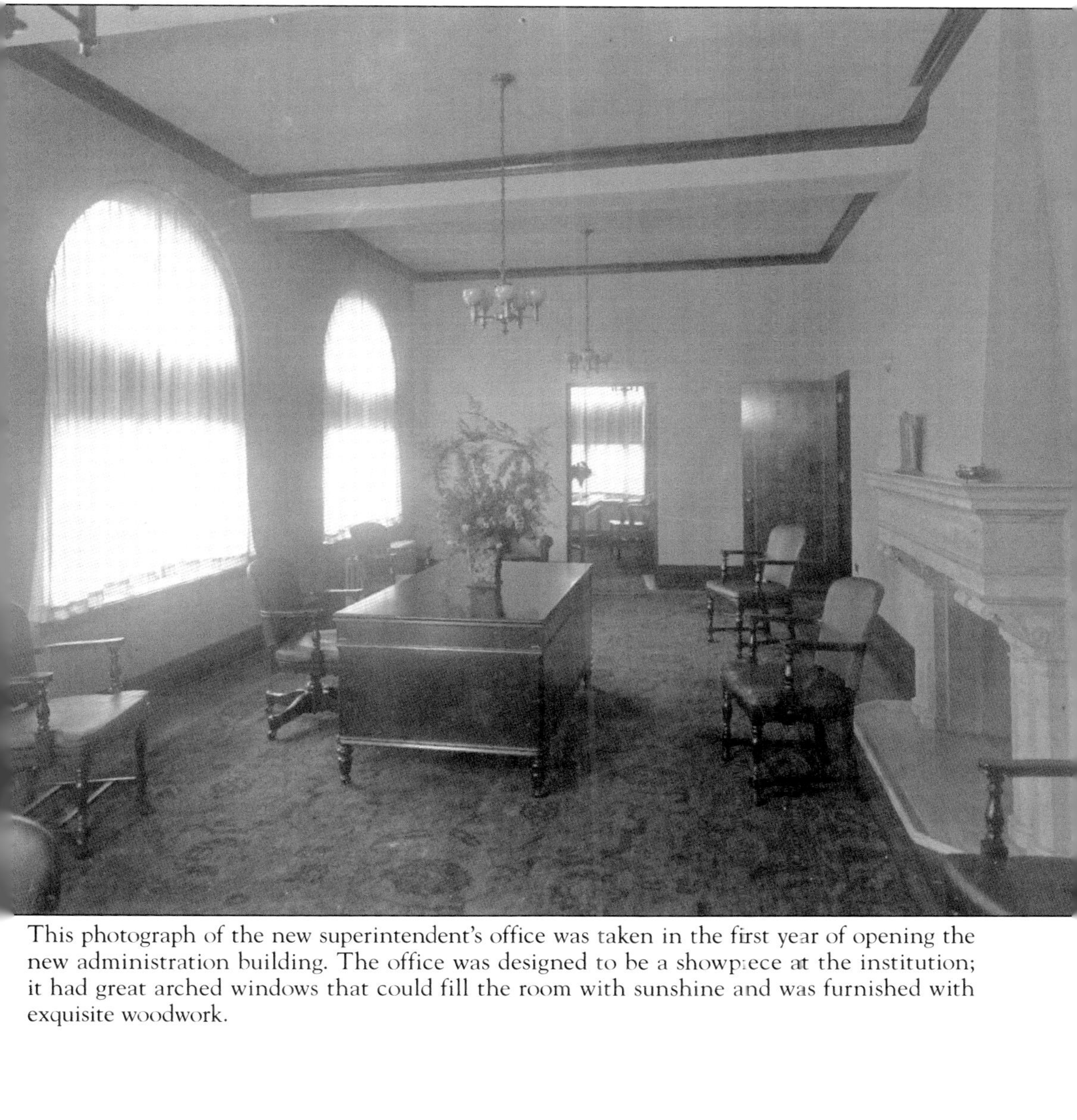

This photograph of the new superintendent's office was taken in the first year of opening the new administration building. The office was designed to be a showpiece at the institution; it had great arched windows that could fill the room with sunshine and was furnished with exquisite woodwork.

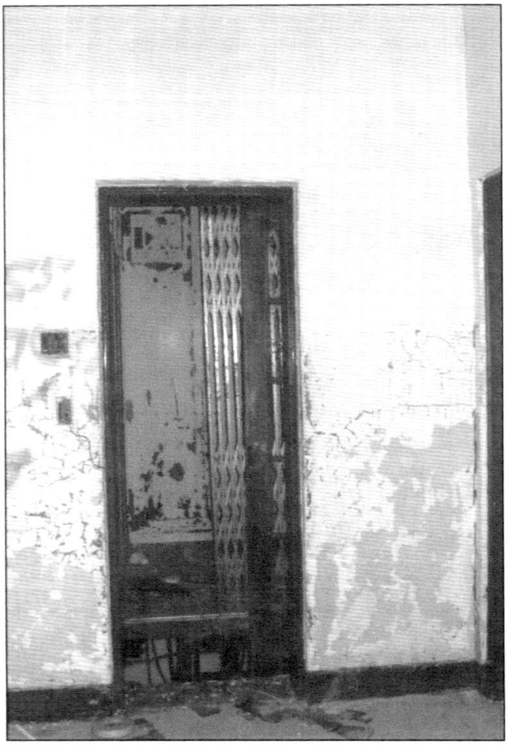

This view shows one of the administration building's two small elevators, which were located in the north and south wings. In 1952, the elevators were revamped to take AC current, along with other accessories in other buildings. Prior to the upgrade, DC current had been used. (Courtesy of Diane Hickman.)

This wooden platform on the fourth floor led to the cupola. The platform was supported by wooden beams positioned below the trusses. It was very rare that anyone was permitted or had reason to go up to the cupola. The metal trusses that hang are stamped "Carnegie C.U.S." (Courtesy of David Flinchbach.)

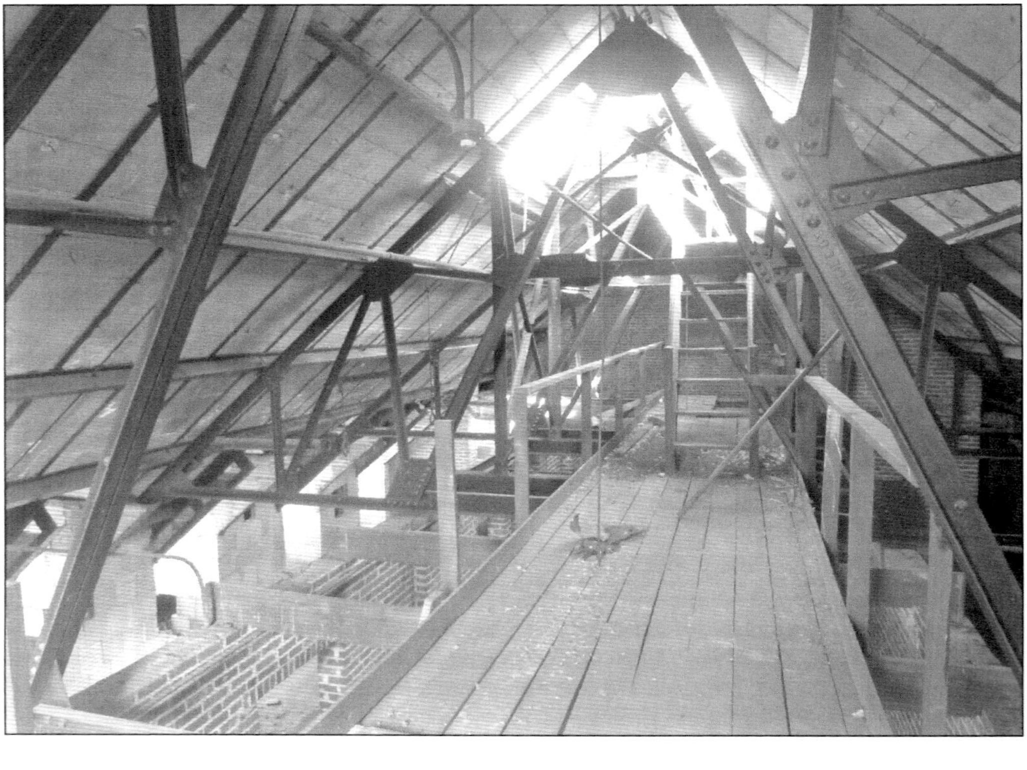

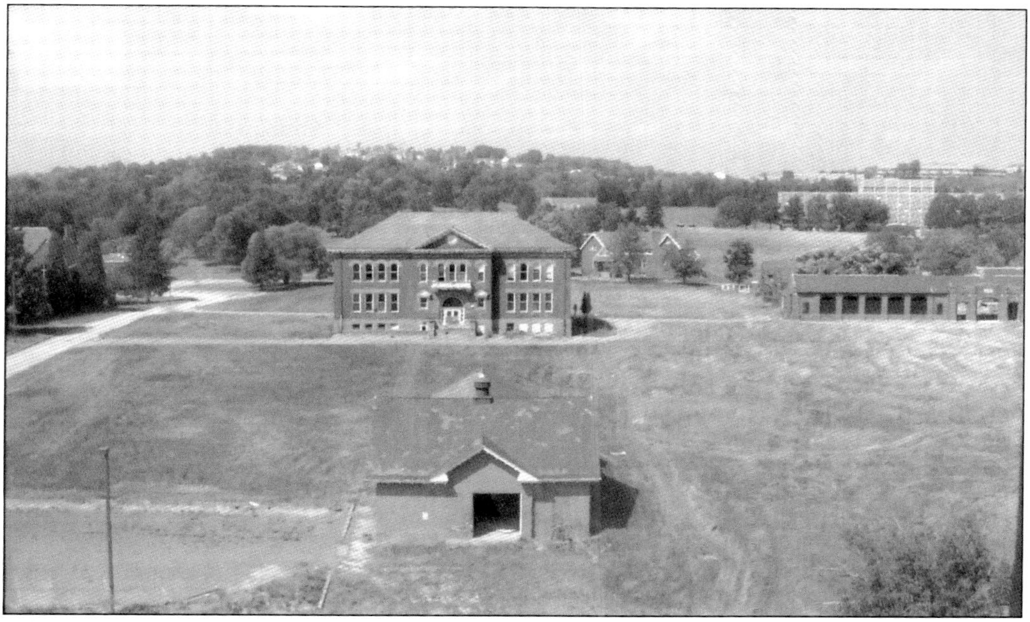

Taken after the institution was closed, this view looks from the cupola to the area behind the administration building. In the center foreground is the garage, which was originally the bakery until a new bakery was constructed into the dietary building. Behind it is the schoolhouse. On the far left, just off the drive, is the old dietary building, while the industrial shop building is on the right and Cottage No. 8 is in the center distance. (Courtesy of Rebecca Brocato.)

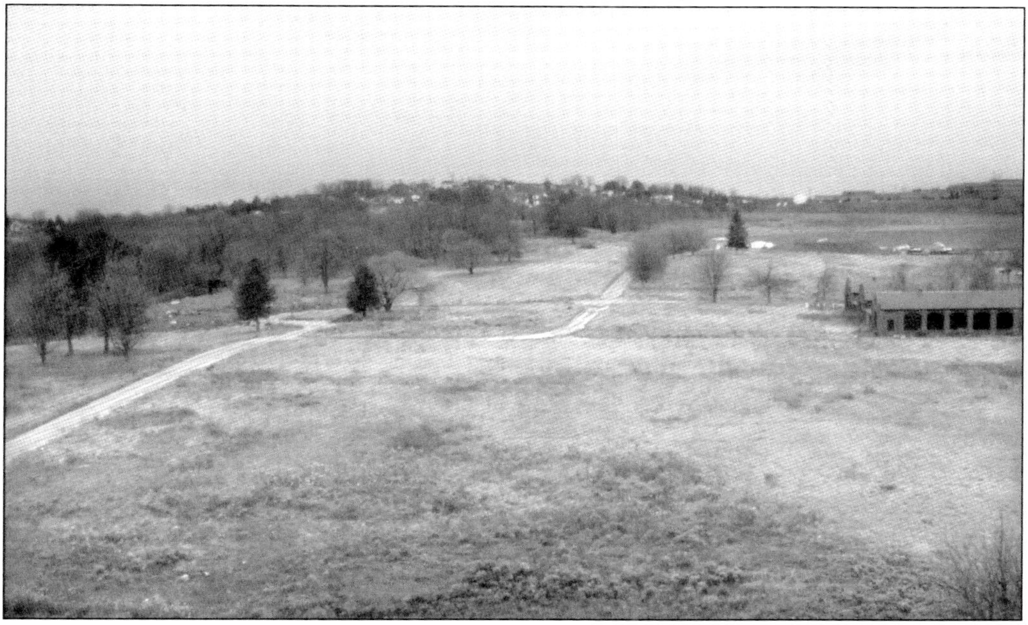

This later view from the cupola shows the removal of nearly all the structures seen above, with the exception of the industrial shop buildings. This photograph was taken in the final days before the demolition of the administration building—it and the industrial shop building were the last two standing structures. (Courtesy of Diane Hickman.)

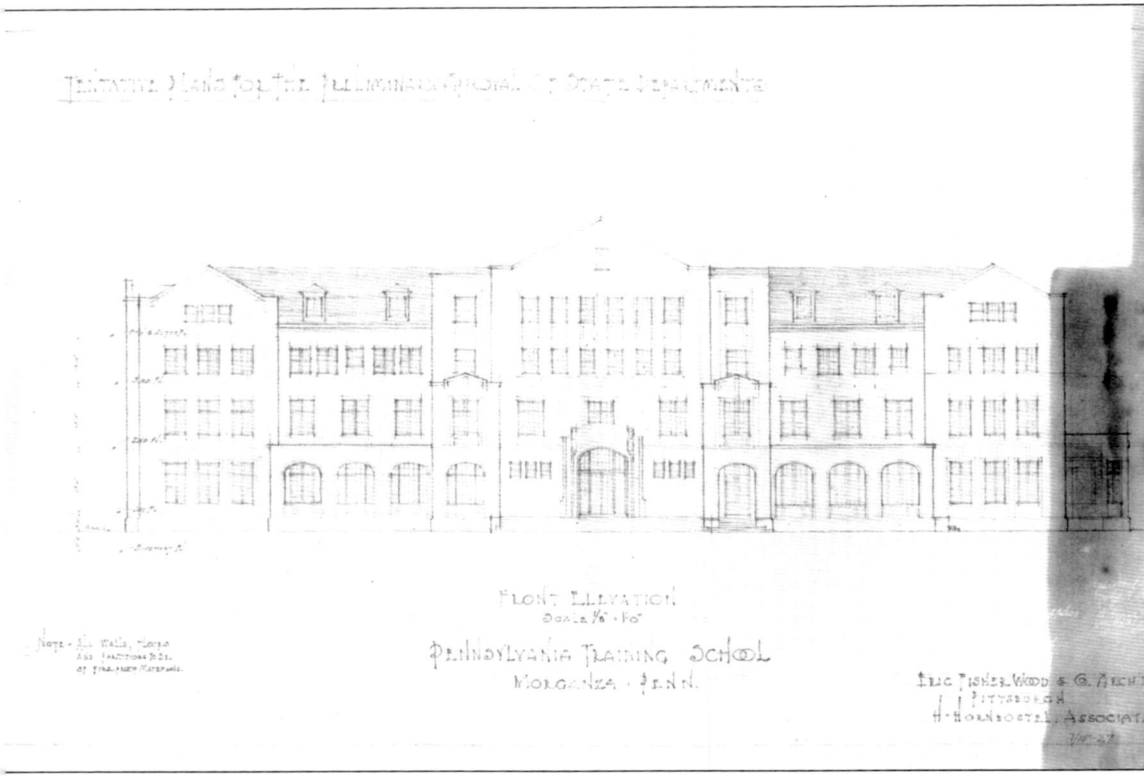

Dated July 15, 1927, this is a preliminary front-elevation sketch of the new administration building. The preliminary sketch did not include the cupola. Also added later were the three distinctive dormers centered just above the entryway. (Courtesy of Carnegie Mellon University Architecture Archives.)

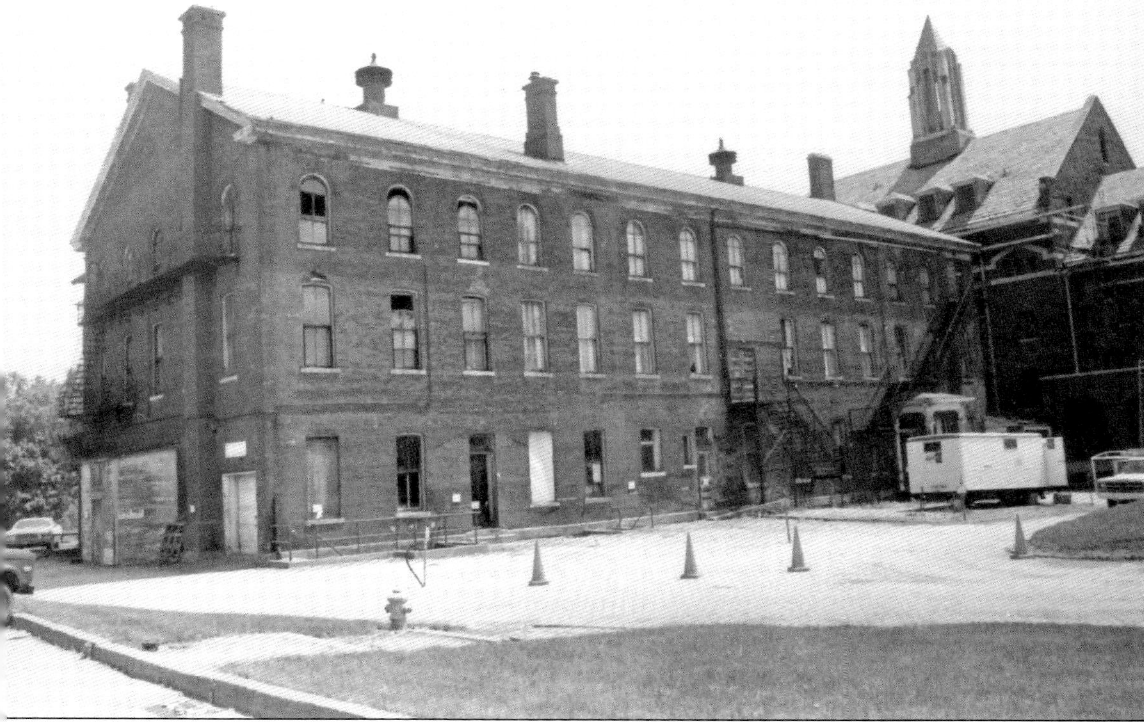

Built in 1890, the three-story brick chapel, also known as the auditorium, connected to the rear of the administration building, which survived the fire in 1927. After the fire, administrative offices were constructed in the auditorium as a temporary solution. The auditorium was one of the longest-standing structures on the grounds before it was demolished in the mid-1990s. (Courtesy of Pennsylvania Historical and Museum Commission.)

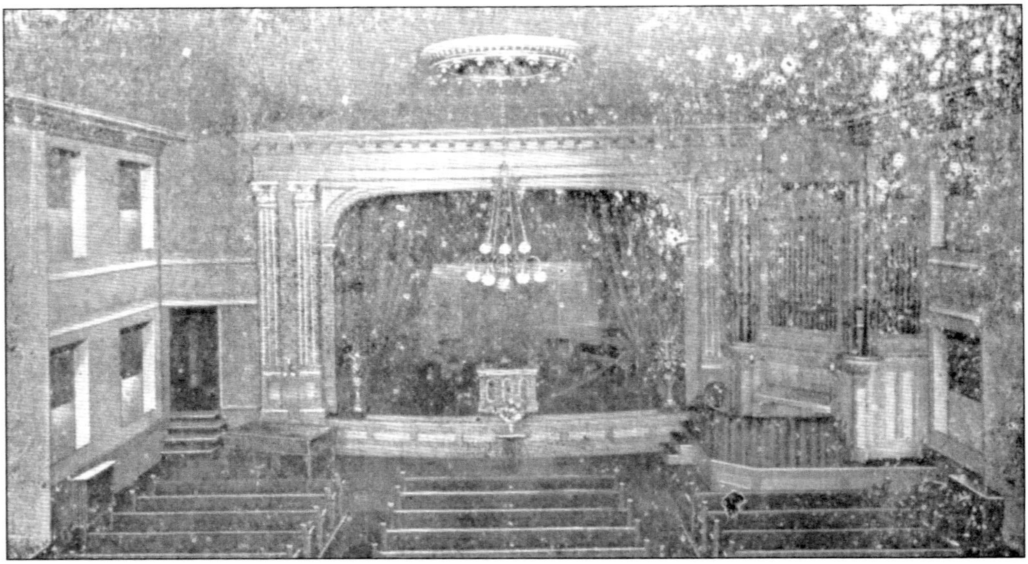

This photograph, taken on Thanksgiving Day in 1906, shows the inside of the chapel. Each Sunday afternoon, a nondenominational religious service was held in the chapel, where all would attend. On the first Sunday of every month, services were prepared by the children rather than by a minister. Each cottage group participated in a different part of the service. This was known as Pep Sunday.

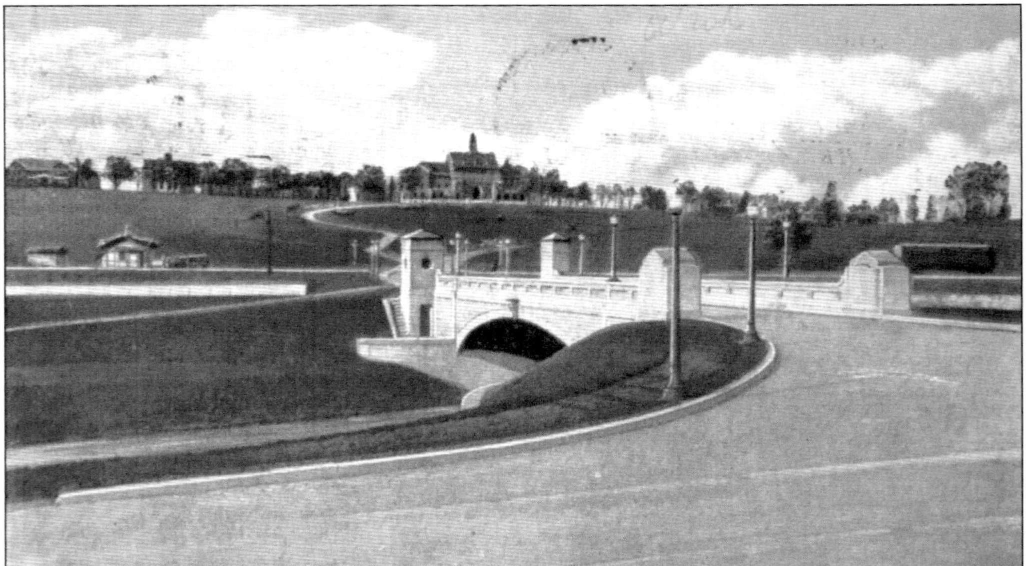

This postcard, postmarked 1932, shows the new administration building on the hill above the front entrance. The message on the back of the postcard reads, "Having a fine time will be home Sunday wish I had another week of vacation the folks here are grand." It was signed, "Elizabeth N." (Courtesy of Pennsylvania State Archives.)

The postcard, dated 1933, showcases the bridge of the Pennsylvania Training School that was built over Chartiers Creek.

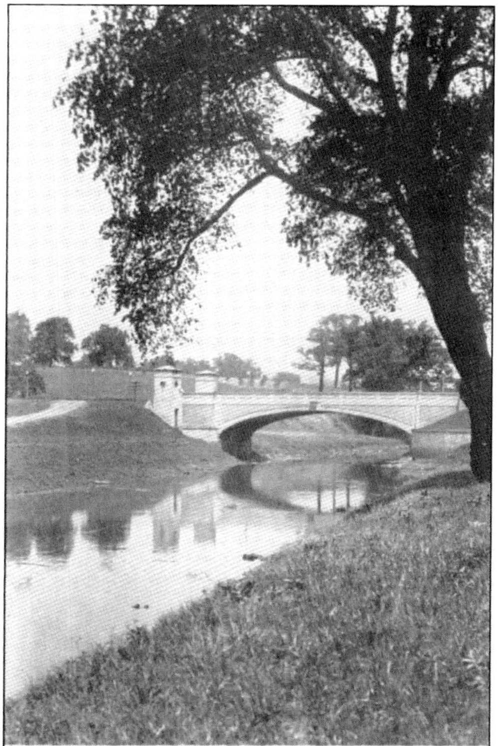

Bridge over Chartiers Creek, Entrance to Penna. Training School, Morganza, Pa.

Located in the girls' department, this cottage, Penn, was likely named after Superintendent Penn, who was the superintendent of the institute when the cottage was built in 1930. His dedication was instrumental to the institute's success. (Courtesy of Diane Hickman.)

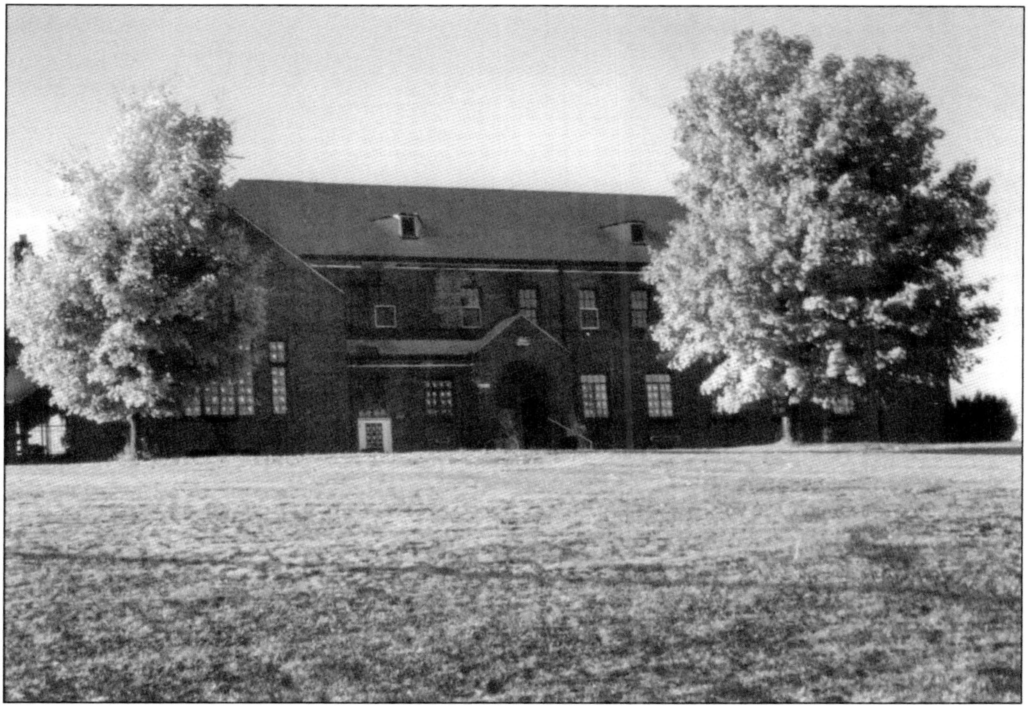

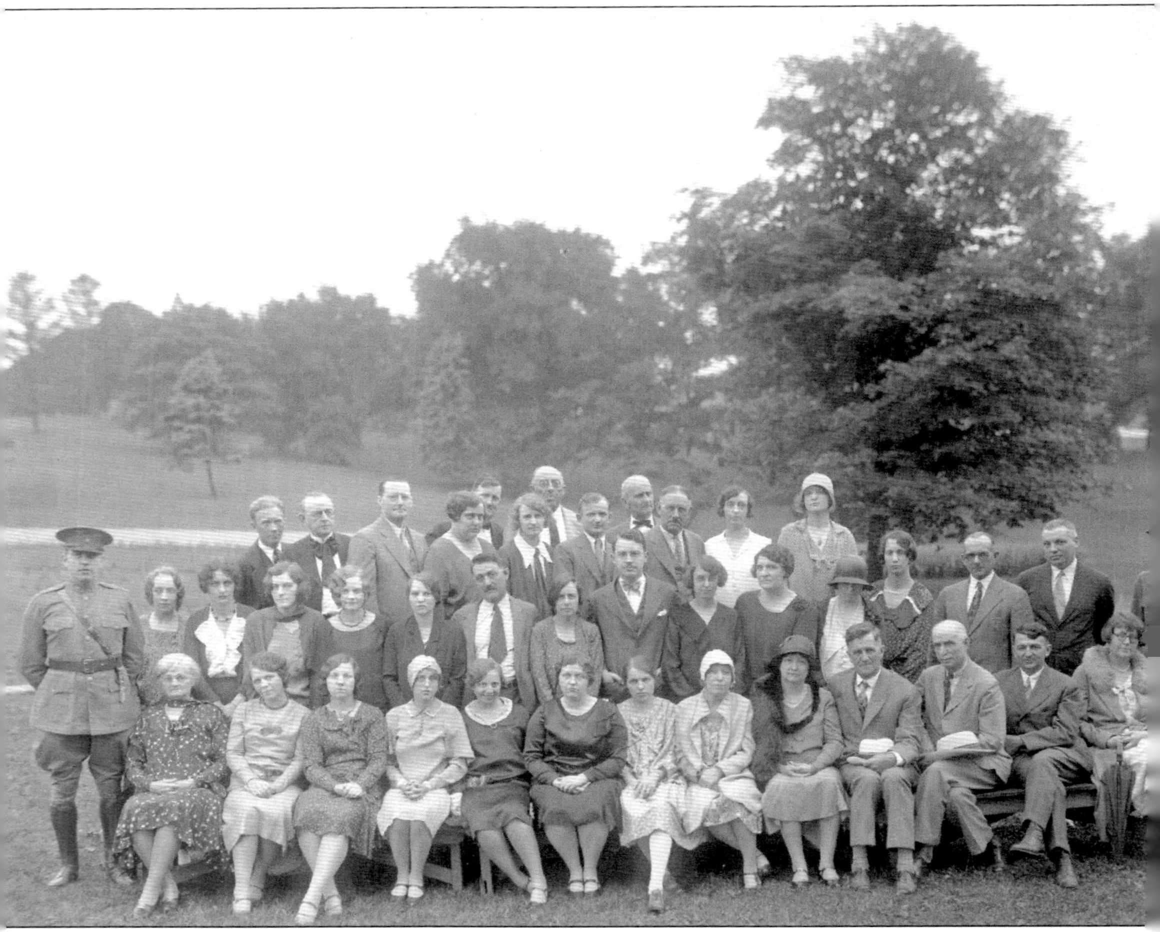

In 1930, there were 100 officers and employees at the training school, many of whom are seen here. The officers included, in no particular order, Hirman Tucker, Robert E. Fagan, C.E. Lockhart, Laura A. Miller, F.W. Glantz, Dr. C.E. Lawson, Mrs. C.E. Lawson, Jessie Tarr, Bessie Sargeant, Marguerite Snyder, Mary D. Secor, Beatrice Jones, Bertha Gaul, Adelaide Wooster, Margaret Suittor, Margaret Fleahman, Angela Schoonover, Maye Orther, Edith Prasse, Eileen Corey, Alma Parks, Mary Sharkey, Elizabeth Fleck, Elizabeth Carter Rugg, G.B. Linah, Helen Ainsworth, Rilla Rogers Bretney, professor J.C. Kerr, Arthur Prasse, Maj. C.A. Fowler, J.W. Considine, T.J. Saucier, Bertha Sturges, Helen Bowman, William Knuth, H.S. Meckley, G.L. Heath, M.M. Miller, P.A. Gille, and Charles F. Lindow. Two years later, the number of officials and employees had increased to 121.

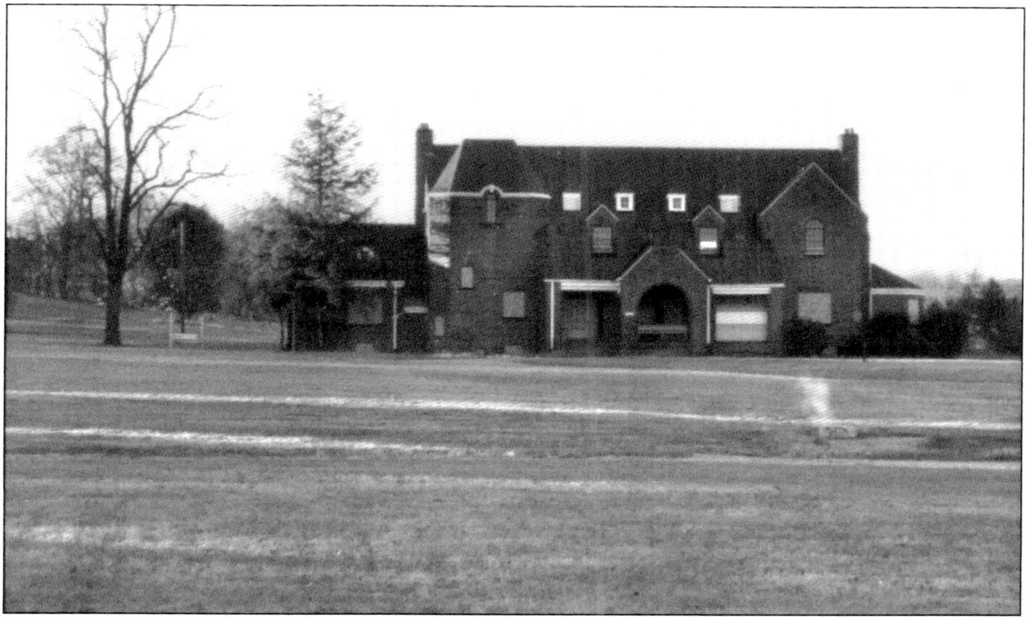

This two-story brick cottage for boys was built in 1930 and known as Cottage No. 9. The foundation was made of concrete blocks. It had a dominant brick structure and a slate roof covered with gabled windows. At this time, there were a total of 14 cottages sprawled throughout the campus. (Courtesy of Diane Hickman.)

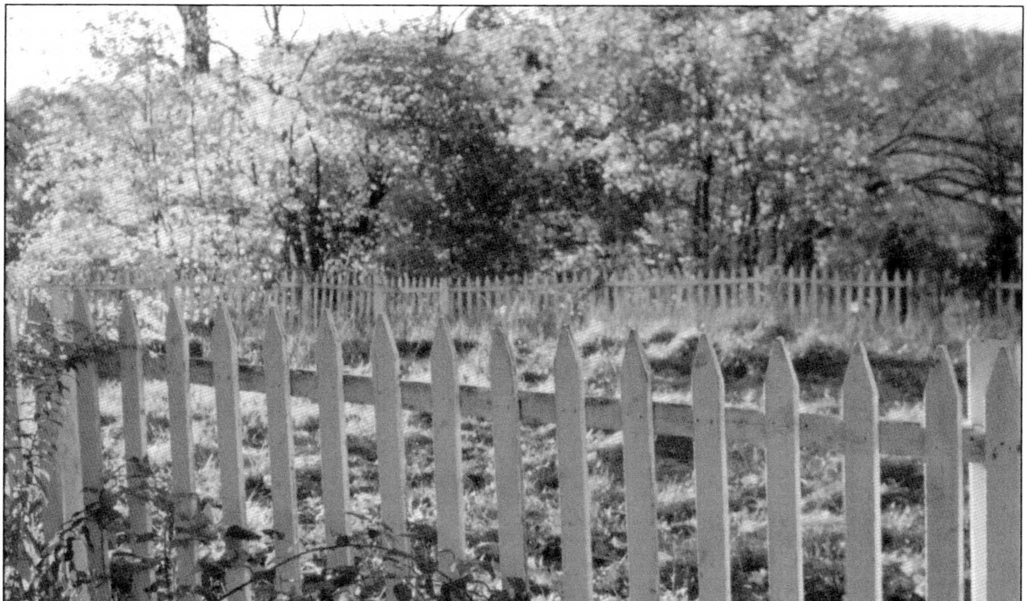

A cemetery with 33 gravestones is located at the far western end of the campus, behind Cottage No. 9, and lined by a picket fence. The graves are marked with a concrete block with a metal plaque. Some only have names, while others have names and age of death. The youngest was 11, and the oldest was 19. The years of death are between 1890 and 1908. (Courtesy of Diane Hickman.)

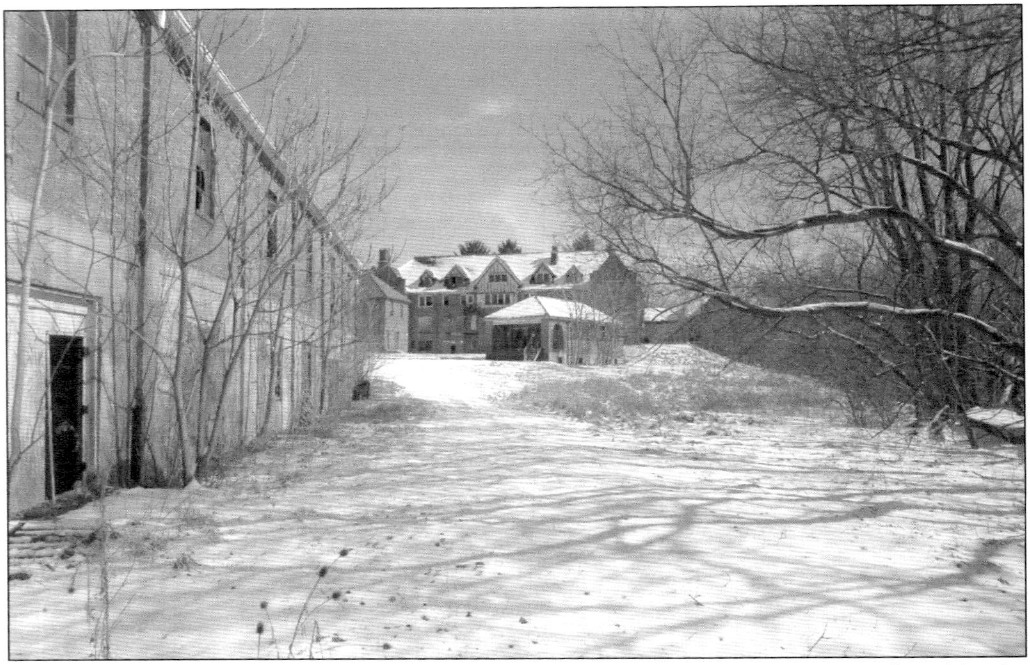

In front of the dietary building (center) was a small cannery. It was built in 1930 and used for the storage of canned food in the winter months. It was one single concrete-floored room with two access doors, one in the front and one in the rear. The porch in front had two nearly 8-foot-by-5.5-foot open archways. The building measured 53 feet long, 21.5 feet wide, and 9.5 feet high. It had its own ventilation system. (Courtesy of Adam Ryan.)

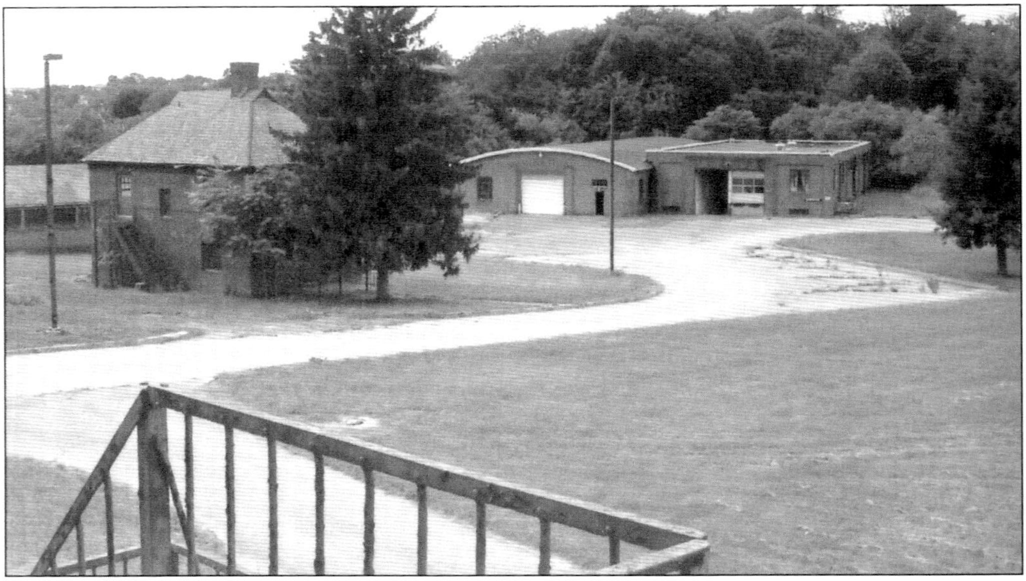

This view looking west from the fire escape of the boys' schoolhouse shows the storage warehouse and garage (right). The garage, built in 1930, could accommodate 40 cars. There was a lower ground floor on the south side, and it had seven doors. The warehouse was built in 1937. Also in view are the cannery (far left) and the annex building (foreground). (Courtesy of Rebecca Brocato.)

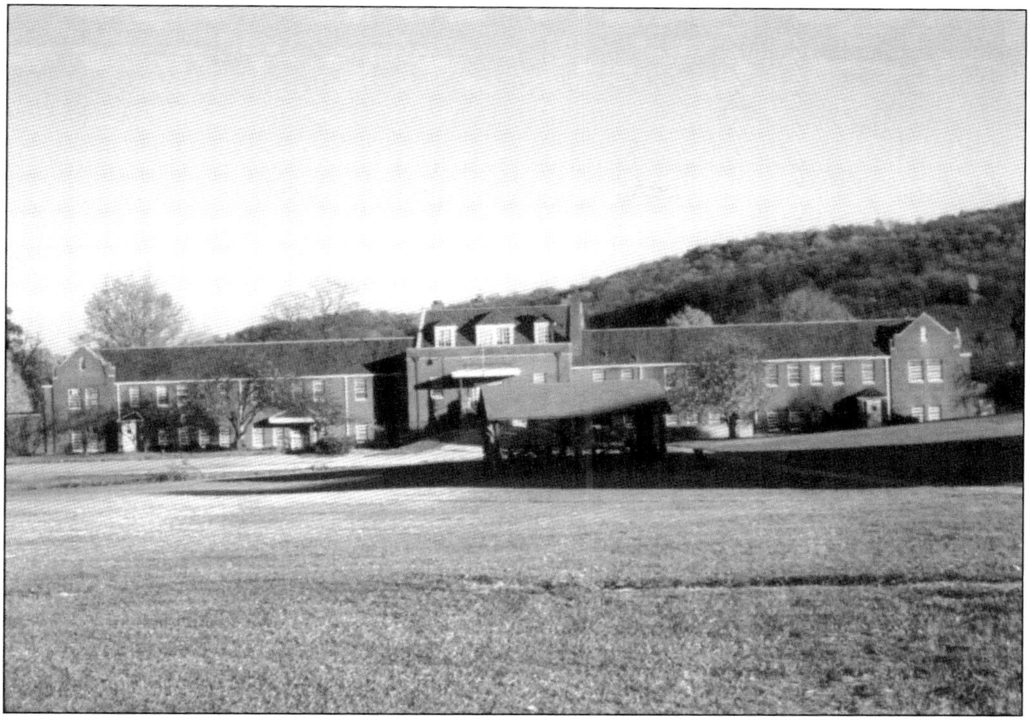

The school hospital, built in 1938, was staffed with four to five nurses 24 hours a day. They had overlapping schedules, with the head nurse typically present during the day, from 7:00 a.m. to 3:00 p.m. Nurses treated simple cases such as puncture wounds, abrasions, and contusions as well as the surgical treatment of burns, cysts, and fractures. (Courtesy of Diane Hickman.)

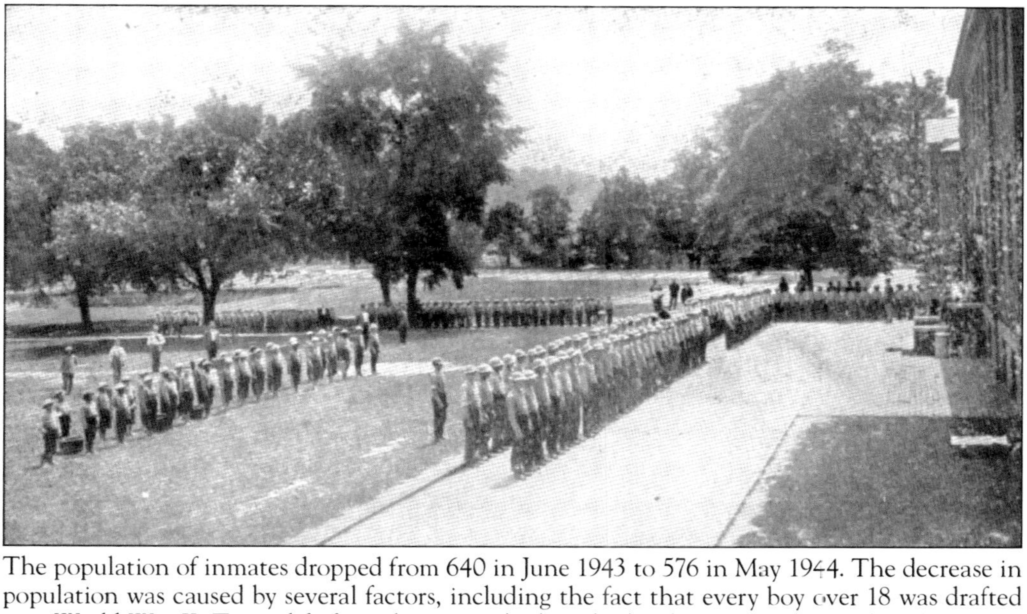

The population of inmates dropped from 640 in June 1943 to 576 in May 1944. The decrease in population was caused by several factors, including the fact that every boy over 18 was drafted into World War II. To qualify for enlistment, the boys had to have a good record at the school and to have been a resident there for six months.

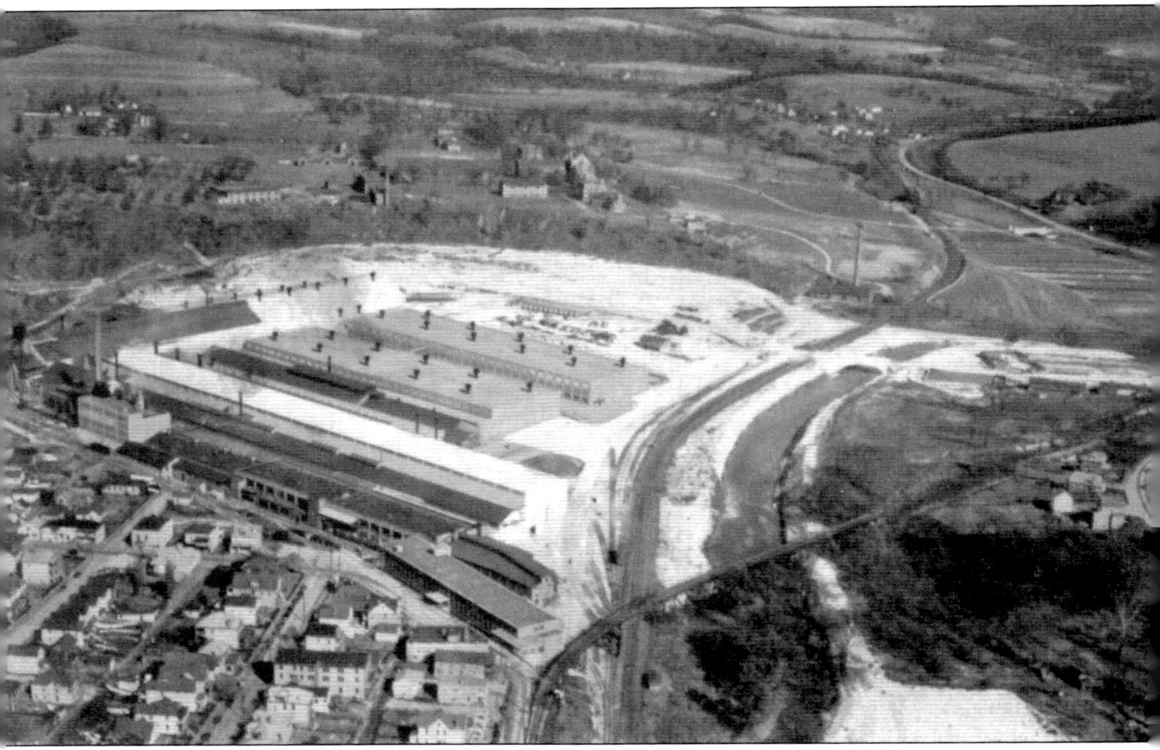

In 1944, a water line was installed at the adjacent aluminum plant by the Defense Plant Corporation. The plant is still adjacent to the former campus and is now occupied by Pennsylvania Transformer. The water line was to be used for fire protection only if needed, and the water was not treated. There was a six-inch tap on the line to be used in case of emergency.

Two

Trades and Activities

The aim of the school was to protect the helpless, reform those who had wandered from the right way, and train the incorrigible to obedience through moral influences, wholesome restraints, education, and the formation of industrious habits. The duties performed were reflected by their earnings upon their discharge from the institution. According to a late-1890s report by the institute, some former inmates went on to become the head of their own shops, showing the institution's high value to the state.

The placement of children into the institution came by several different means. The majority of inmates brought under the control of the institution came because of parental neglect, cruelty, and domestic conflict resulting from second marriages, especially marriages with two sets of children. The convict inmates, who had been convicted by magistrates, mayors, and courts, were of several types: "(1) Those committed by reason of incorrigible or vicious conduct. (2) Those committed as consequence of vagrancy. (3) Children of vicious parents, who from moral depravity or otherwise, are incapable or unwilling to exercise the proper care over such incorrigible or vicious youth. (4) Boys and girls who through circumstances or bad company, are not yet hardened to sin, and who appear capable of being reformed and of becoming respectable and useful men and women."

Upon entry, inmates were interviewed by a psychologist to explain the background story of their life and delinquency. After a physical examination was done, the delinquent was given a Stanford Achievement Test to determine placement in schooling. Once a child became familiar with their routine, he or she chose a trade that best suited their mental and physical fitness. The trade could be changed if it did not seem satisfactory to the individual. It was believed that the trade chosen would be used after leaving the school.

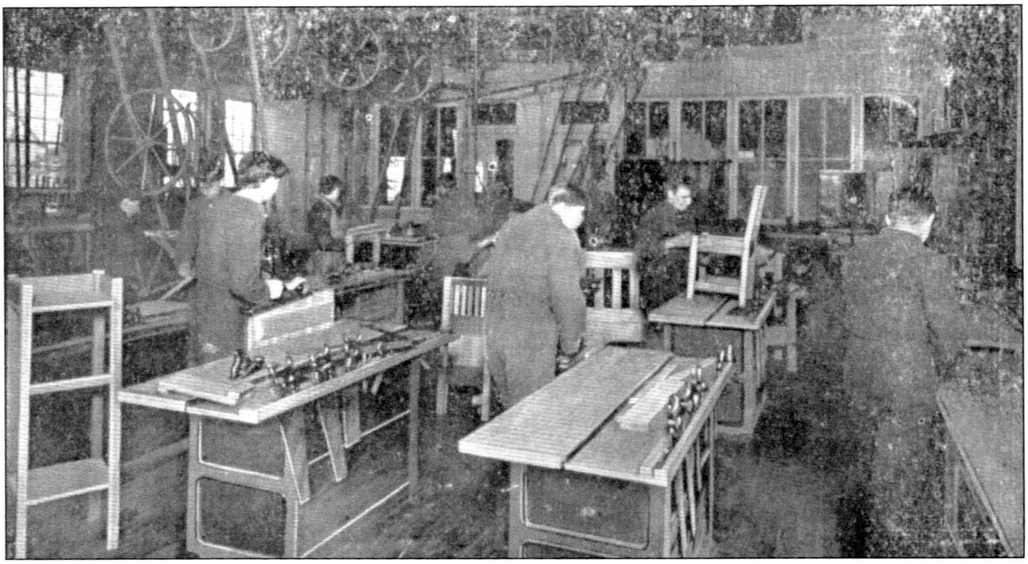

By 1909, the Pennsylvania Reform School had what was considered the most advanced industrial department in a school for delinquents in the country, equipped with the latest equipment in their industrial department. Unshielded belts and power machinery were used by the boys.

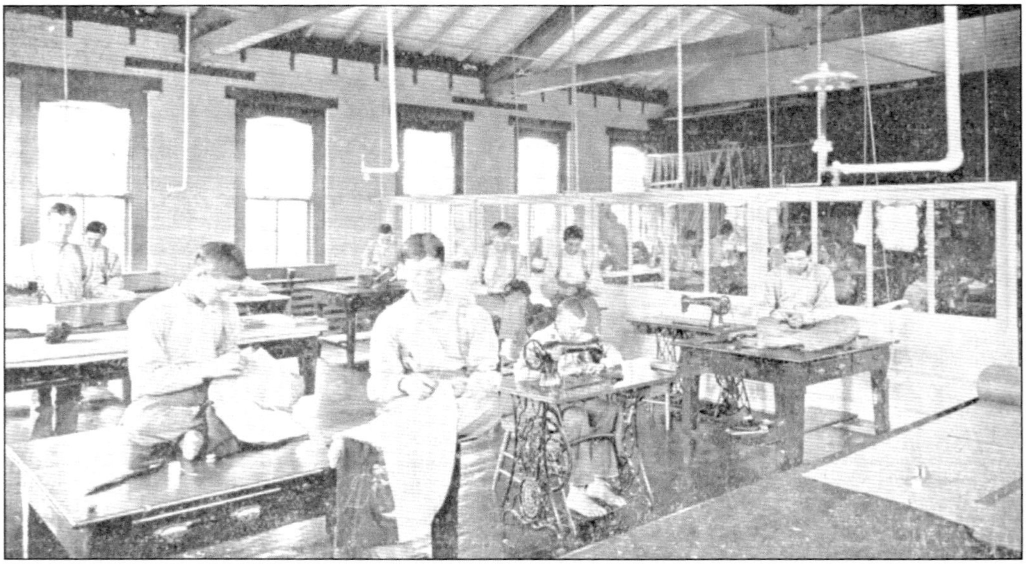

The tailoring department was one of the biggest departments for the boys to be employed in. They made all the clothes for the boys at the institution, with the exceptions of shoes and socks. They also made working clothes, band uniforms, and suits. A suit would be made for an inmate about to be paroled and would be specially tailored for each individual.

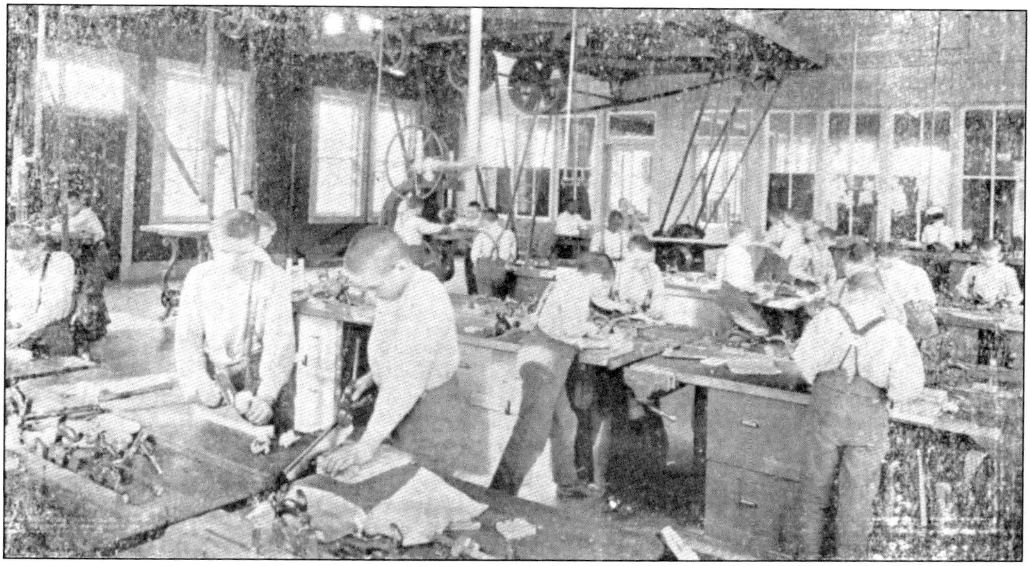

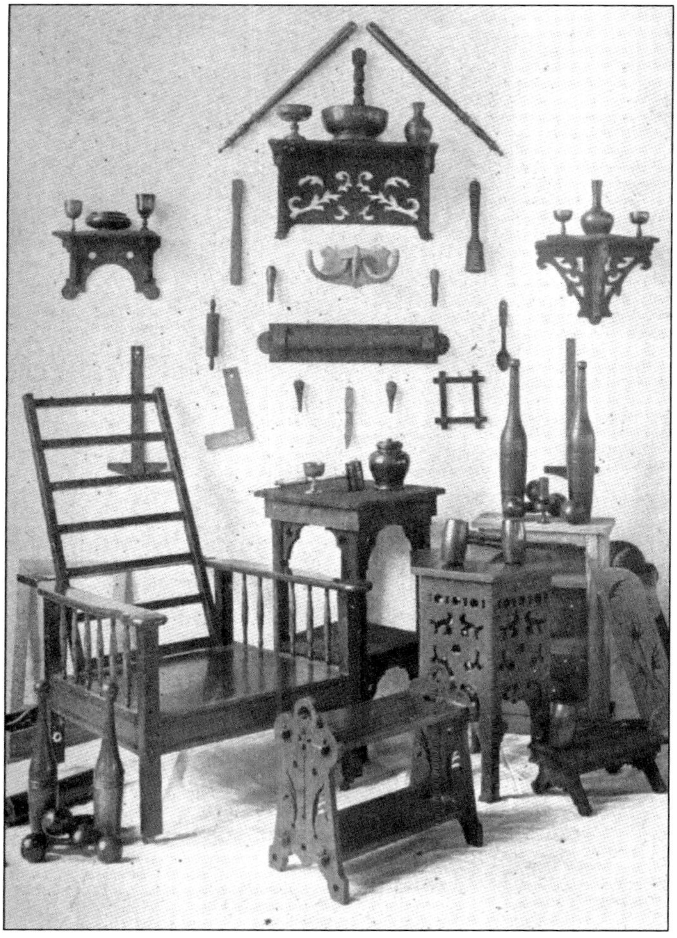

Carpentry students were used extensively at the school, especially with the repair and upkeep of structures but also to help construct new buildings. The boys were shown how to follow instructions and learn the uses of various tools. The carpenters' union recognized the work of the school and counted the number of months a boy spent at his trade towards an apprenticeship.

Seen here are items made by the woodworking department. The course consisted of 20 exercises. The boys were responsible for their personal tools and for the shop's tools, which included crosscut saws, band saws, planers, lathes, scroll saws, and grindstones. A supplemental course in wood turning was also offered. Some of the items seen here are a wooden spoon, a footrest, a T square, a chair, and a rolling pin. (Courtesy of Pennsylvania State Archives.)

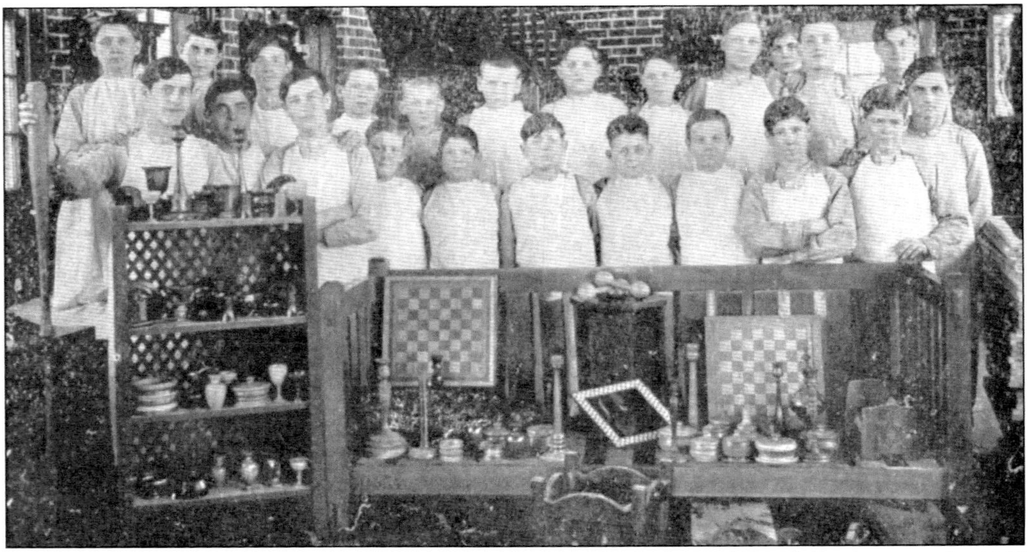

Male inmates are seen here displaying projects they made in the industrial department. In 1945 and 1946, vocational training was given more consideration, and a hobby shop was started in connection with the carpentry department. A proposal was also made for a general course in automobile repair and maintenance.

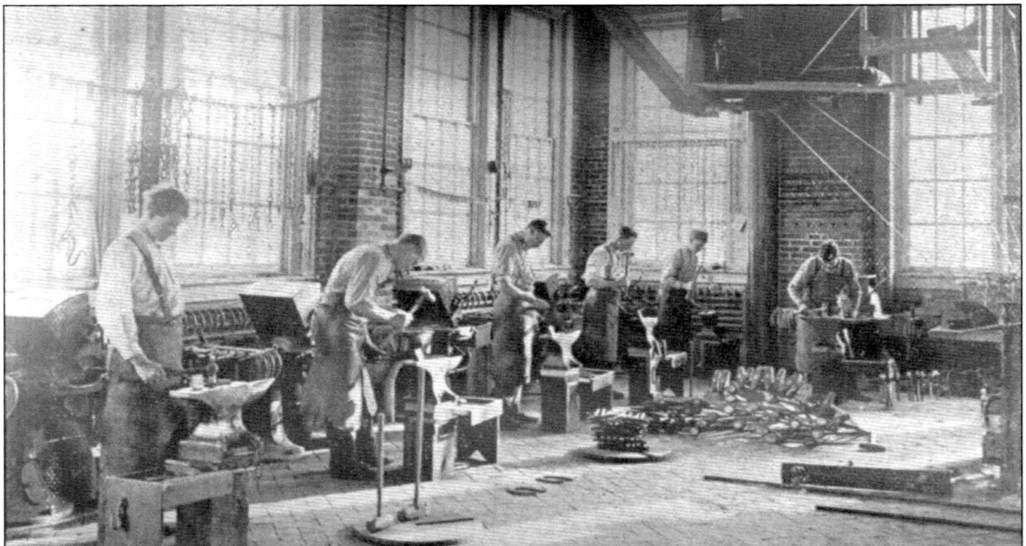

Seen here is just one of the many lines of work the boys were taught. Many larger and stronger boys worked in the blacksmith department. Students in the blacksmith department created horseshoes, constructed iron tools, and learned the skills to repair farm equipment.

Seen here are projects completed in the blacksmith course, which had five parts: (1) the introduction of the names and uses of tools, the making of fire, position when working, and handling of work; (2) introduction to the forging of various items, including hooks and welded rings (shown); (3) learning to make tools; (4) making ornamental ironwork, like the umbrella stands shown; and (5) horseshoeing, creating them as well as fitting, pulling, and driving. (Courtesy of Pennsylvania State Archives.)

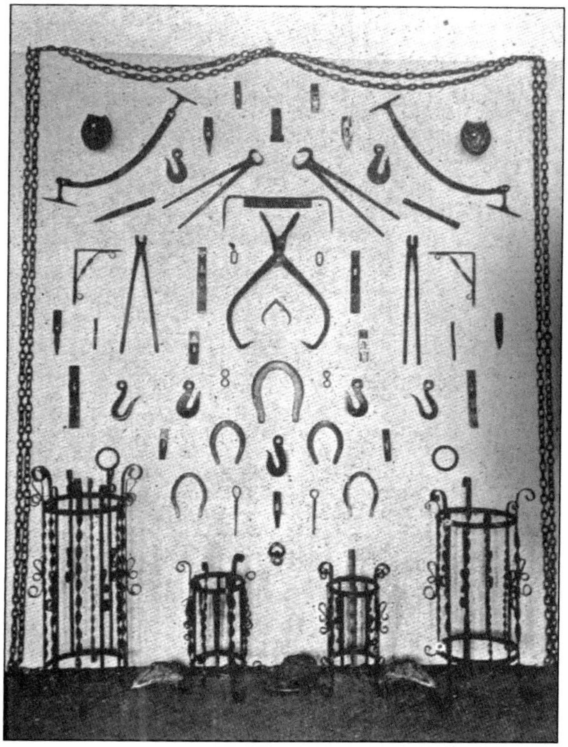

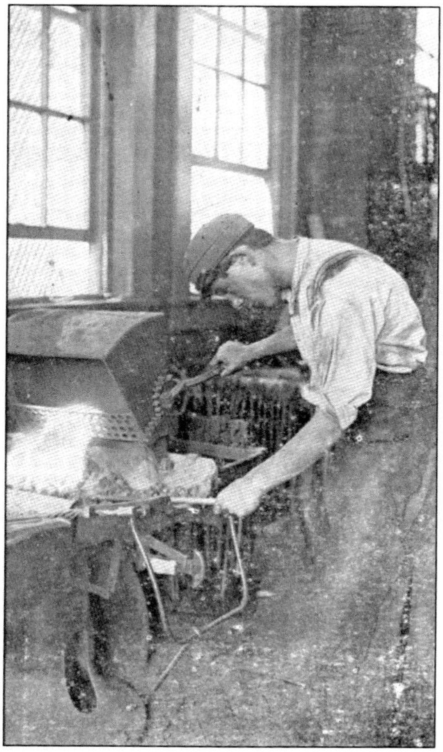

In August 1954, a boy was struck in the head by a piece of broken pipe in the blacksmith shop, causing a laceration to his skull. After nearly two weeks in the school's infirmary, he was released and sent back to his daily routine. Five days later, he became violently ill and was sent to the Montefiore Hospital, where he died 30 minutes after he arrived. An autopsy showed that he had a fractured skull that caused a hemorrhage in his brain. A modernization to the machine shop equipment was then declared necessary, and the legislature opened an investigation into the school.

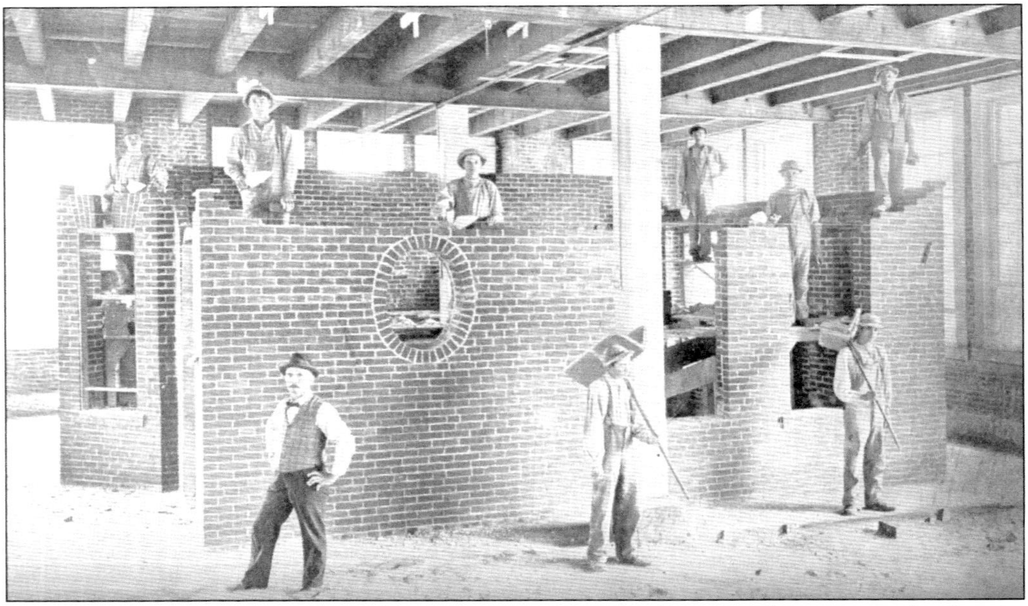

Bricklaying was another trade taught at the institution. The boys would practice in the shop by constructing walls and fireplaces. They learned how to pour concrete and lay brick. Many of the brick roads that ran through the institute's grounds were laid by the boys as well as fireplaces and walkways. They would also lay bricks for the construction of new buildings.

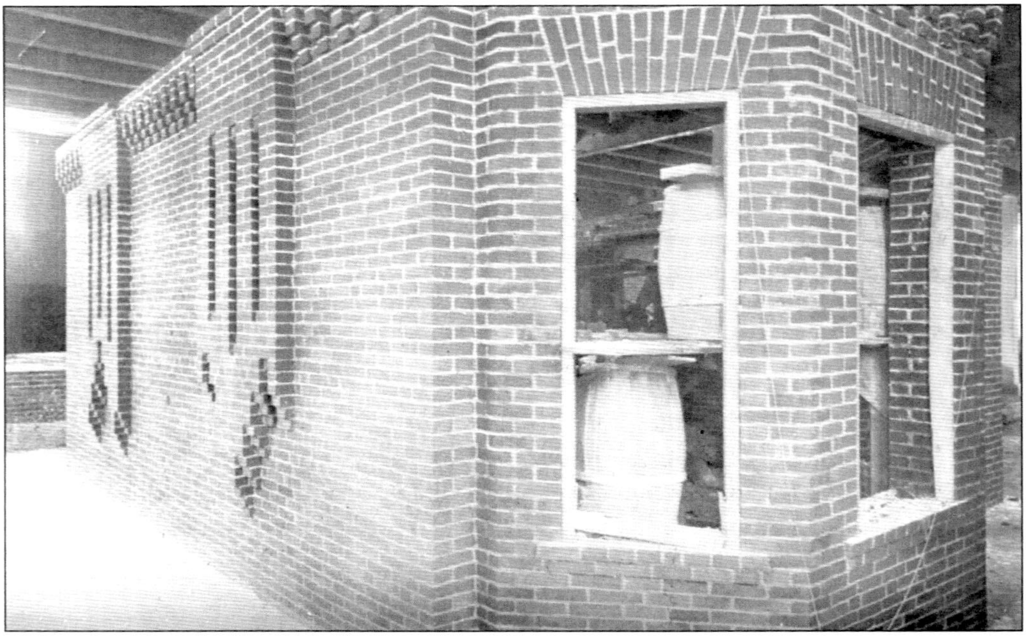

A finished project by the bricklaying department is seen here. The department's course had five parts: (1) the naming of tools, holding a trial, cutting and taking up mortar and spreading it, and building using line and a plumb rule on 8-inch and 12-inch walls; (2) the construction of corners and intersecting walls; (3) the construction of piers and flues; (4) the building of arches, fireplaces, and chimney tops; and (5) construction of a building implementing all courses of 1–4.

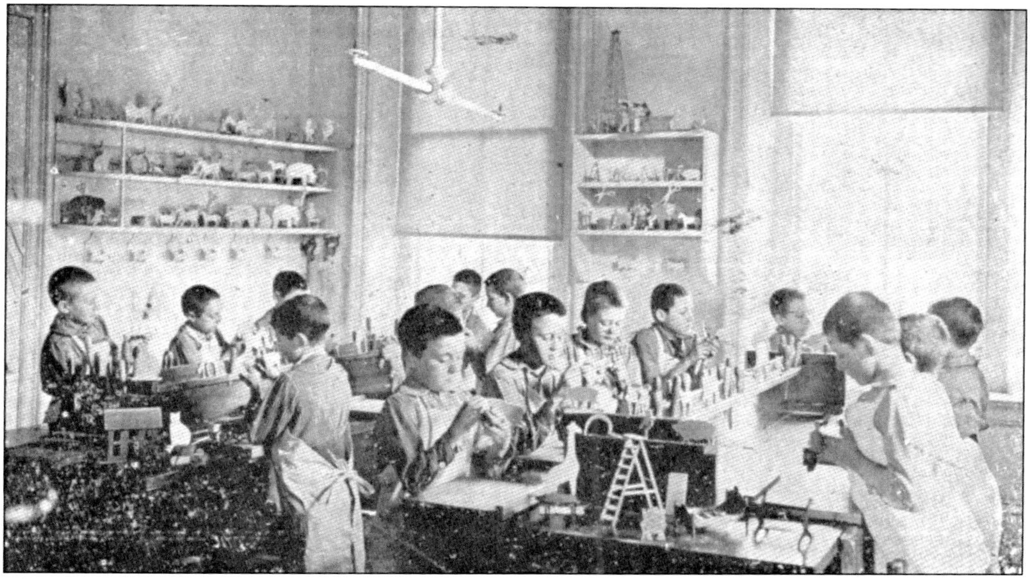

The smallest boys attended school all day, but a portion of their day's session would be spent in what was known as the workroom, where instructions were given on manual work. They worked with paper, basketry, and woodwork. The boys would be given materials of odds and ends with which to construct useful articles such as birdhouses, bookends, and toys from old boxes.

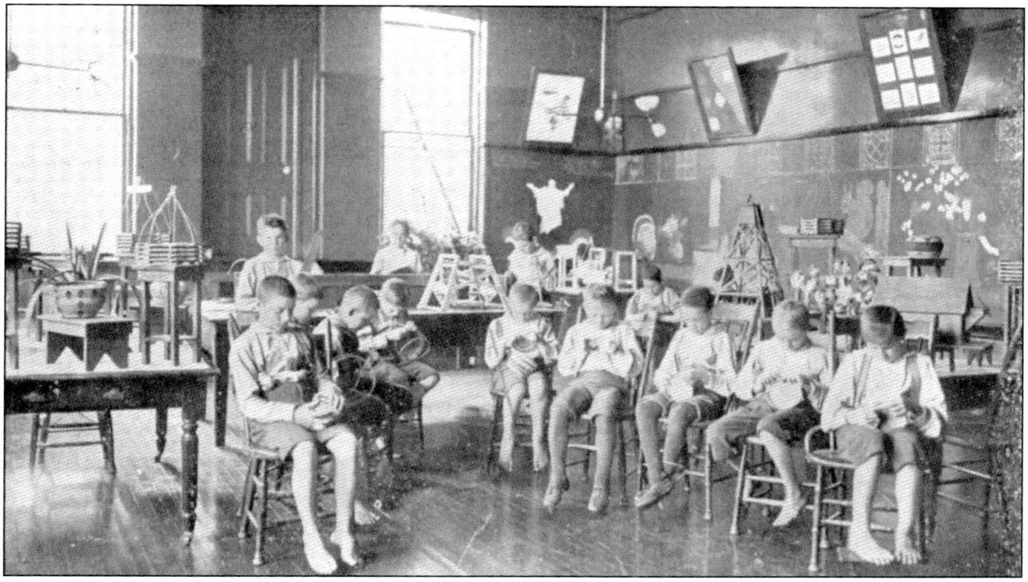

Another view of the workroom shows boys arranged in two rows. On the left table, woodcrafts were made by the class. Projects would get incrementally more difficult, starting with basic wood-making skills and then introducing more tools and materials into the education given to youths ages 9–15.

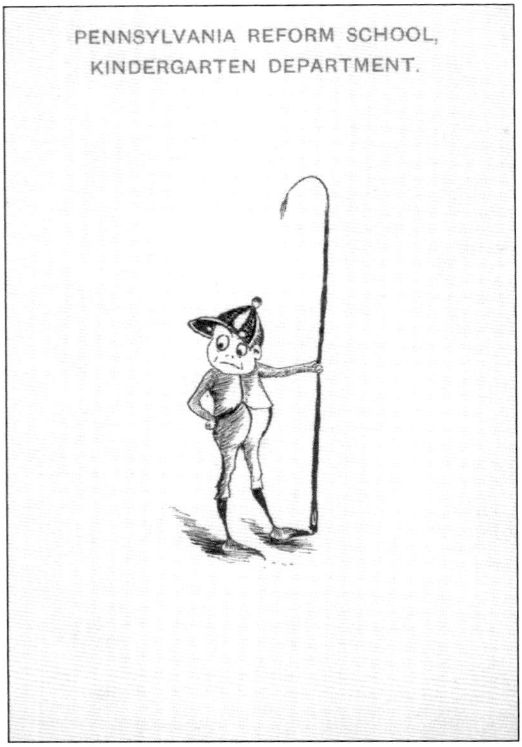

This cartoonlike figure of a boy holding a curved cane was drawn by a student in the kindergarten department with an ink pen on a heavy paper material.

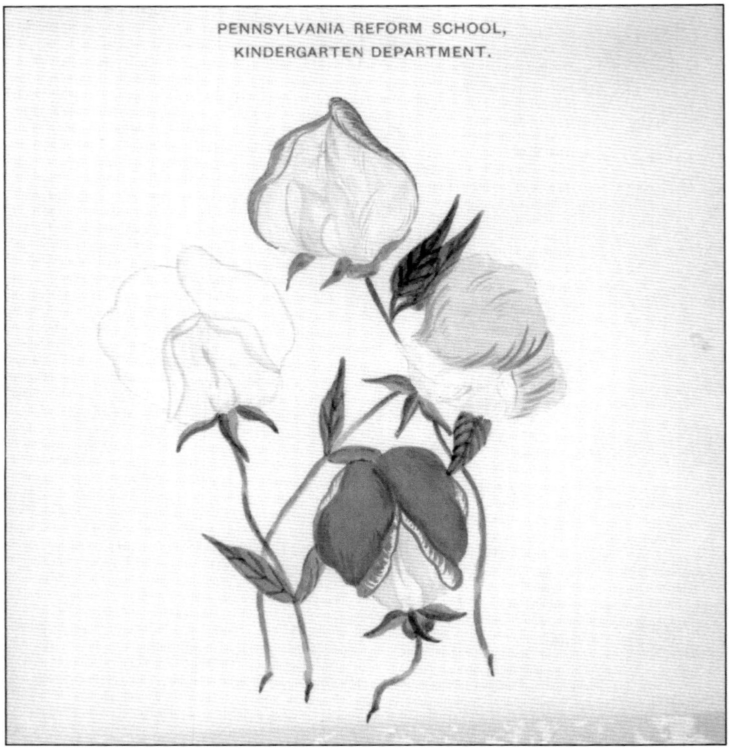

Another drawing made in the kindergarten department shows an arrangement of flowers. The flowers were colored and shaded with bright, vibrant colors.

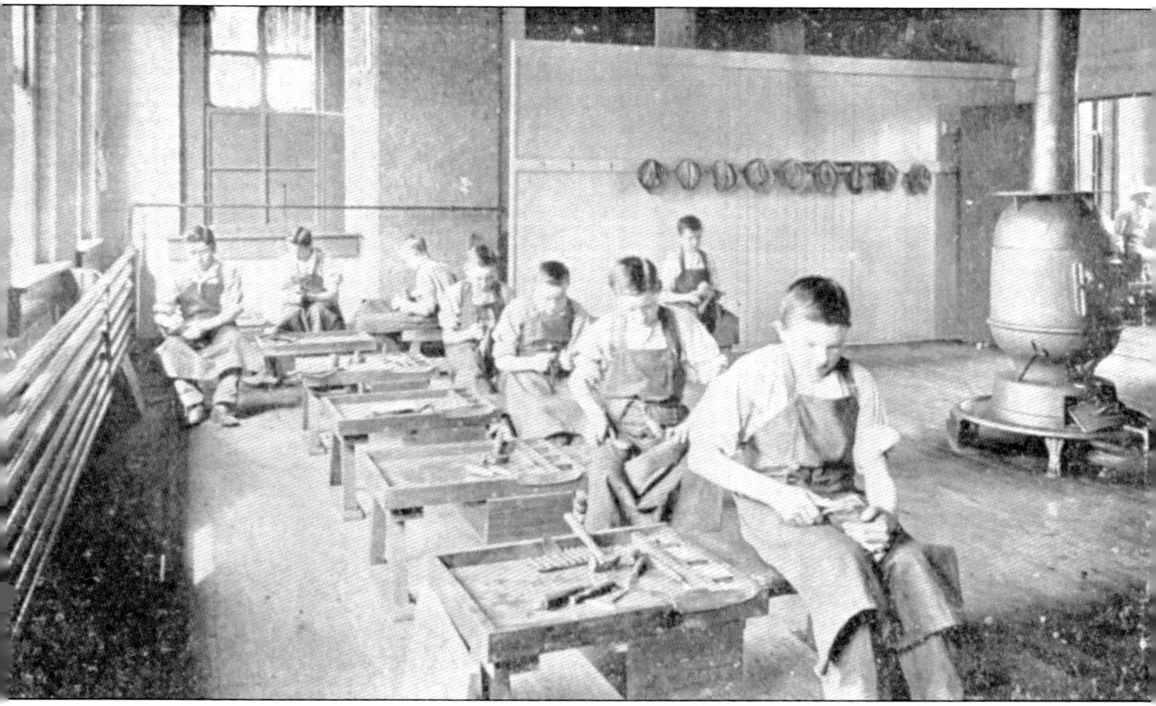

The boys employed in the shoe-making department felt they would have an opportunity to work with a shoe repairer or one day own a shoe repair shop of their own. All the shoes for the inmates were made by the shoe department as well as shoe repair. Most boys of Italian heritage worked in the department.

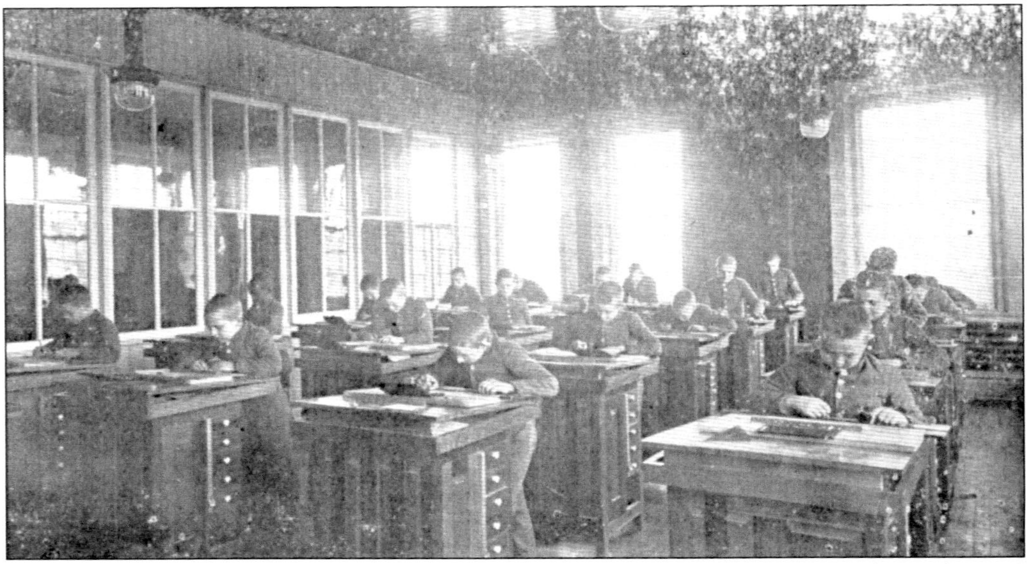

By 1890, the Pennsylvania Reform School had four classes of 16 boys who were taught mechanical drawing. The school provided drawing tools, including compasses, dividers, ruling pens, T squares, triangles, draughtsman's scales, and pens and pencils. The boys were responsible for keeping the tools in good working order.

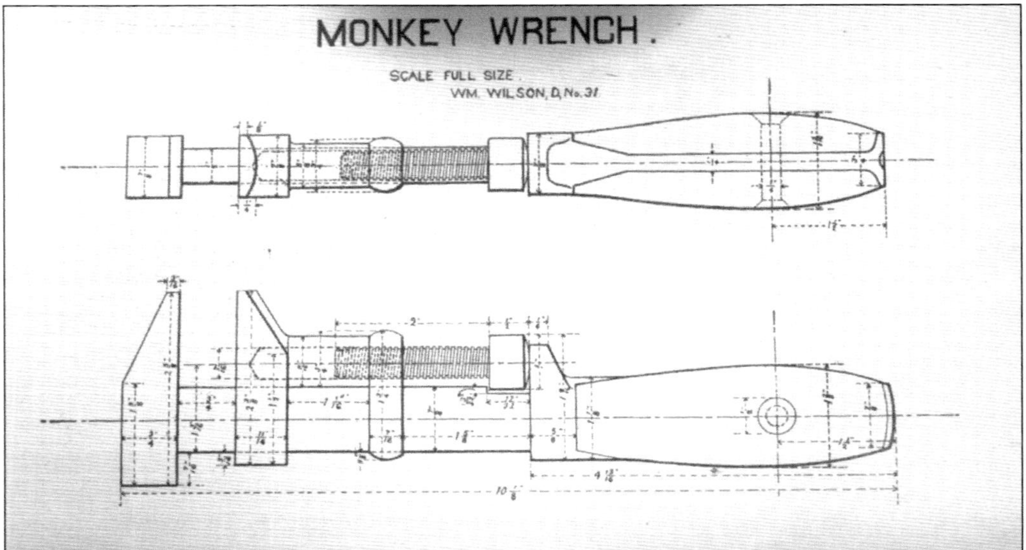

This drawing of a monkey wrench was part of a project in the mechanical drawing department. The course had 36 exercises, with subjects in plain geometrical figures, projection of solid geometrical figures, development of surfaces, and screw threads, standard bolts, wrenches, pipe fittings, valves, and other parts used in the shops. (Courtesy of Pennsylvania State Archives.)

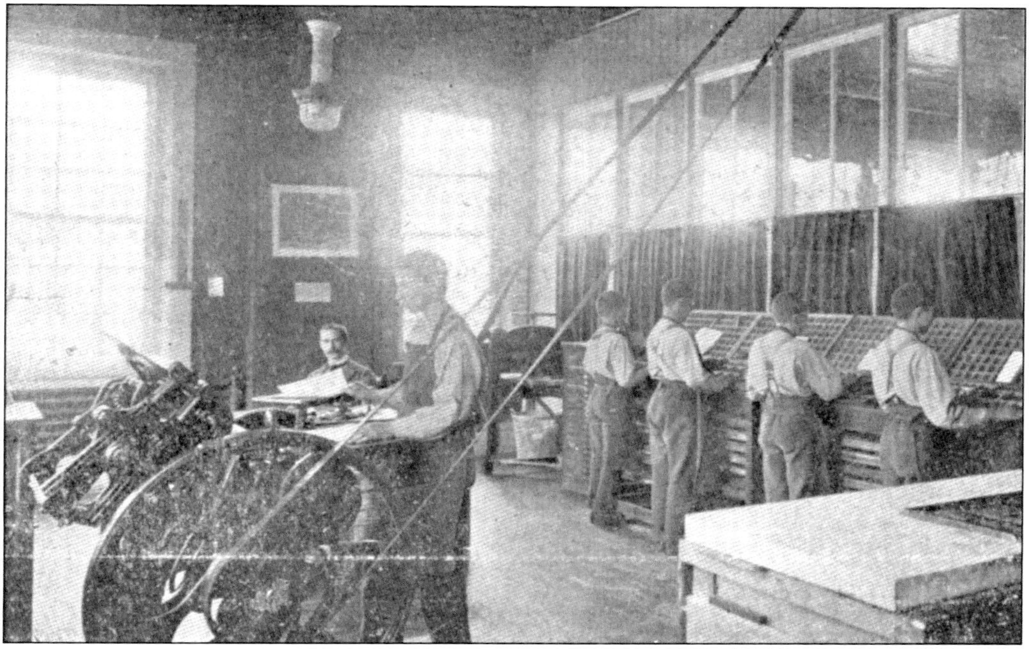

Boys who worked in the printing department learned to set type, feed and operate presses, and bind books. The printing department printed school programs, reports, and forms used in the offices as well as other special works such as name cards and the school paper. The school's biennial report was also printed and bound there.

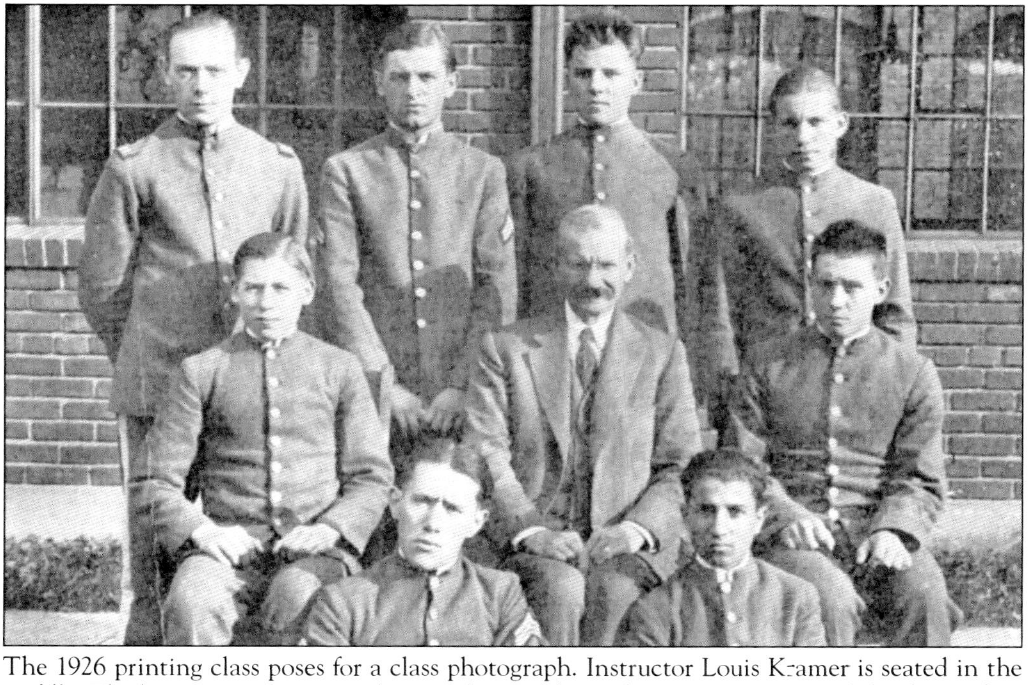

The 1926 printing class poses for a class photograph. Instructor Louis Kramer is seated in the middle. The boys are, in no particular, Stanley Barkley, Robert Barr, George Habil, John Jordan, John Koncik, Philip Saba, Warren Sert, and William Stuart.

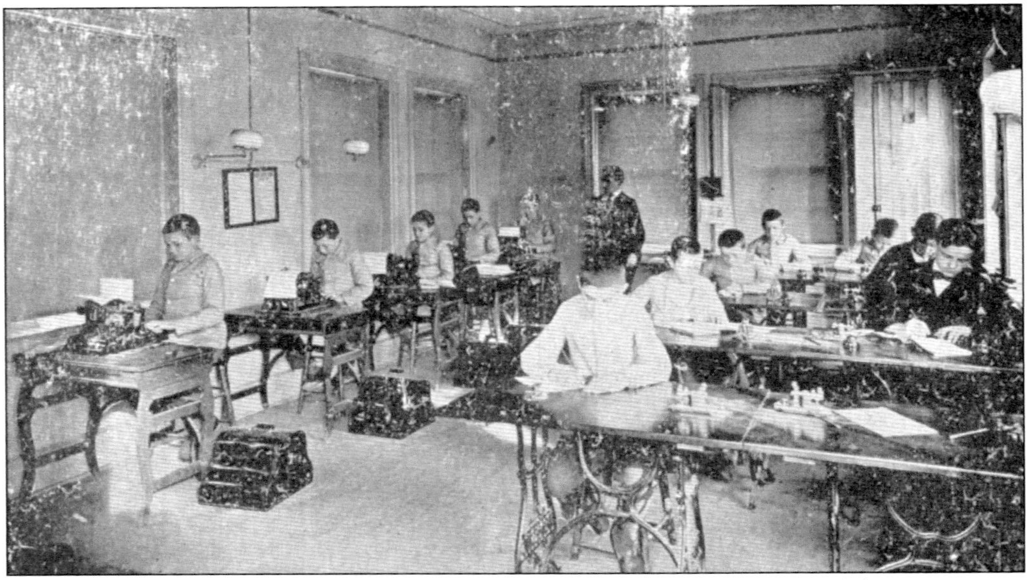

Boys are seen here at work in the clerical department. The deputy secretary of the Department of Welfare, Clement W. Hunt, commented in the 1932 biennial report that the report, made by the school, contained not a single typographical error. He mentioned that if all institutions would present reports so well, it would make for a much easier review of a facility.

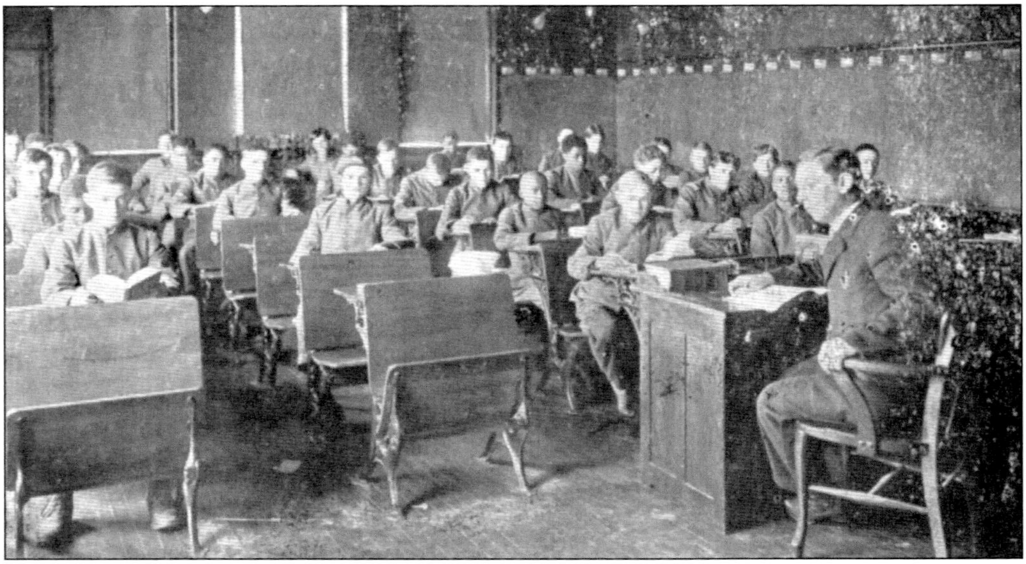

When it came to academic schooling, a standard educational achievement test was given to every child. As children had different ability levels, it was important to place them in a class with those of similar learning abilities rather than strictly by age. A student's score on the exam and the records from the student's previous schools were put into consideration in determining their proper grade placement.

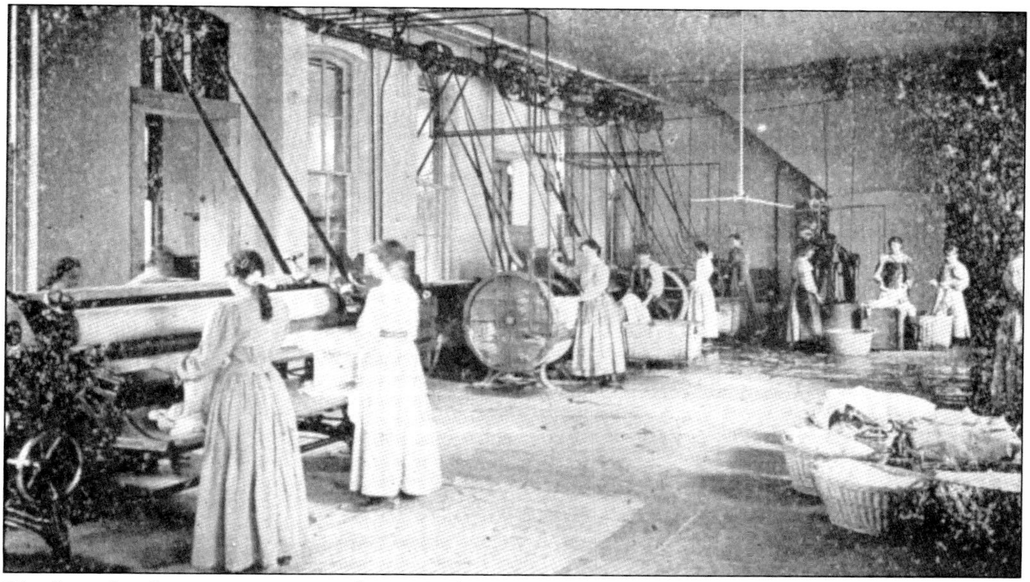

The laundry department is seen here. Girls were given the latest technology to wash and iron clothes. They used tumblers in combination with drying racks where heat was produced. A large mangle and a small press also were used. The girls were responsible for doing the laundry for the entire institution.

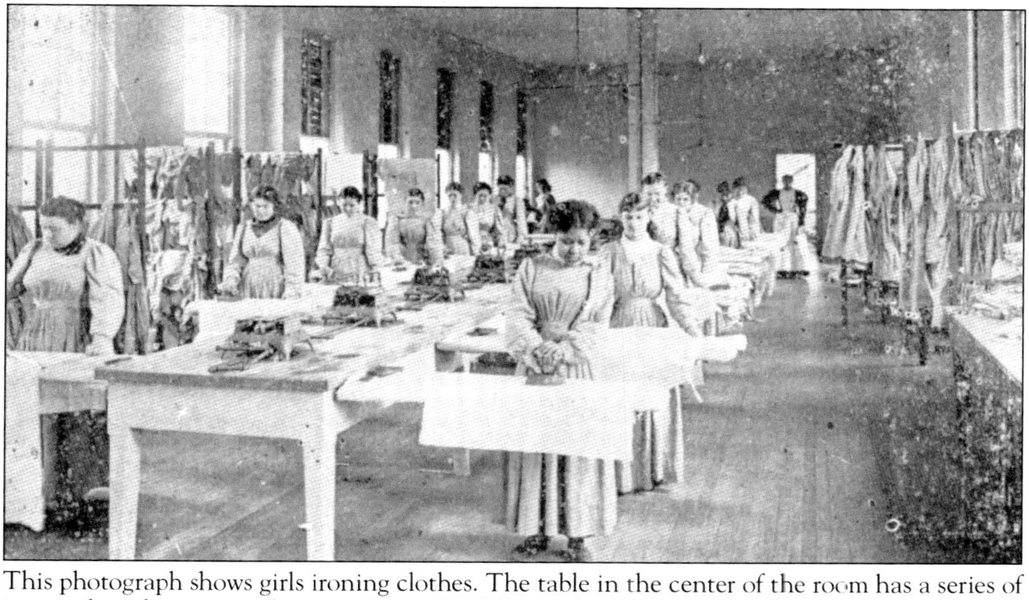

This photograph shows girls ironing clothes. The table in the center of the room has a series of ironing boards connected to it and runs the full length of the room. It was likely constructed by the boys' carpentry department.

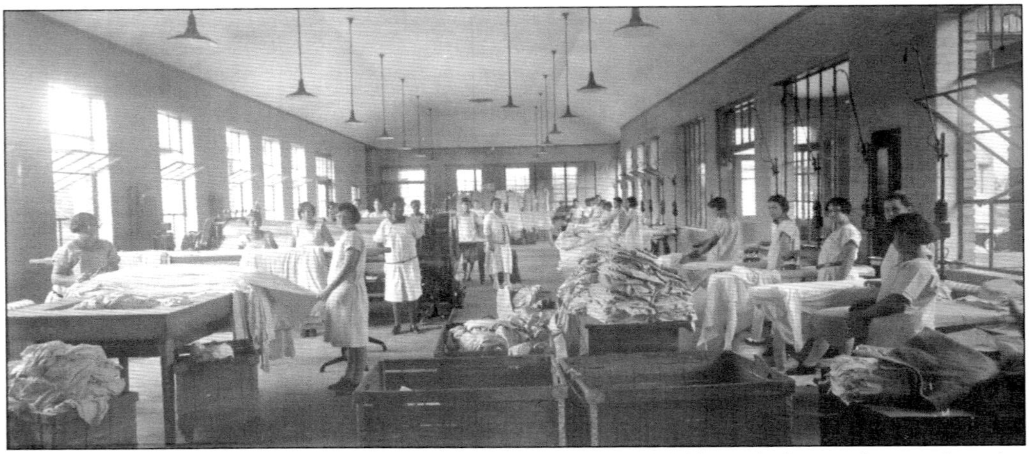

This view of the laundry room in 1930 shows girls sorting and folding clothes in the new laundry building. Constructed in 1926, it was designed in a similar style as the first building, but it could accommodate linens of bigger sizes and it was upgraded to include the latest equipment.

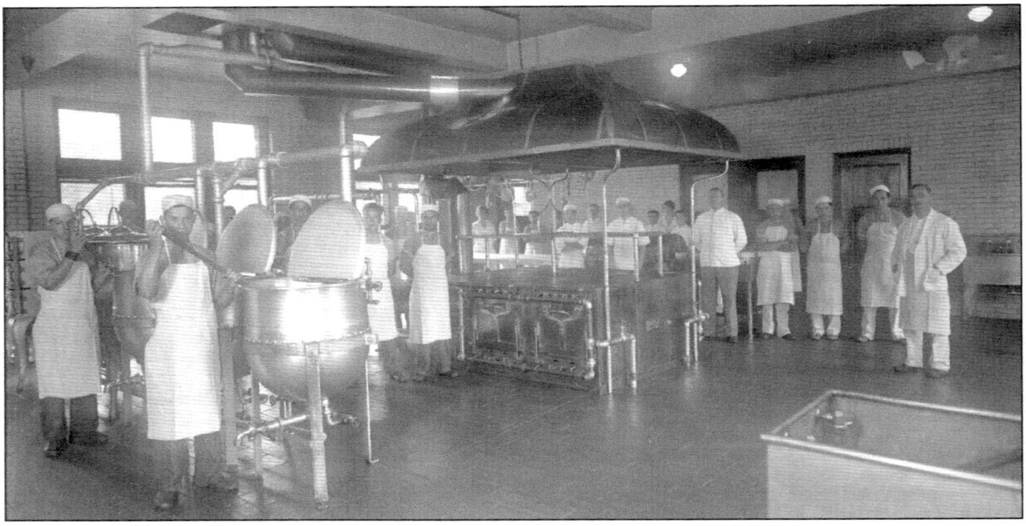

Boys are seen here working in the bakery. Originally located behind the administration building, it was moved to a smaller structure constructed next to the dietary building. The two buildings were connected by an underground tunnel, the bakery had a small boiler plant capable of heating both buildings, and the basements were made of fireproof material.

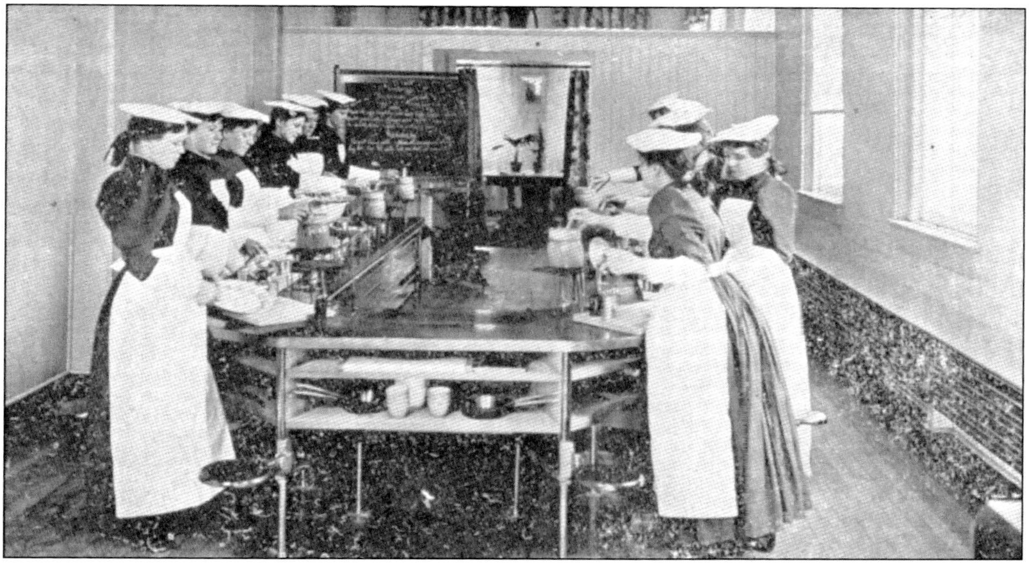

The photograph shows girls in the kitchen preparing a meal. Unlike other tasks performed at the institution, baking was taught to both genders. Breads, pies, and pastries were all made in the well-equipped bakery and kitchen at the institution. Experienced bakers instructed the children in the art of baking.

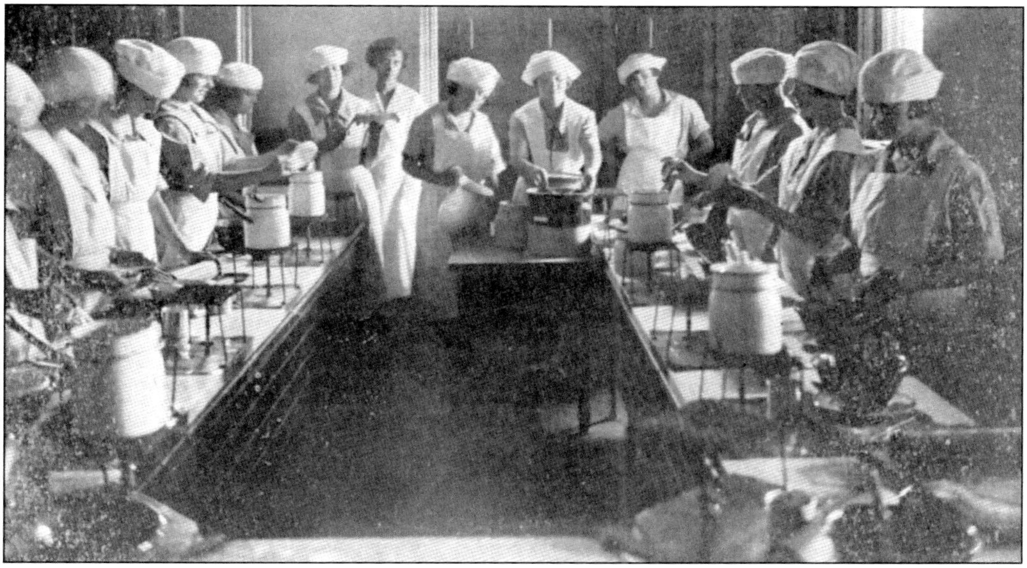

Domestic science classes were taught to classes of 12 girls. According to a school report in 1908, the pupils were taught in morning classes from 9:00 a.m. to 11:30 a.m. or in afternoon classes from 2:00 p.m. to 4:30 p.m. In the 1907 fruit season, 400 glasses of jelly and 130 quarts of marmalade, jam, ketchup, and canned fruit were prepared by girls in the domestic science department.

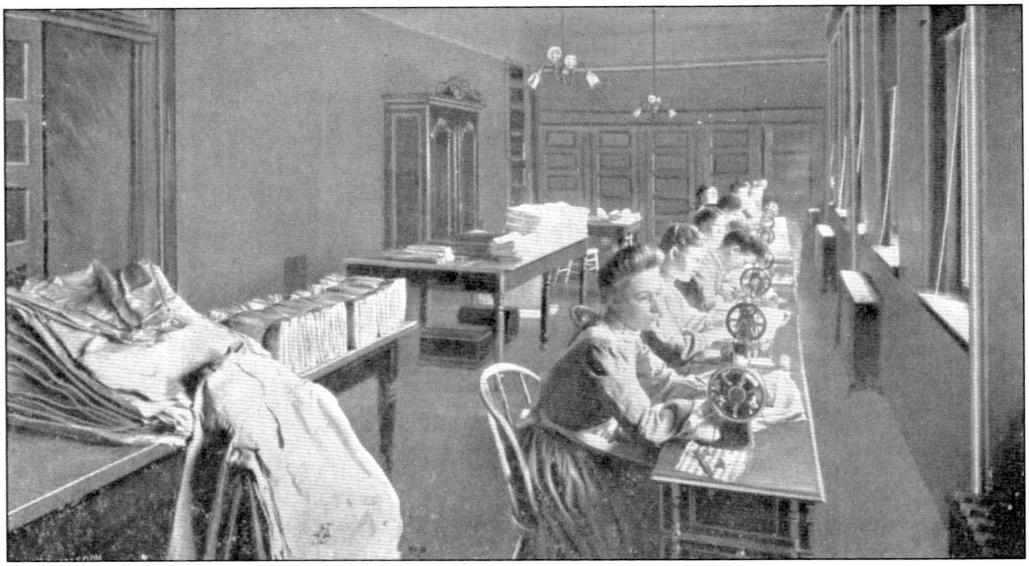

Some girls were taught sewing, knitting, basketry, drawing, designing, crocheting, embroidering, art, and some woodwork. The sewing department made dresses, gowns, and boys' shirts. In 1944, additional sewing machines were secured by the Department of Welfare. Curtains were made for cottages that featured vibrant colors, helping to boost morale during wartime. In 1947, a total of 712 dresses were made, and 900 were made in 1949.

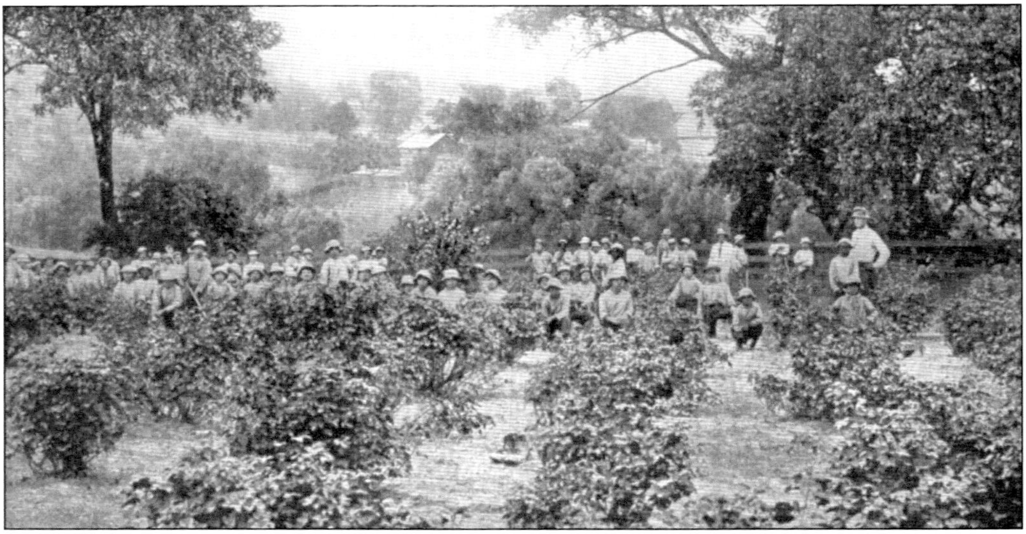

Boys are seen here tending to the gardens. Boys did much of the gardening and farm work for the entire institution. In 1930, the production of crops was as follows: oats, 110 acres; wheat, 18 acres; potatoes, 40 acres; corn, 75 acres, clovers and alfalfa, 206 acres; Timothy hay, 54 acres; garden truck, 40 acres; small fruits, 3 acres; and orchards, 50 acres. In preparation for the next spring, the upcoming year's early spring plantings included 5,000 tomato plants, 15,000 sets of celery, 10,000 cabbages, and 2,000 cauliflowers. In the late spring, there were 50,000 cabbages, 5,000 cauliflowers, and 40,000 celery. Other crops planted throughout the year included 5,000 Brussels sprouts, 4,000 peppers, and 1,000 broccoli plants.

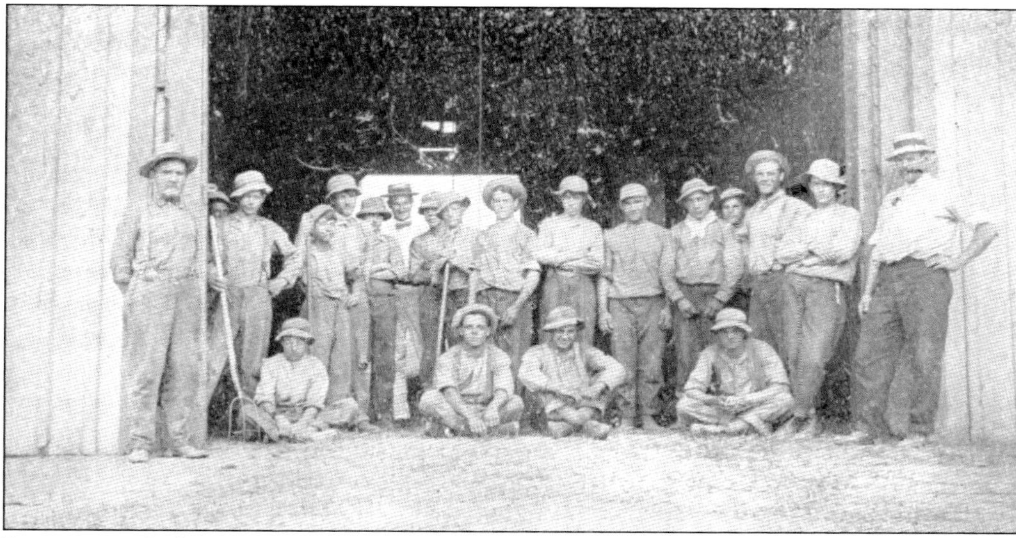

Farming was the biggest department at the institution. In 1906, of the 495 inmates at the institution, 135 boys worked in farming. Besides the typical practice garden work of necessary grains, fruits, and vegetables, the farm also raised poultry, sheep, hogs, cattle, and other livestock. By the mid-1940s, a piggery was added. During World War II, the farm was instructed by the governor of Pennsylvania to produce as much as possible. The farm program produced $67,485 worth of farm products between 1943 and 1944.

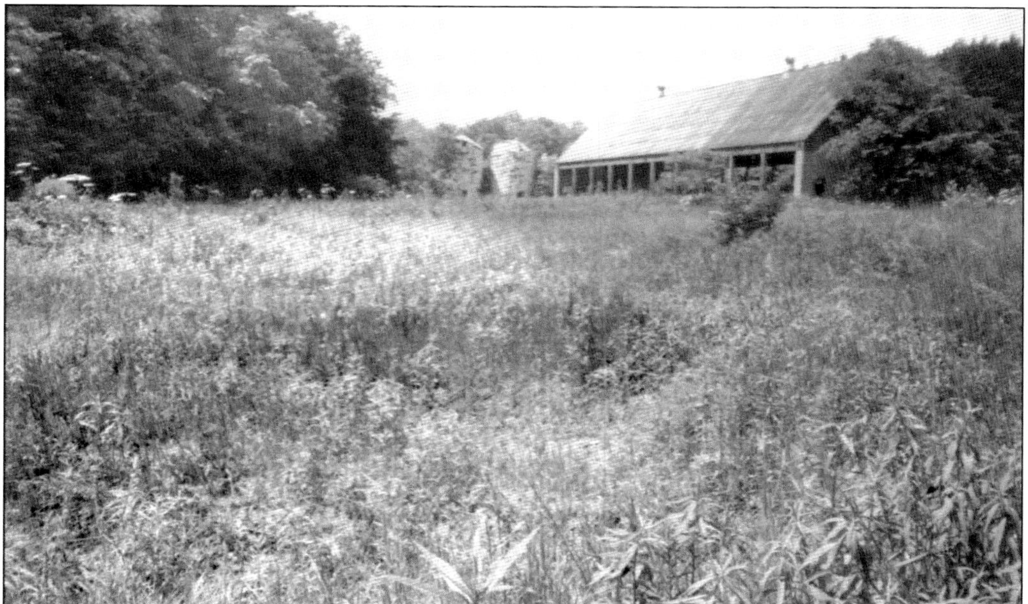

This view shows one of several barns once located on the training school grounds. In 1953, one barn, two storage buildings, and tons of grain were destroyed by fire. It was reported at 4:00 p.m. after being seen from a larger two-story barn. Before the school fire department arrived, 30 cattle were moved from the basement shelter to the cattle yard. The barn had been built in 1888, but it was remodeled a few years before the fire with a new foundation, flooring, and roofing. (Courtesy of Pennsylvania Historical and Museum Commission.)

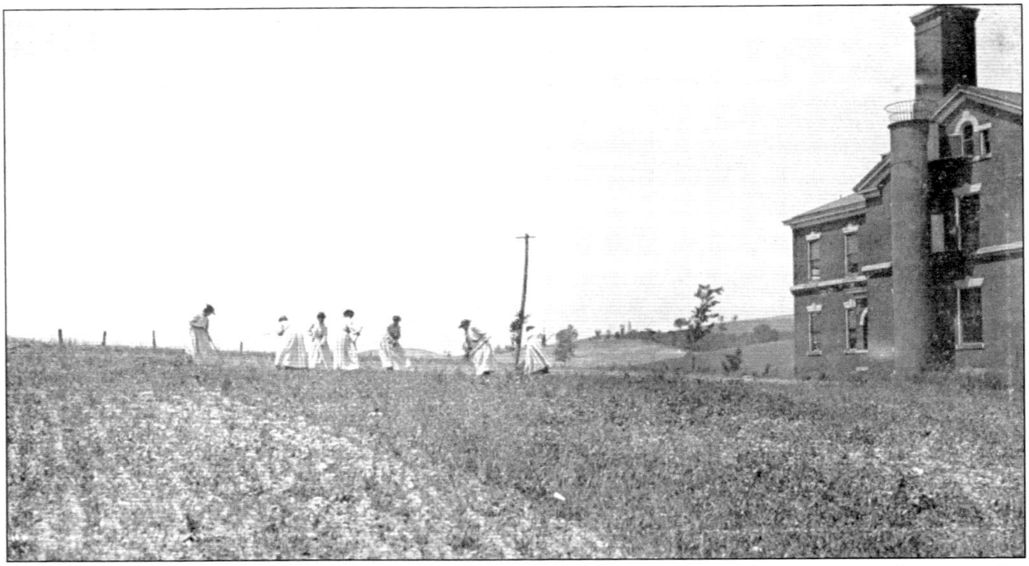

Girls are seen wearing long, flowing dress skirts with blouses and working in a garden near the girls' main building. Girls not only tended vegetable gardens, but also planted flowers and groomed gardens, helping to maintain the aesthetic of the grounds.

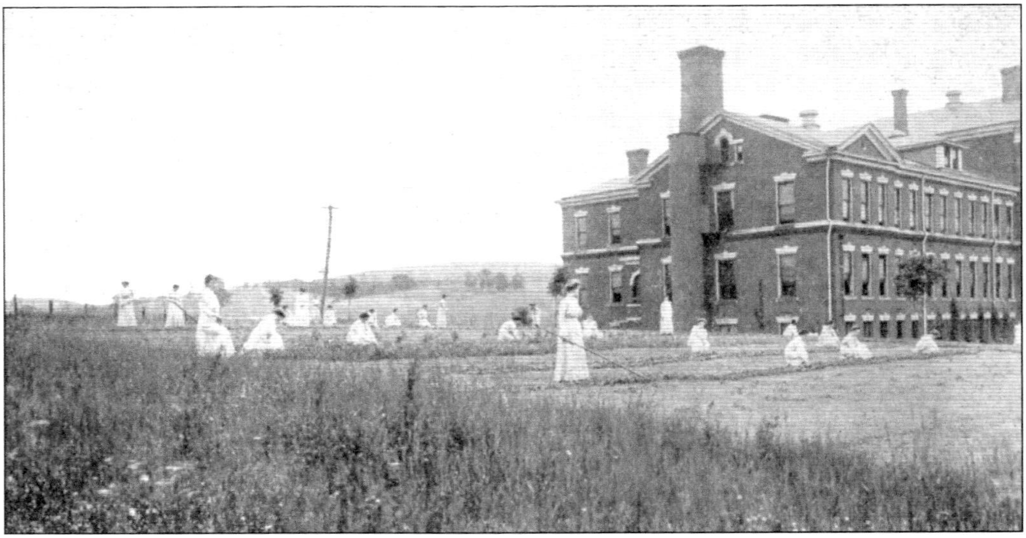

Another view of the gardens near the girls' main building shows more girls working in the garden. According to records from a biennial report by the school, girls did not begin gardening work until around 1912, when just six girls worked in the gardens. A report in 1914 showed that the number of girls working in the gardens had risen to 18. The majority of gardening was done by the boys; 100 of them worked in the gardens in 1914.

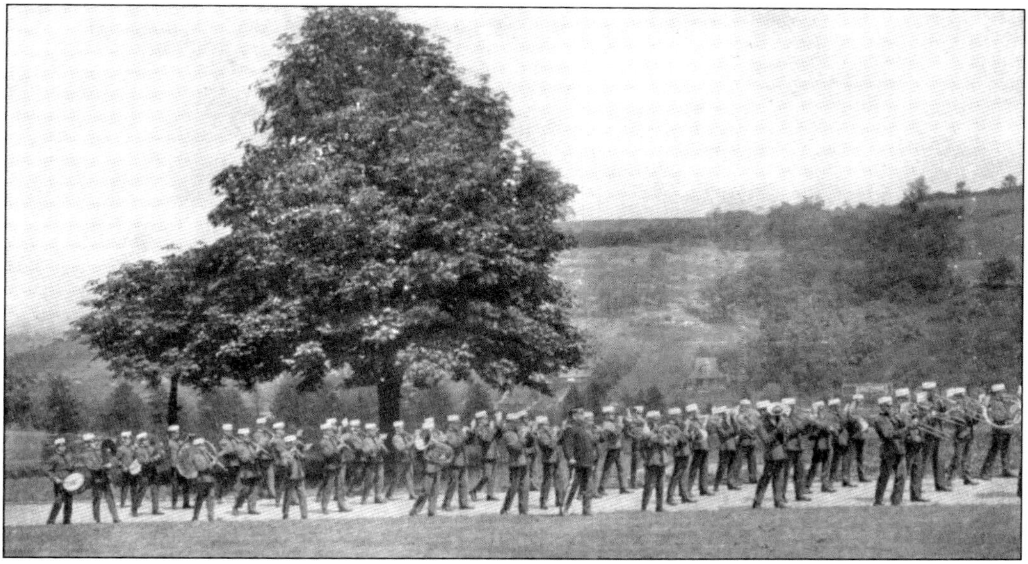

The cadet band was made up of 30 to 40 pieces. Upon leaving the school, many of the cadets found that their musical education led them into good positions. Some boys led orchestras of their own; some of them with high-standing musicians in leading organizations throughout the country. The orchestras played regularly for chapel services.

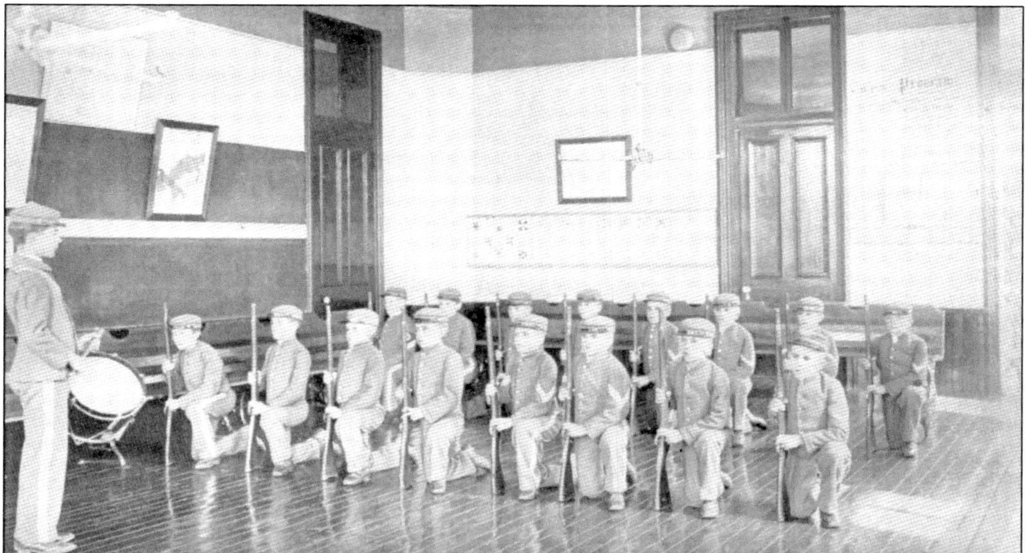

An Army-trained drill instructor supervised and directed the boys. The routines taught to the boys were the United States' infantry drills. Directions were taken by selected student officers. Over the years, boys who showed aptitude for this work assumed the responsibilities and duties of battalion adjutant.

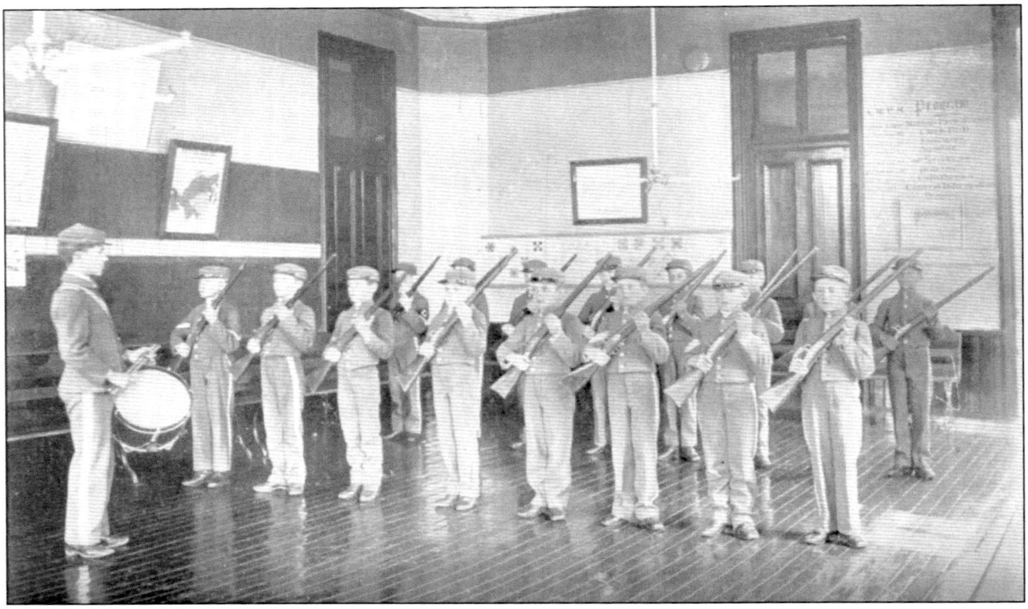

Cadets were taught that honor was always a virtue of true soldiers and that this virtue was no less necessary in civilian life. The training would teach an individual that soldiers and citizens are alike: both are obedient to regulations and laws and must respect those in authority. Many boys went on to hold responsible positions as noncommissioned officers and bandsmen in the US Army because of their training at the school.

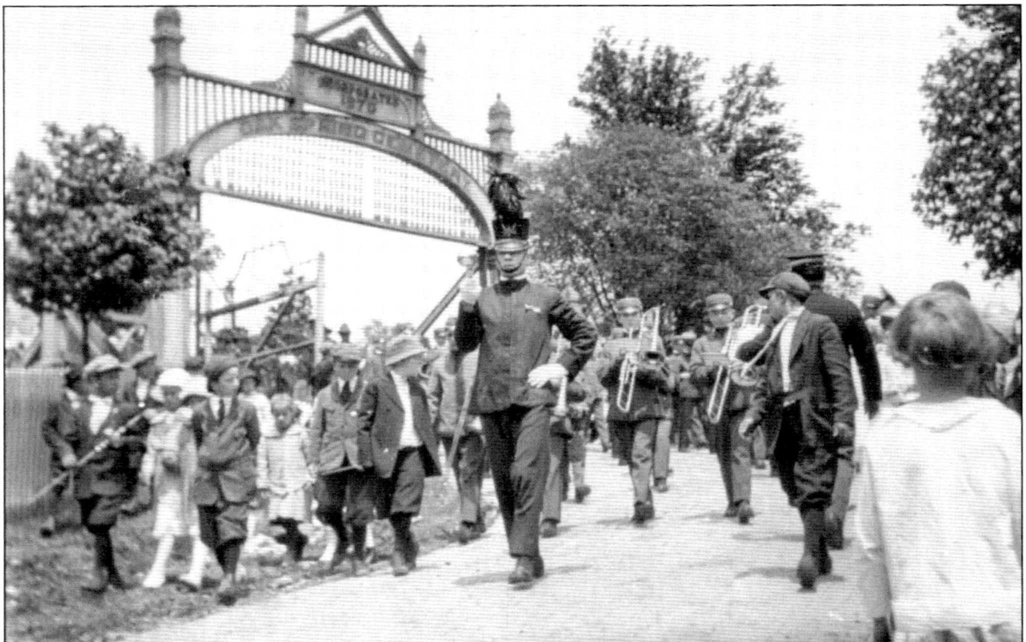

The Pennsylvania Training School cadets march in the 1917 Memorial Day parade at the Oak Spring Cemetery. The cadets would often perform outside the school at holiday parades, concerts, and other occasions.

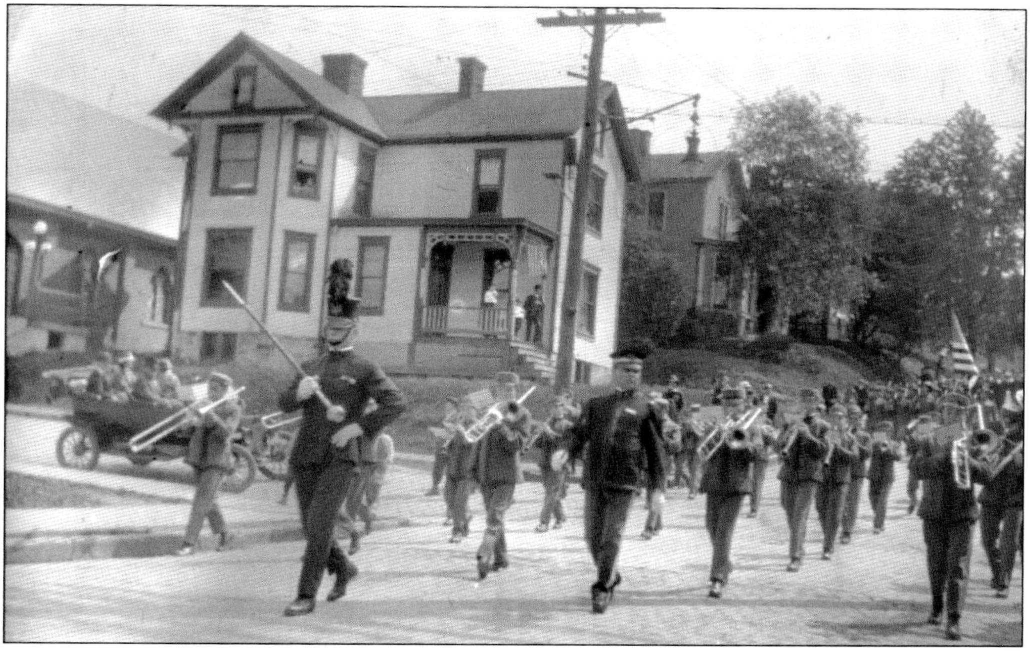

The Pennsylvania Training School band often marched in local parades. The picture shows the band marching on College Street in Canonsburg during the 1917 Memorial Day parade.

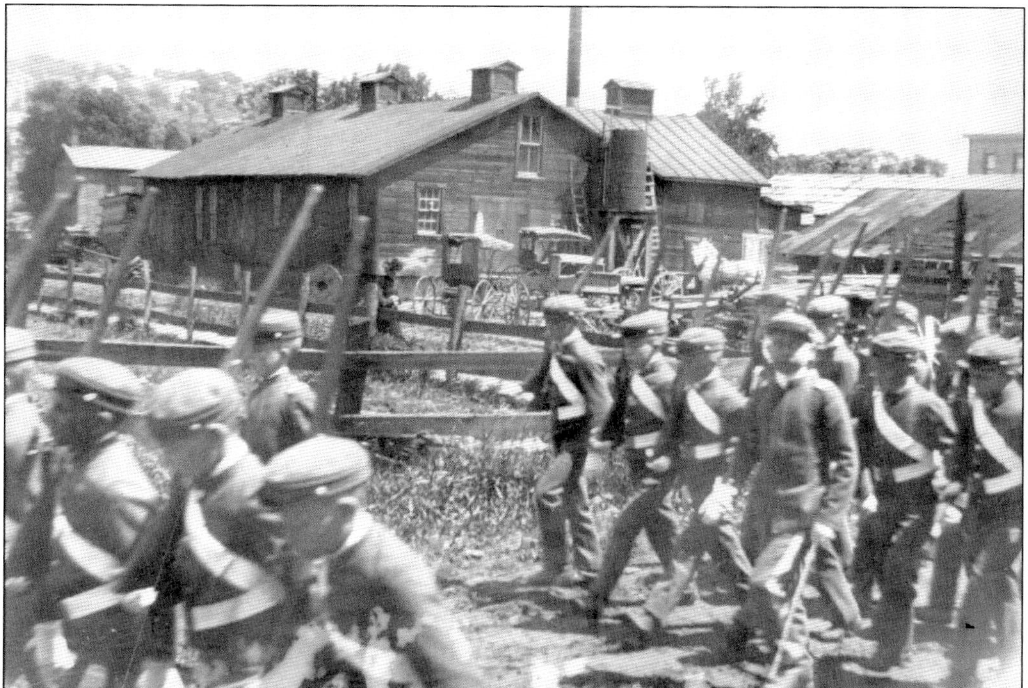

Boys march in their cadet uniforms in front of the Taylor & Crawford lumberyard on Harrison Street in Canonsburg. The cadets were taking part in the Canonsburg centennial parade in 1902. The photograph was taken by Howard Taylor.

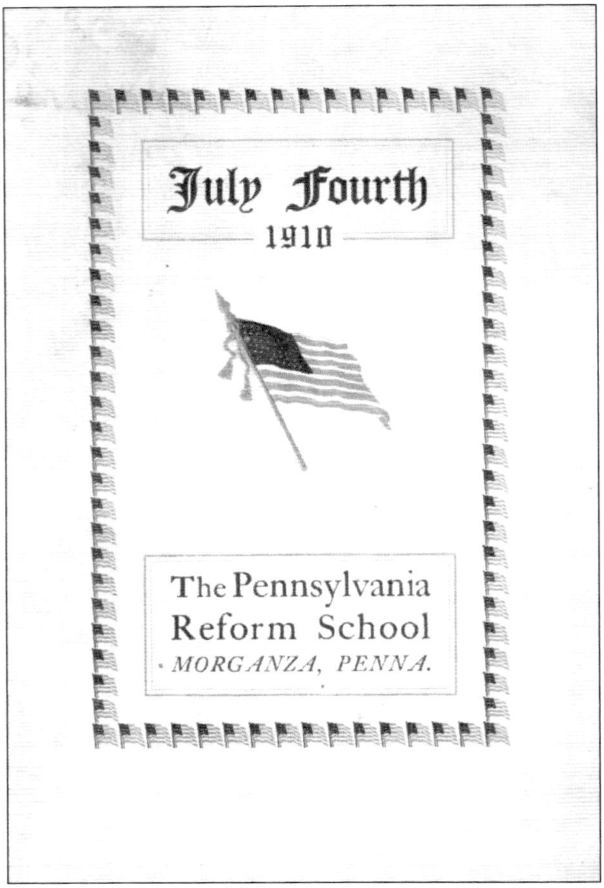

The 1910 Fourth of July pamphlet, printed by the school's printing department, is 24 pages, with the center two pages detailing the schedule of the day's events. It also contains details about the institution and the history of the Fourth of July.

The Fourth of July celebration was a big event for the school. Great preparation was taken with the buildings, grounds, and equipment for the event. The all-day event started with a parade of the cadet corps at 10:30 a.m., led by the institution band. Regimental review and competitive drill followed. The afternoon program began with speeches by the superintendent and the head of the board of trustees. Athletic events, drills, calisthenics, musical numbers, and other features also marked the afternoon program. In the evening, there was a concert by the school's orchestra in front of the administration building.

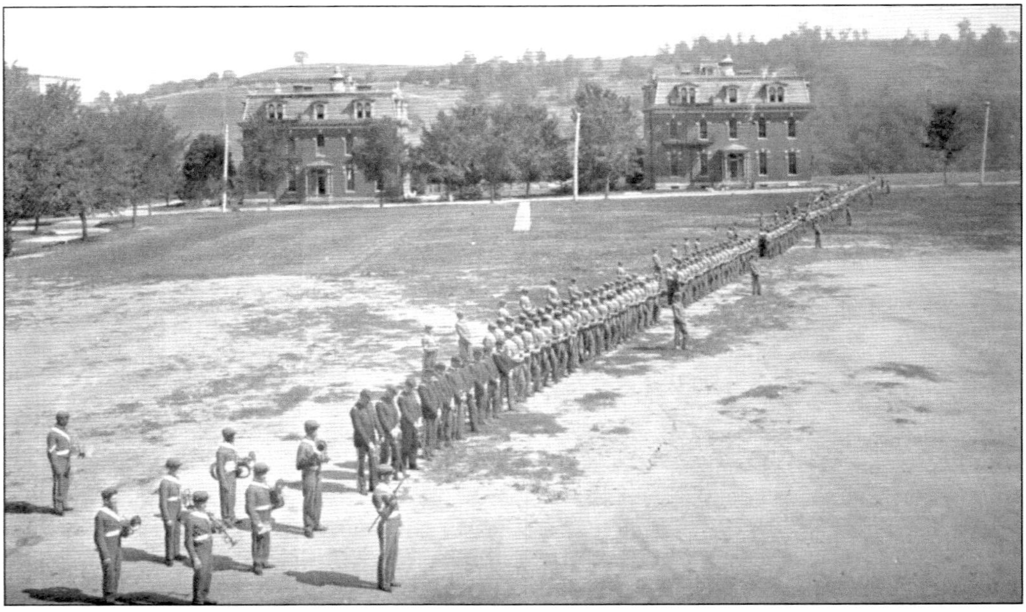

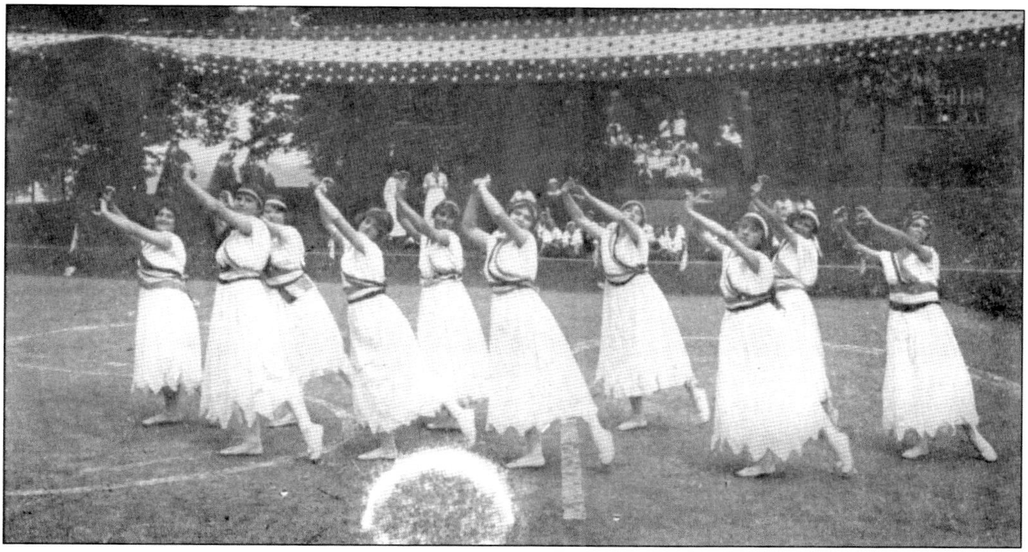

This group of girls performs a dance routine during a celebration day. The girls of the institution often performed folk dances, quadrilles, minuets, and field drills at Fourth of July celebrations.

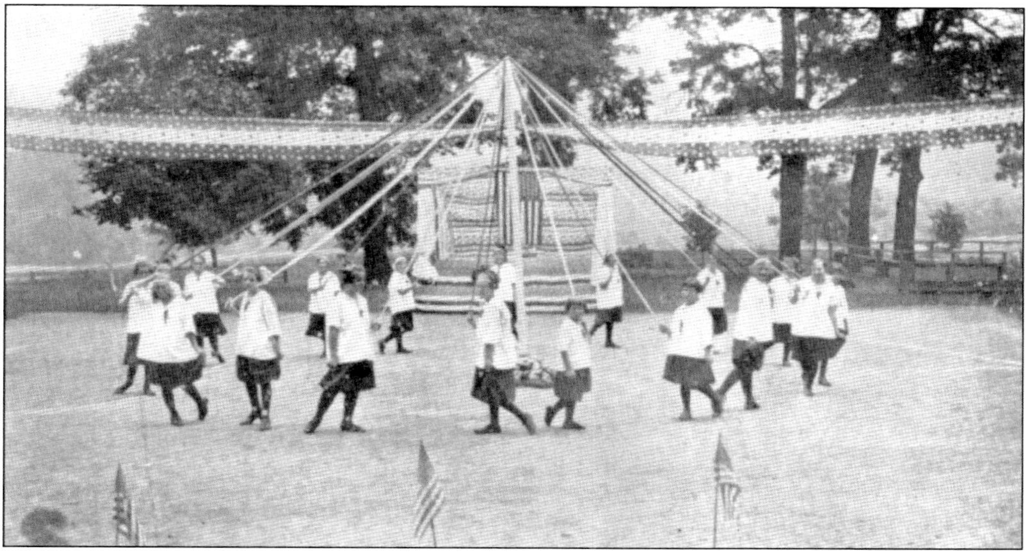

Here, girls take part in the Maypole dance on May Day, each of them holding a ribbon attached to the pole. The ribbons were intertwined and were woven either onto the pole itself or into a web around the pole. The dancers then retraced their steps to unravel the ribbons.

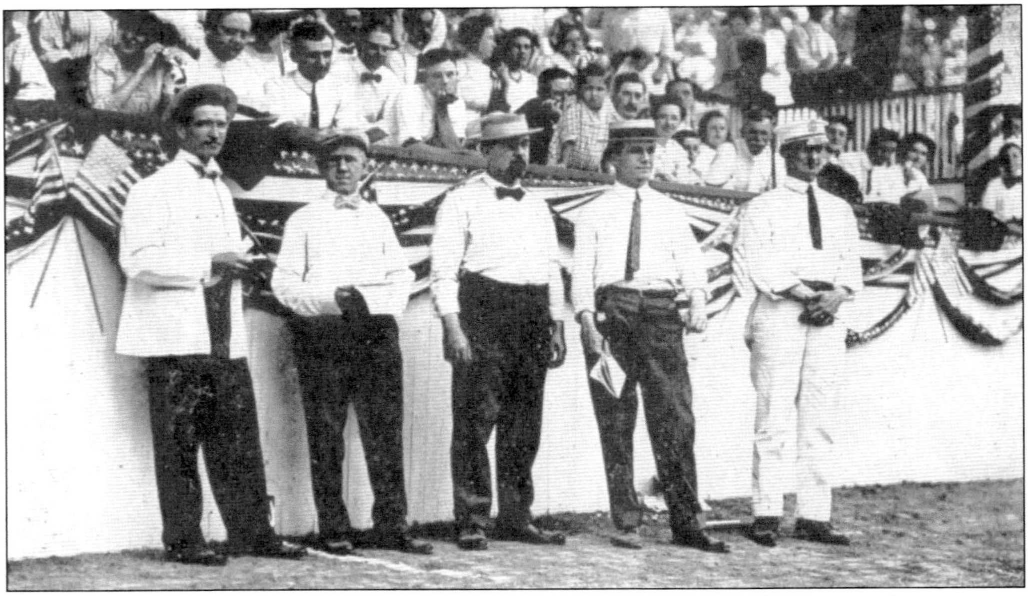

The athletic events at the Fourth of July celebrations were competitive. The picture shows a group of judges with some of the many spectators who came to watch the spectacle.

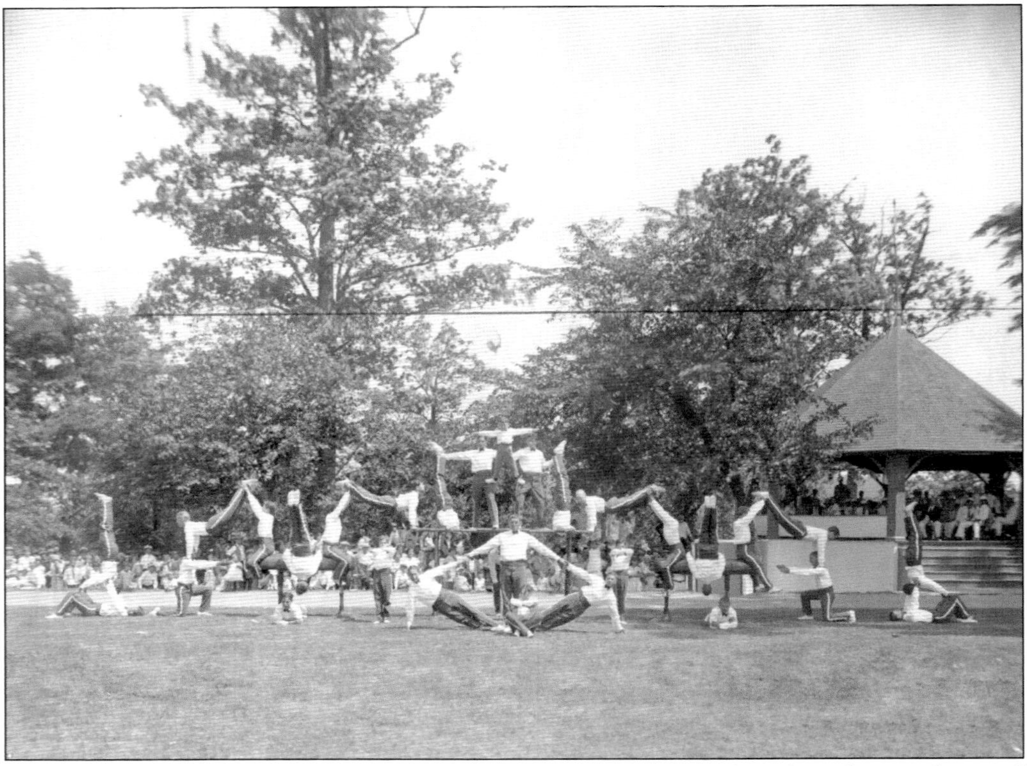

This large group of boys performs an intricate gymnastics routine. The talented group shows off their skills in front of a large audience, likely at a Fourth of July event. The boys held the difficult gymnastic tableau long enough for a photograph to be captured.

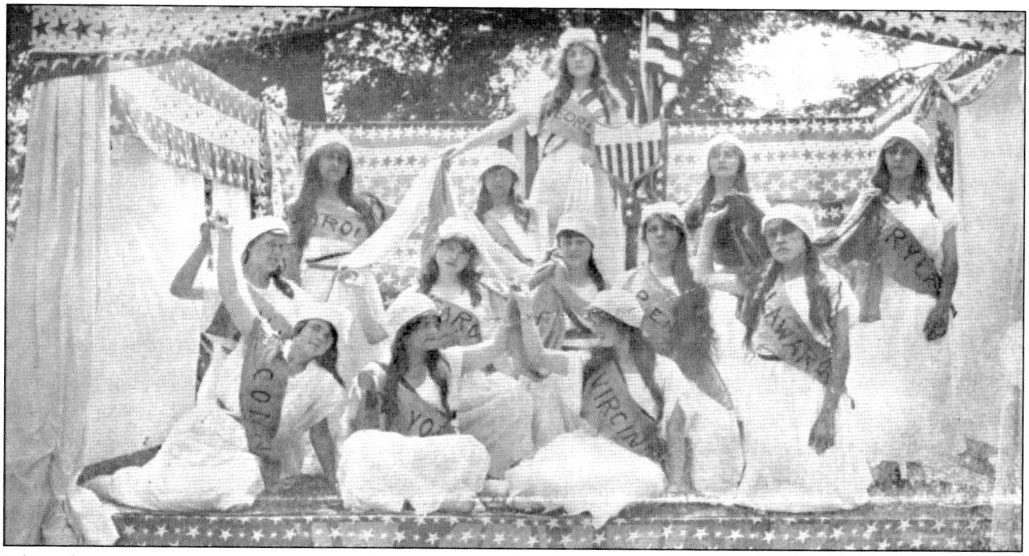

This photograph shows a pageant show during a Fourth of July celebration. Pageants were common at events like these. In 1945, a pageant show was presented by Protestant chaplain William R. McKim. More than 100 girls modeled a variety of clothing made in the girls' division, including street dresses, house robes, lounging robes, garden costumes, waitress dresses and aprons, and work and play suits.

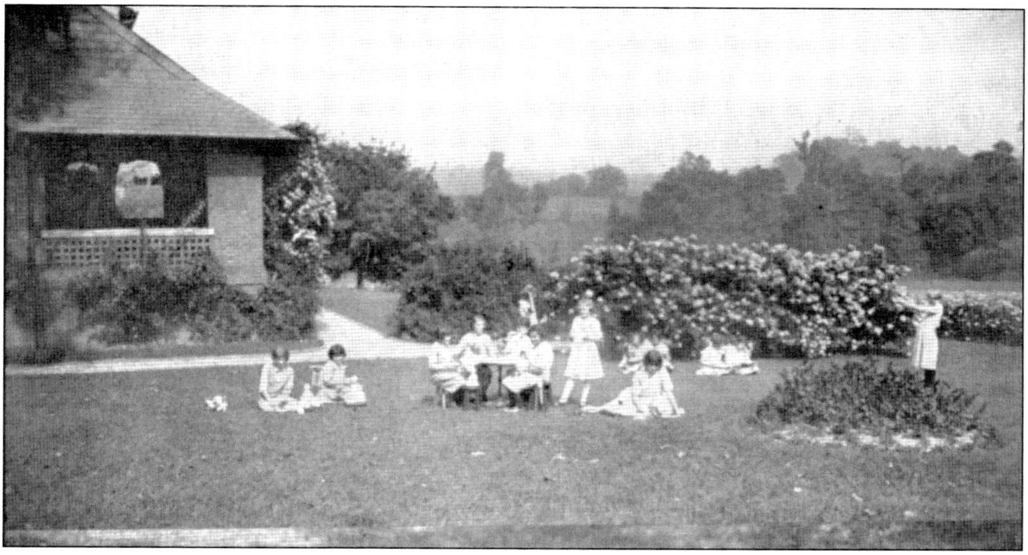

Girls are gathered on the lawn of a cottage for an outdoor party. Girls were typically never seen with boys, as the school did not allow them to speak to or mingle with one another. The only time they were seen in the same place was in the chapel during services or entertainment, according to a school's biennial report in 1892.

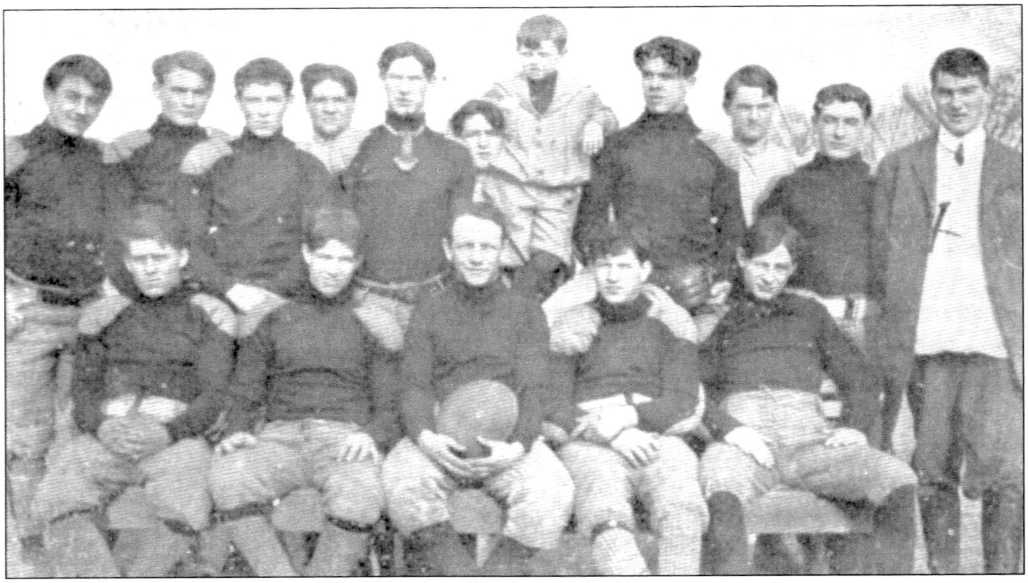

Prior to 1908, Morganza athletic teams competed only with other cottages' teams within the institution. In that year, varsity teams were formed in different sports by selecting boys with the best abilities from all cottages. The varsity teams faced outside schools in games. On October 27, 1908, the Morganza football team defeated Washington & Jefferson Academy 11-10 after only two weeks of practice. In the following year, Superintendent Penn secured coaches from Washington & Jefferson. The first-class coaches whipped the team into shape, and they were not scored on the entire season. That year, they played the Canonsburg Scholastics, Washington & Jefferson Academy, and Washington High School.

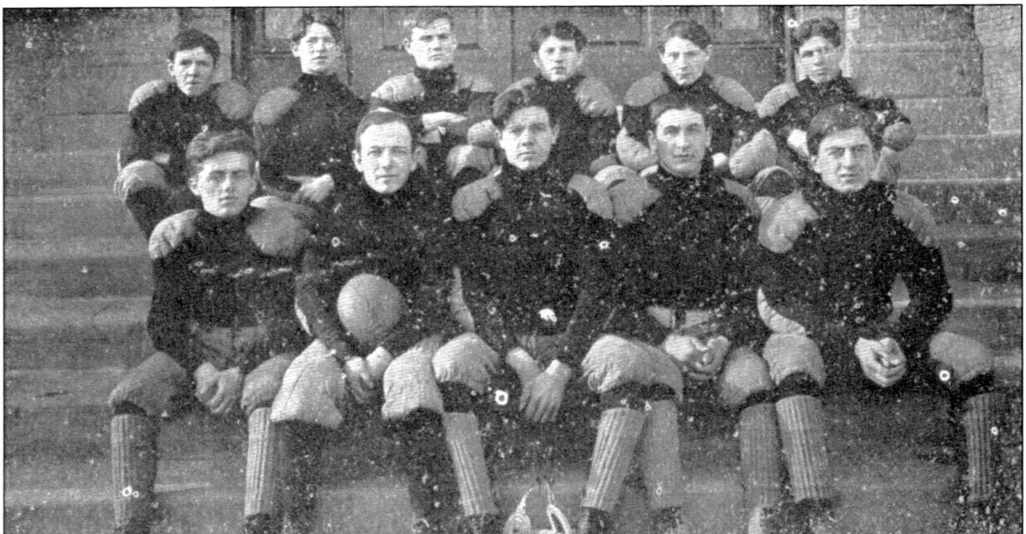

The football program was dropped in 1945 and then reinstituted in 1953 by Supt. George Miles. In 1954, the team won its season opener against West Bethlehem 19-0. Morganza's average linemen weighed in at 160 pounds, those in the backfield weighed an average of 155 pounds, and the team was considered "rather light" for teams playing during this time. Teams they faced included West Bethlehem, Centerville, and Chartiers High Schools.

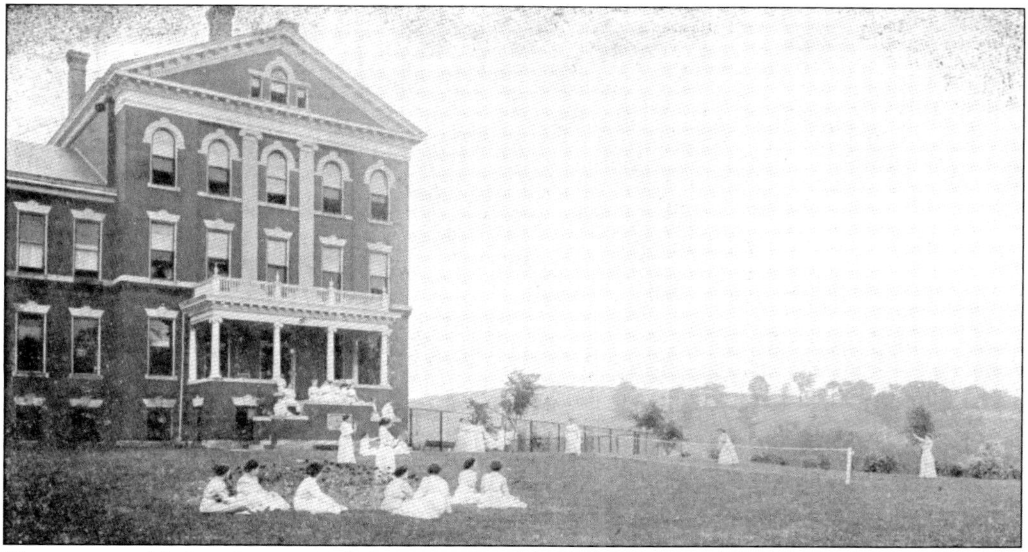

This picture, likely taken around the opening of the girls' main building, shows girls watching a game of tennis. By 1910, tennis courts were constructed as part of the girls' department.

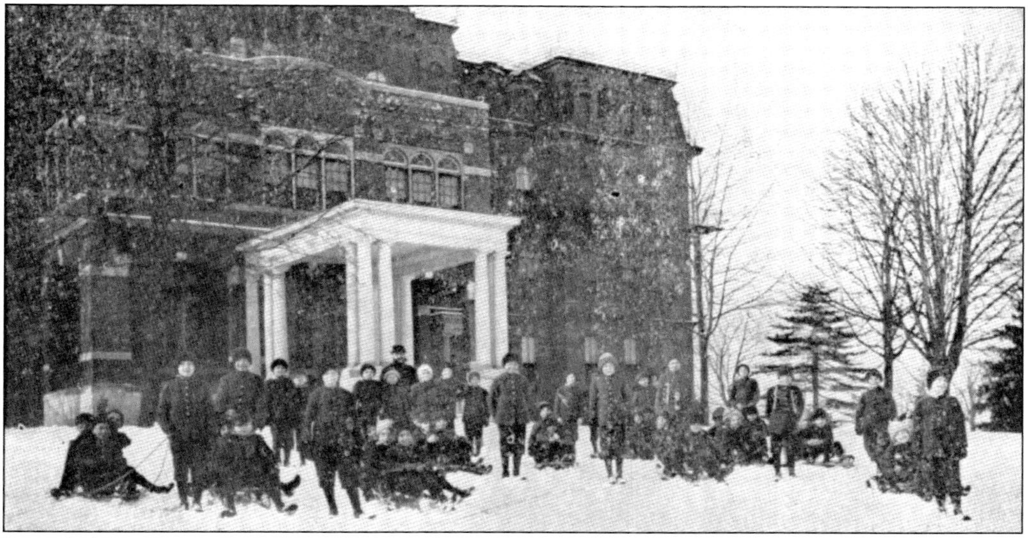

Boys sledding on a snowy day pose for a photograph in front of the administration building in the early 1900s. Recreation time was given to the children at the end of each weekday and for half the day on Saturday. Sunday was considered a quiet day, with children spending time in their cottages before going to the chapel service in the afternoon.

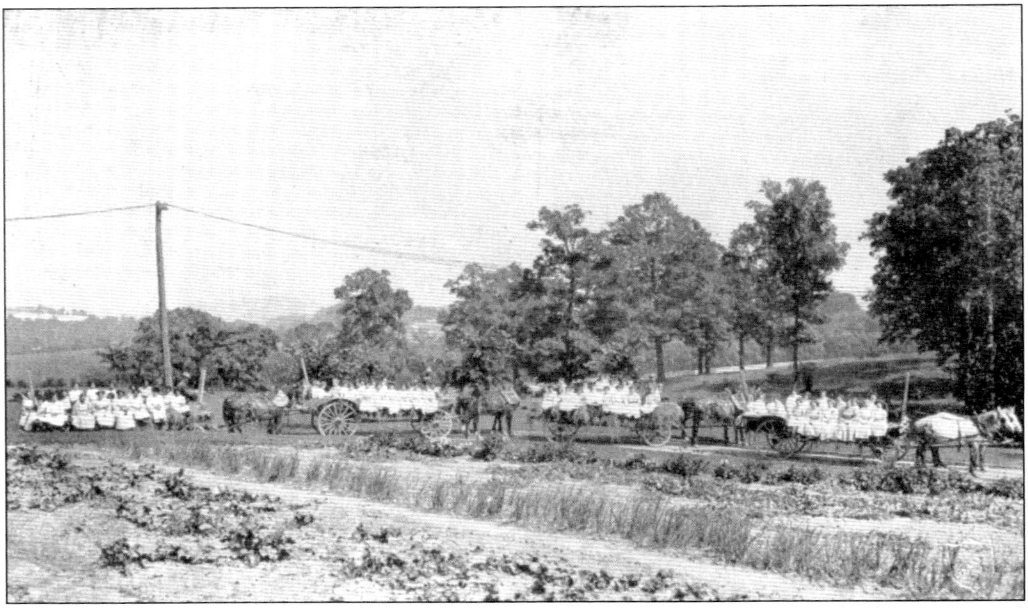

Girls enjoy a hayride through a garden area on a clear day. In the 1890s, wagon sheds were located to the west behind the administration building, where the boys' schoolhouse was constructed. By 1907, they were relocated farther west of the schoolhouse.

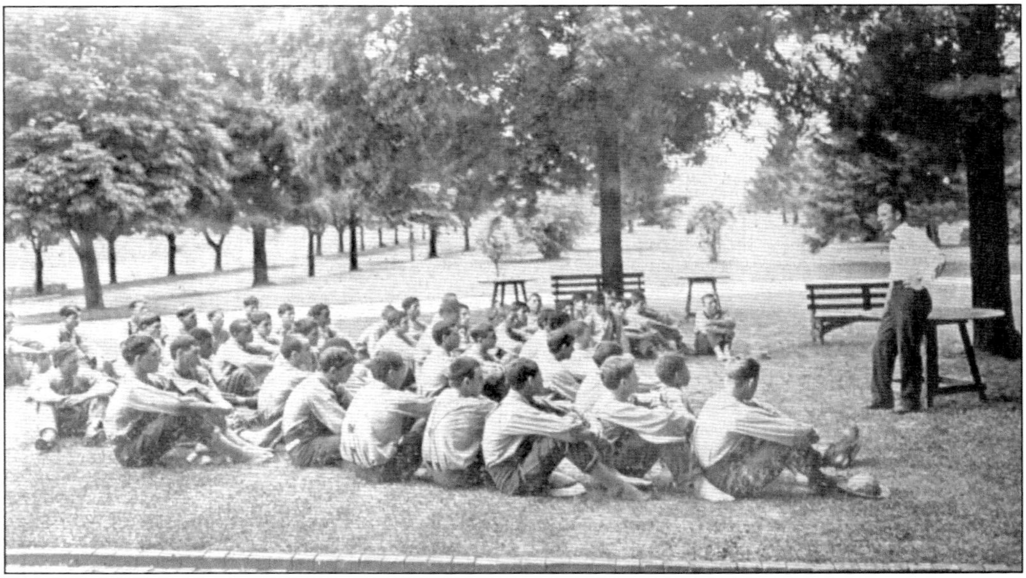

Boys sit on the lawn for a club meeting. In 1930, the Penn Booster Club had 130 members, all boys. The club's purpose was to foster a closer understanding between the school and the boys, making for a friendlier, kinder spirit among them. A club member aimed to be loyal, courteous, obedient, and anxious to boost his school, his cottage, and his brother.

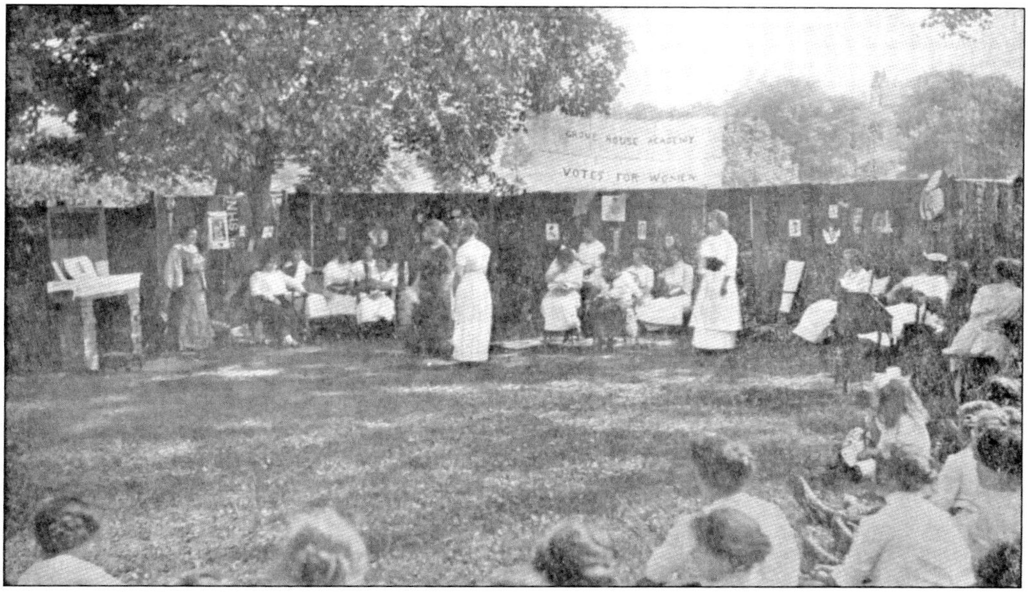

A group of girls performs a play appearing to represent the right of women to vote, which was ratified in 1920. In the photograph, a partitioned wall is used to hang various props, and the sign behind it reads, "Grove House Academy Votes for Women."

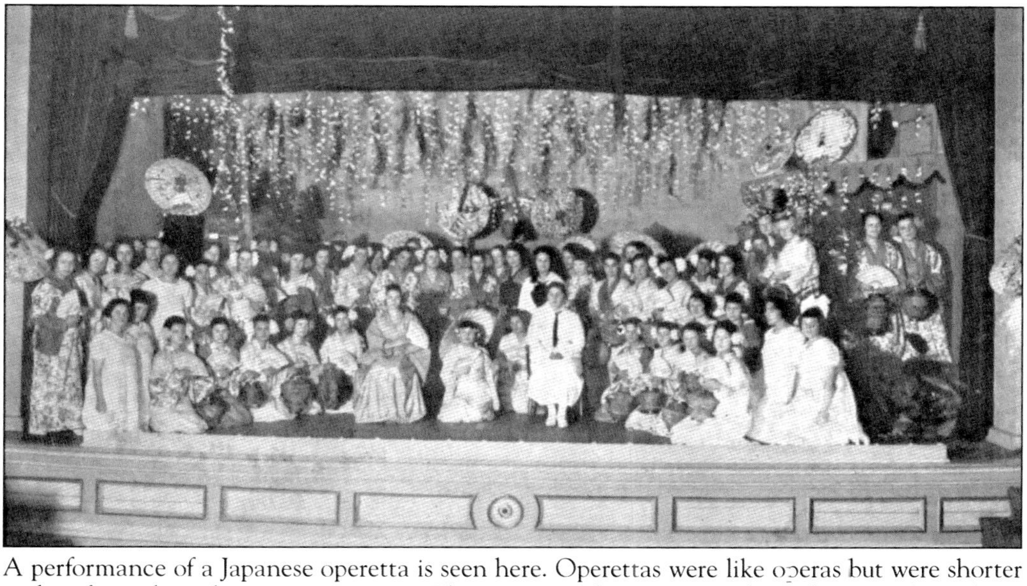

A performance of a Japanese operetta is seen here. Operettas were like operas but were shorter and performed in a less serious manner. There were performances in the auditorium throughout the year. By the 1940s, movies were shown as well. The auditorium had a seating capacity of 1,000 people.

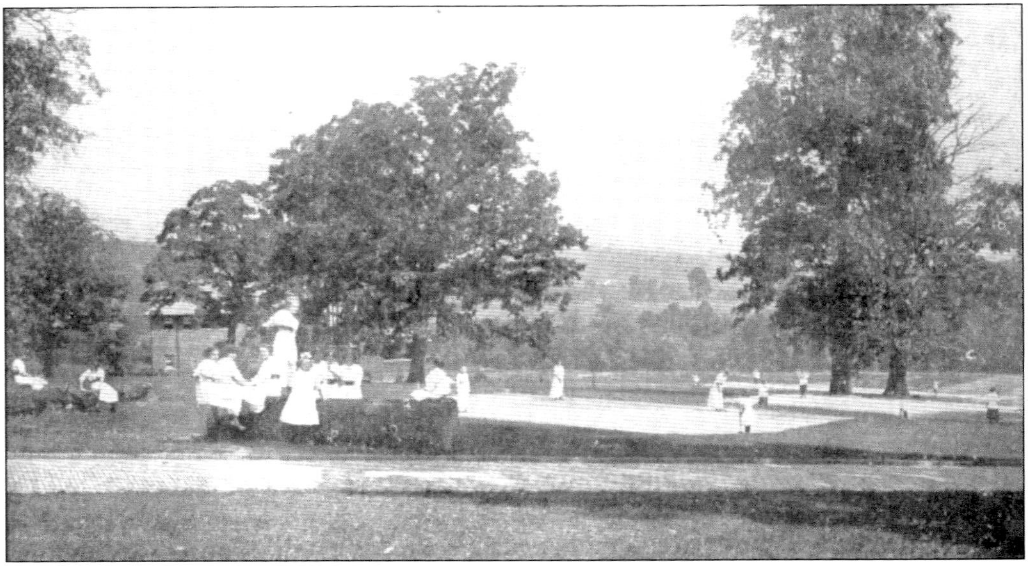

This picture shows a view of the tennis courts located in the girls' section of the campus. Besides tennis, girls also played volleyball, corner ball, and indoor and outdoor basketball. The physical training department was supervised by a trained instructor—a woman for the girls and a man for the boys.

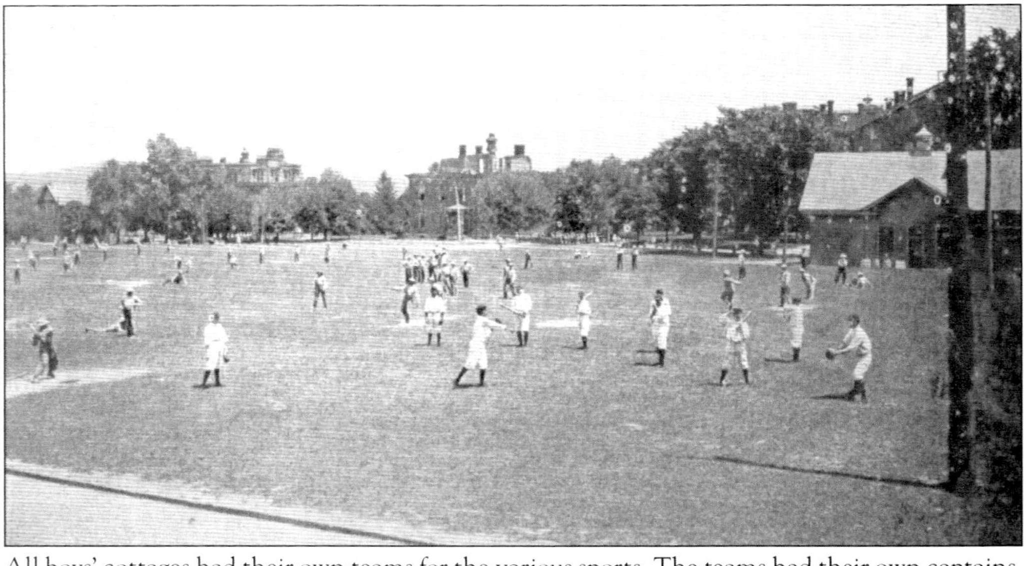

All boys' cottages had their own teams for the various sports. The teams had their own captains, a code and system of plays and signals, and their own cheering section. Most of the time, the cottage teams met on Saturday afternoons, when the playgrounds were busy as the cottages strived for supremacy. The gold saber trophy was awarded to the winning cottage.

Three

TRANSFORMATION

The decision to change the institution from a juvenile reformatory to a home for the mentally handicapped and emotionally disturbed was likely influenced by a sequence of events. In March 1955, an investigation was issued by the Democratic state legislators, William J. Lane and Elmer J. Holland, into charges of "irregular treatment of inmates." There were reports of girls being contained in cells with no toilet systems and little to no food. Secretary Harry Shapiro made a hasty trip and found no brutality; however, he referred to "highly disturbed children" in the detention rooms as being "neglected."

A few months later, in September, a boy died from a shop-related accident in the industrial department. Around this time, a 15-year-old girl had escaped and reported stories of beatings and cruelty by officers at the institute. The state senate voted 39-4 to stage a surprise investigation by reporters Chester Harris and Pat McCormick, a photographer for the *Pittsburgh Sun-Telegraph*, and P.L. Prattis, a member of the board of trustees. The investigation discovered that several girls were being contained in cells in the hospital of the institute in conditions similar to those that had been described earlier. In 1955, an act provided funds for the construction of three new institutions for the mentally handicapped. A submission from the Department of Welfare was then approved in November 1956 for one at Morganza.

In January 1956, the legislators had reported that events at the training school bordered on brutality and that the board of trustees should have or did know of the events. The legislature then made recommendations about the future of the institution. One recommendation was to make Morganza a boys-only institute, which never happened. By 1960, the Pennsylvania Training School underwent another name change and was known then as the Youth Development Center. In December 1962, Western State School and Hospital, a facility to care for the mentally handicapped and emotionally disturbed, opened on the grounds near the Youth Development Center.

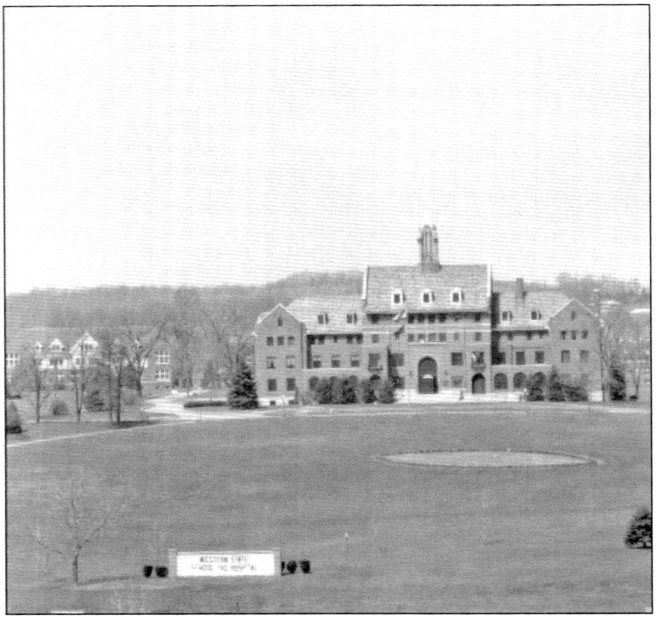

Two patients were admitted to Western State School and Hospital on its first day, in December 1962, followed by two more patients the following day. Dr. Jens A. Dalgaard, the director of Mental Health Services for children for the Department of Public Welfare and Health, was the acting superintendent of the new facility. He stated that just a small number of patients would be admitted at a time. A census of the patients would allow for the addition of more staff if needed as the number of patients grew. At the opening, a staff of 100 was hired, including three doctors and seven full-time registered nurses.

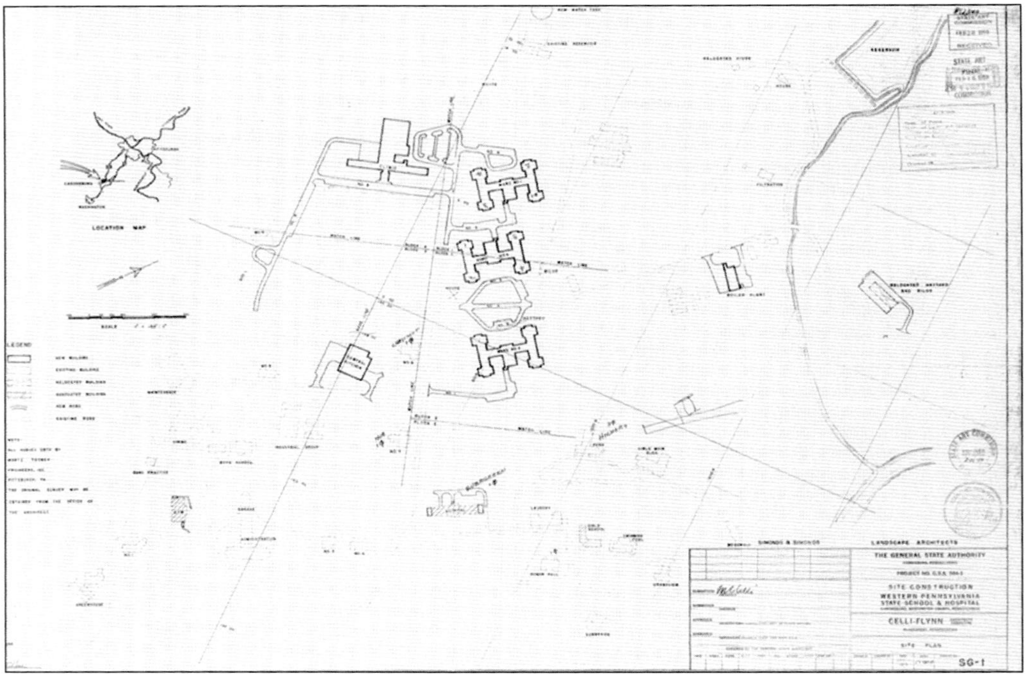

In 1955, an act of the state legislature provided for the construction of three new institutions for the mentally handicapped and emotionally disturbed. The number was increased to four and approved in June 1957. The locations of the new institutions would be in White Haven, Philadelphia, Edensburg, and Canonsburg. This 1959 blueprint shows the proposed plan for Western State School and Hospital, which called for the construction of a seven-story clinic building, three single-story ward buildings, a newer boiler house for steam heating, and a central kitchen. It would be located on the property of the new Youth Development Center. (Courtesy of Adam Ryan.)

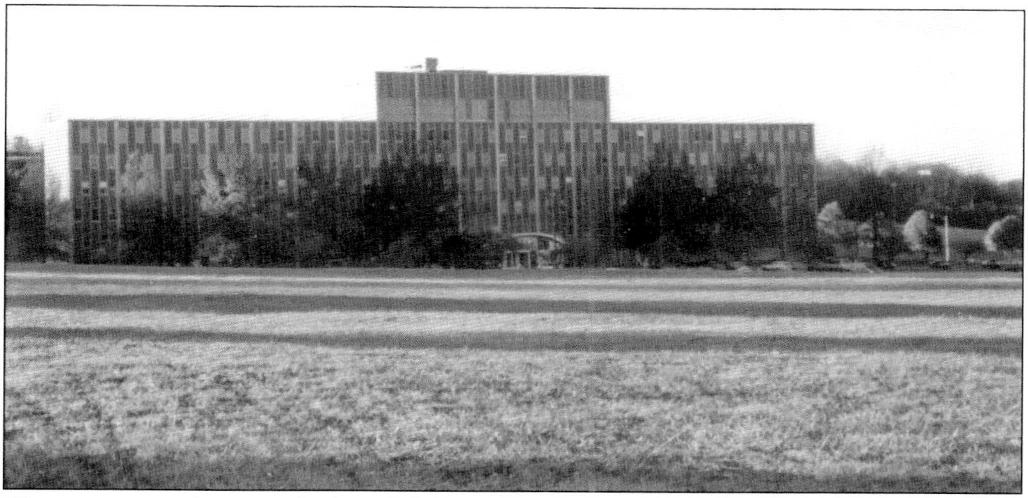

The seven-story clinic was built and dedicated by Gov. David L. Lawrence in 1960. With 204 beds, it opened as a diagnostic treatment center for the institution. The clinic also provided in-patient services for the psychotic and emotionally disturbed. The basement of the clinic included maintenance corridors, clothing storage rooms, and a recreational area. On the first floor, there were administrative offices, clinical laboratories, a dental clinic, a pharmacy, a library, classrooms, and a medical records room as well as social services, occupational therapy, physical therapy, therapeutic recreation, volunteer services, psychology, x-ray, speech and hearing, steno-pool, central supply, and various specialty clinics. New admissions, intensive care units, and classroom and activity areas for treatment service were housed on the second, third, and fourth floors. The fifth and sixth floors housed the emotionally disturbed, preadolescent males and females, and adolescent males. A resident cafeteria, conference room, and beauty shop were all located on the seventh floor. (Courtesy of Diane Hickman.)

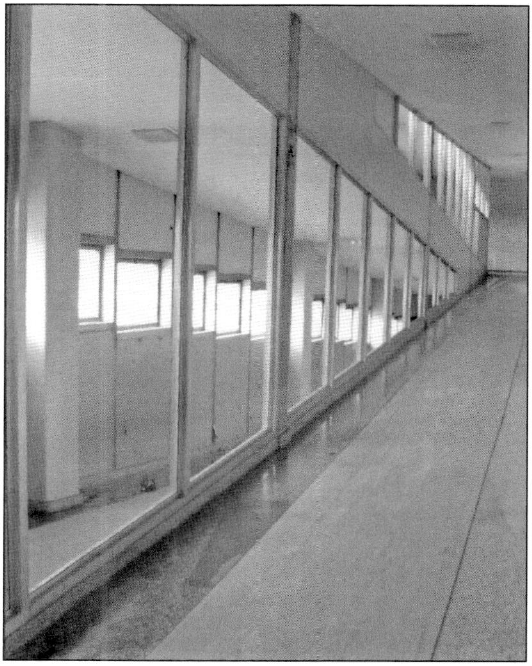

One unique feature of the clinic building was the unique ramp on the northwestern edge that connected to each floor. The ramp could be noticed from the outside of the building, marked by the stepping of windows that led from one floor to the next. The ramp connected to all seven stories of the clinic building, allowing nurses to easily move patients by wheelchair from floor to floor. (Courtesy of Rebecca Brocato.)

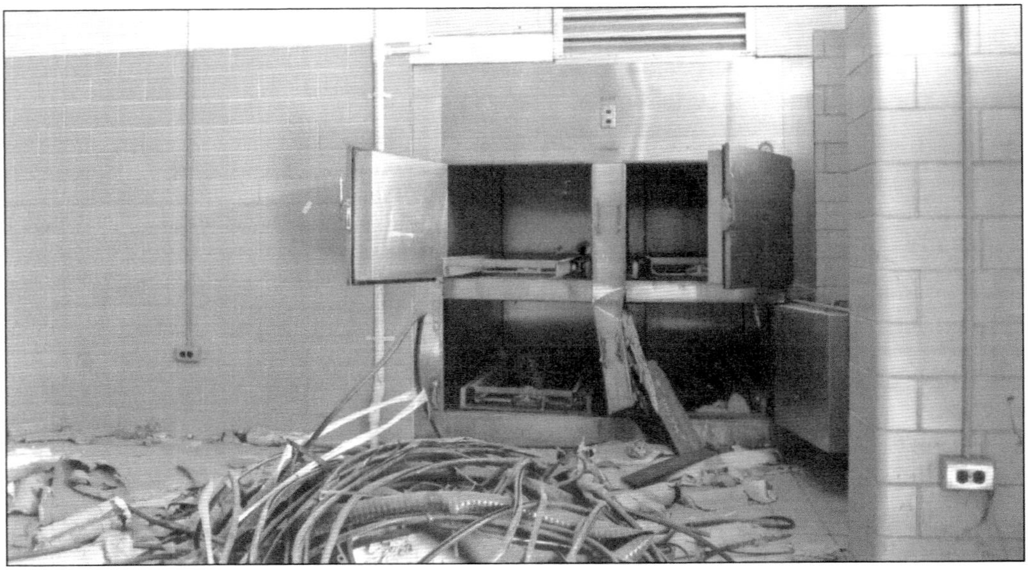

Located in the laboratory area was a morgue, with four refrigerated holding compartments and a hearse entrance. The compartments were almost never used in the way many would think. Instead, the coolers, which contained proper refrigeration, were mainly used for storing items that needed to be kept cool. (Courtesy of Adam Ryan.)

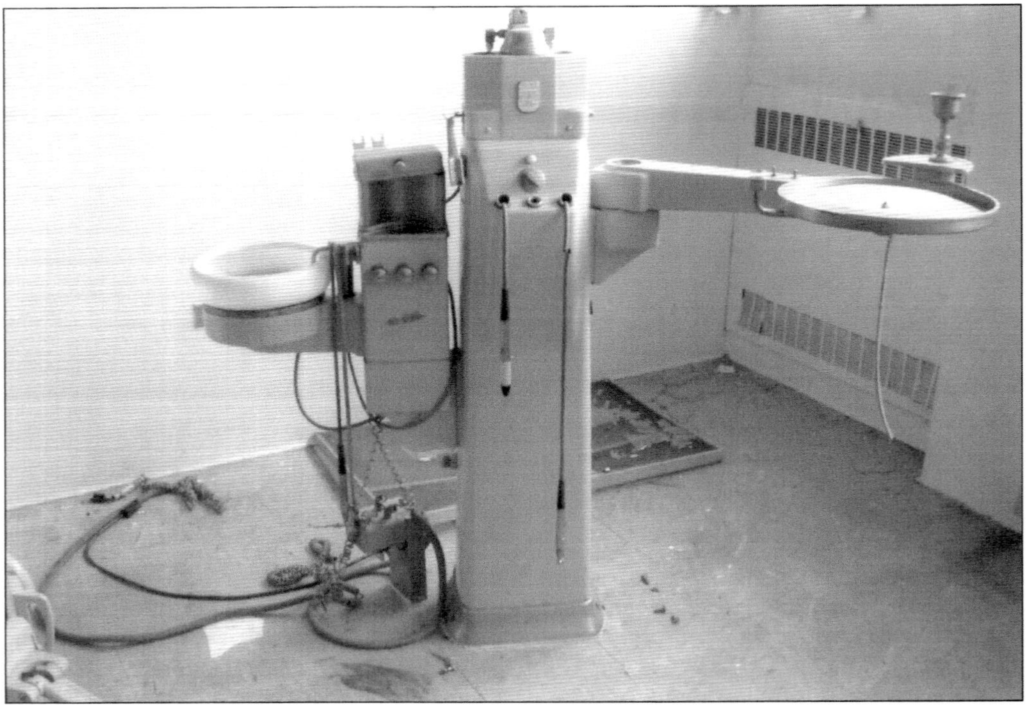

Another department on the first floor was the dental suite, which contained two dental chairs, one equipped for radiography and one for oral surgery. In addition, four dental hygiene chairs, darkroom, workroom, waiting room, and patient restrooms were all located in the dental suite. (Courtesy of Rebecca Brocato.)

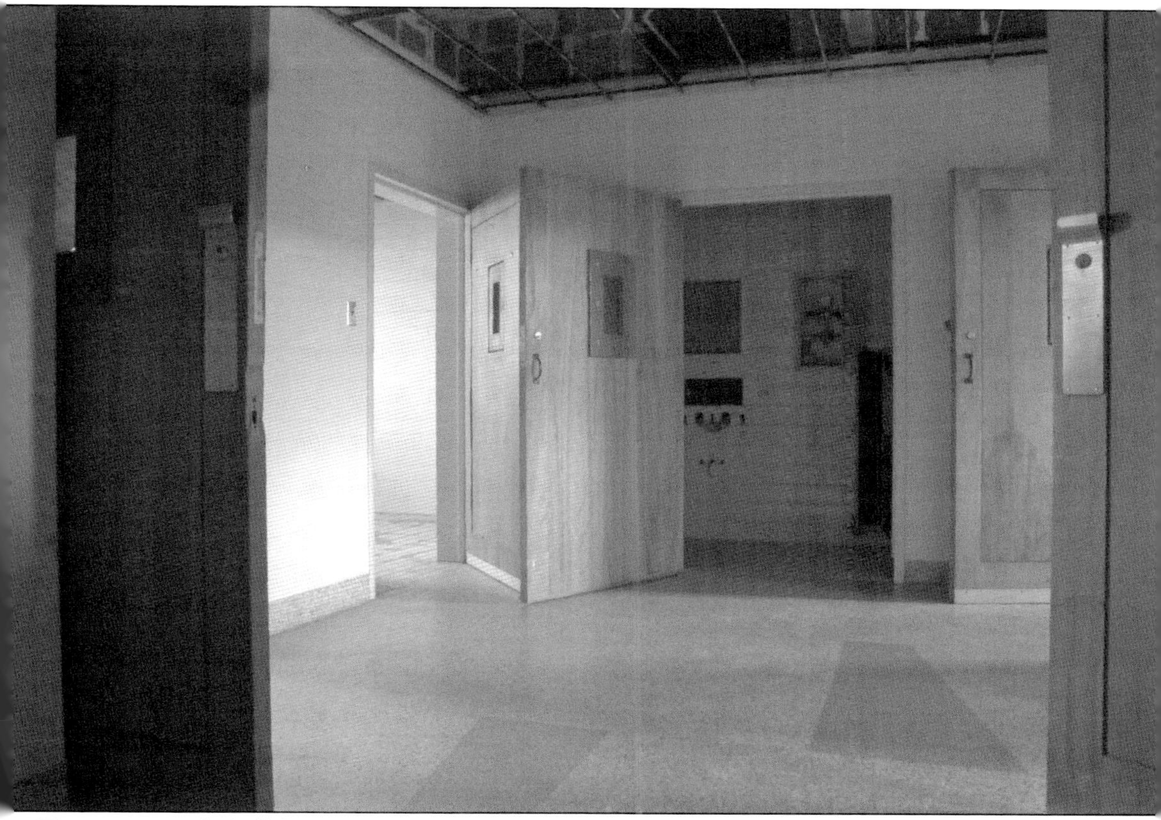

This is a view of a hall from a patient's room located on the fifth floor of the clinic building. Since the floor was used for patients who were emotionally disturbed, wooden frames were added to windows in the doors. The frames reinforced the window glass to prevent patients from breaking them. (Courtesy of Adam Ryan.)

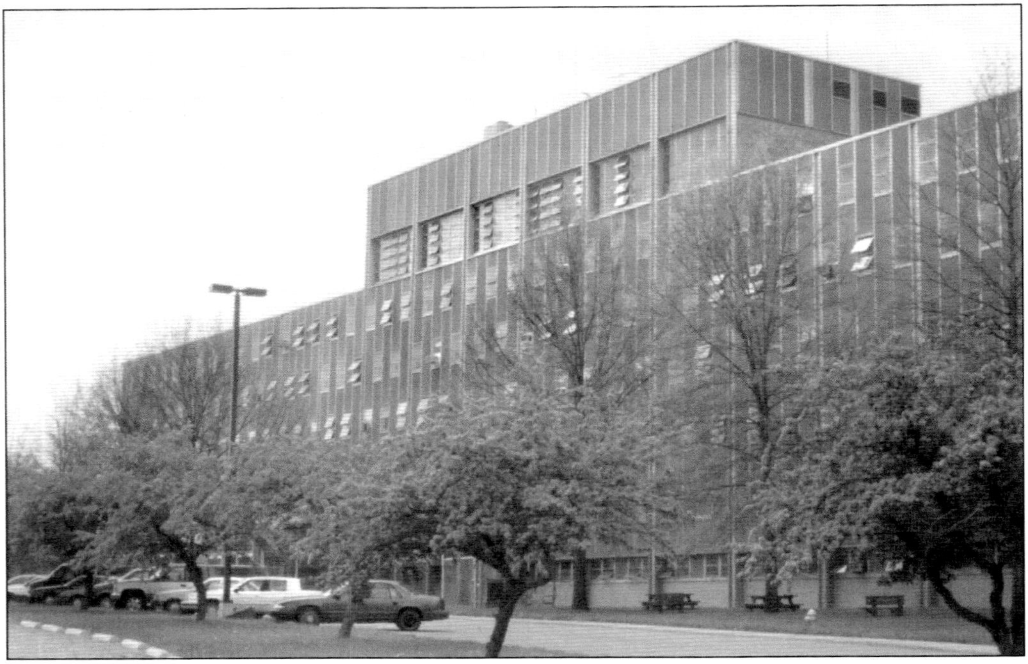

Buildings were named Cedar, Pine, and Spruce. The name designations had no significance other than to give a name to the building. The clinic, however, was not given a name originally. A contest was held among the staff to name the building, and Sherwood Towers was chosen. (Courtesy of Diane Hickman.)

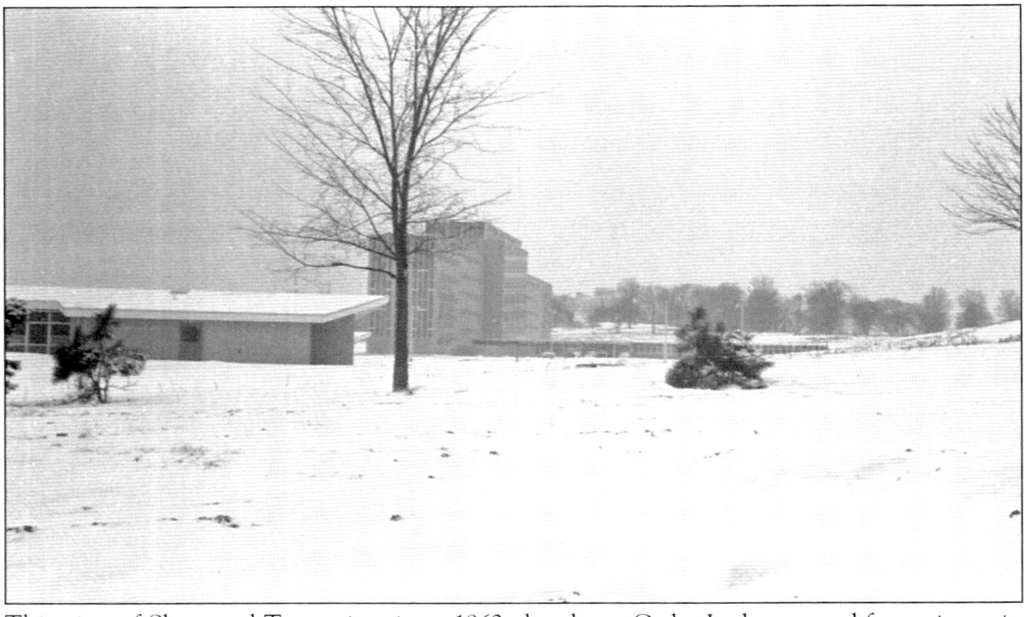

This view of Sherwood Towers in winter 1962 also shows Cedar Lodge, a ward for patients, in the left foreground. The single-story ward buildings featured curtained walls with large, square aluminum windows. The interior featured pastel ceramic brick, terrazzo floors, and raspberry-colored carpeting.

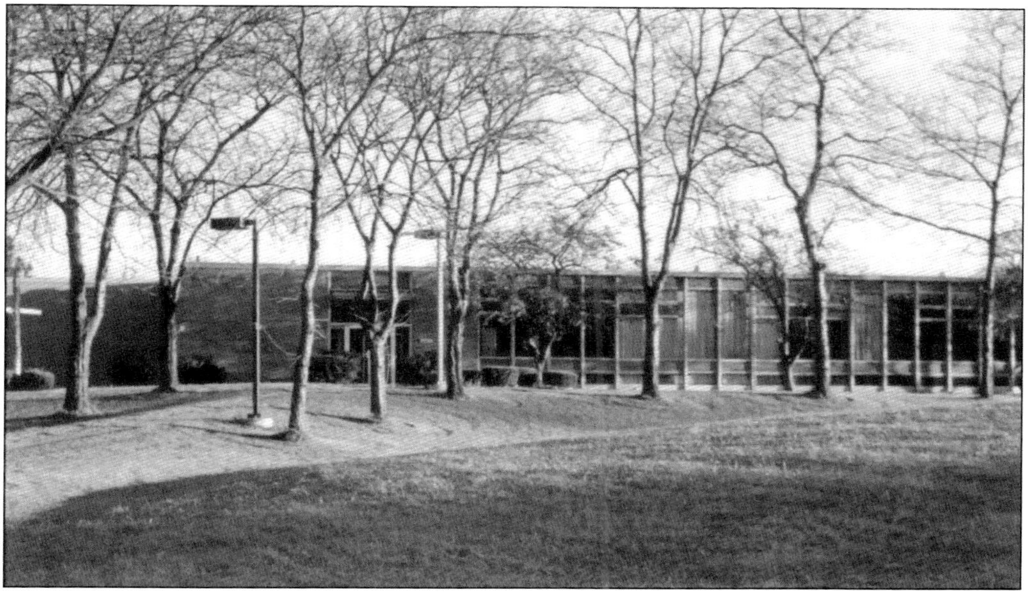

Constructed in 1960, the new kitchen was located centrally to all the surrounding buildings. The food was cooked and prepped at the central kitchen and then moved by truck to the surrounding buildings. When the food arrived, it could be readied quickly in the each building's kitchen. (Courtesy of Diane Hickman.)

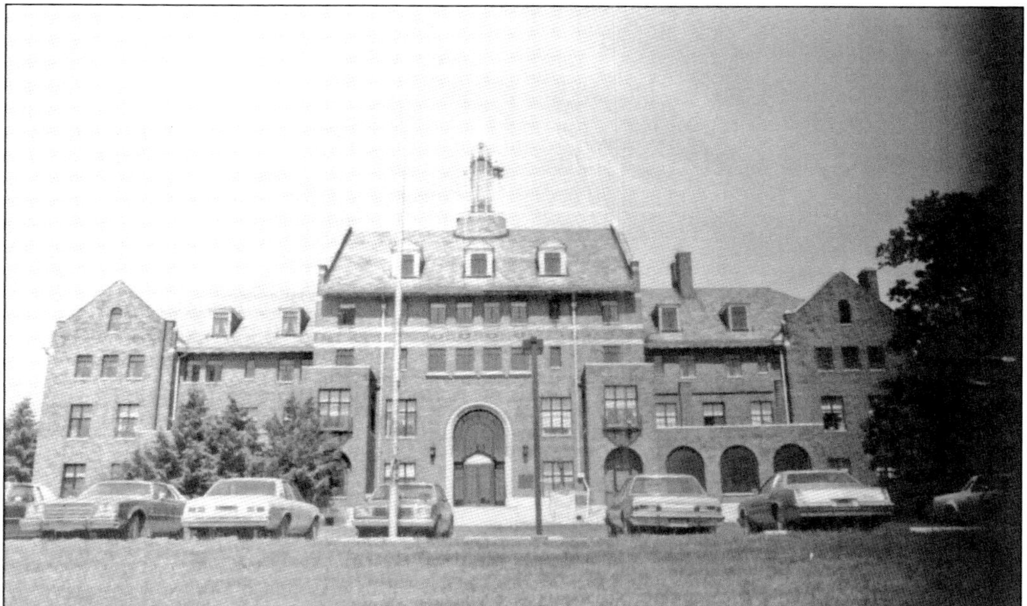

In 1968, the Youth Development Center was phased out and all of the remaining delinquents were sent to other youth development centers, one in Waynesburg and the other in New Castle. Approximately 30 boys and girls were transferred during the closing. Western State School and Hospital then used the grounds of the old institution, seen here in 1983. The administration building and some of the cottages were renovated for new uses. (Courtesy of Pennsylvania Historical and Museum Commission.)

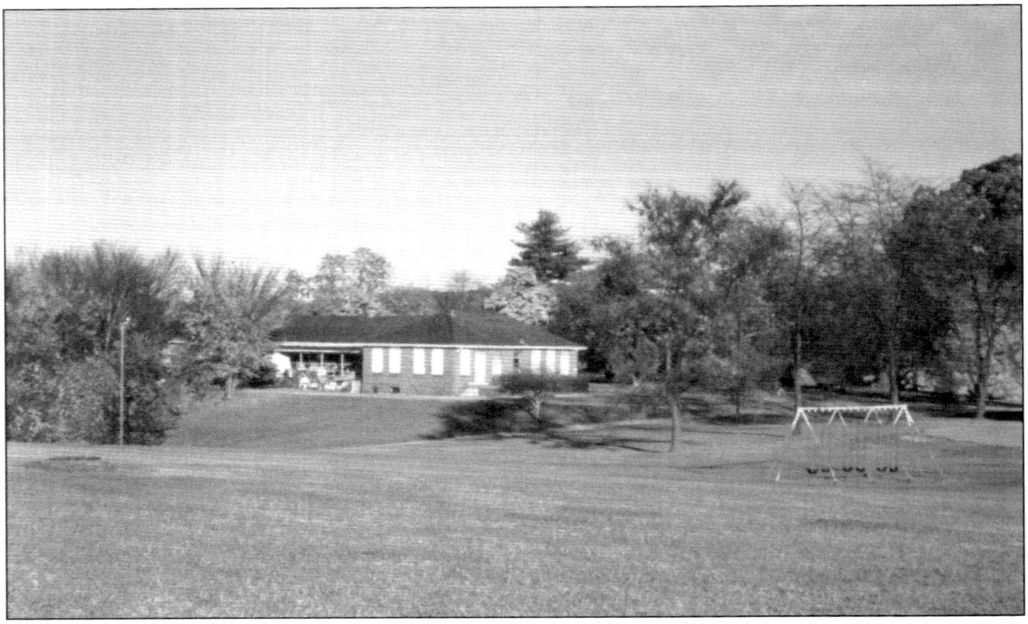

The laundry building, constructed in 1926 and seen here, was adapted for reuse. In March 1968, roughly 99,490 pounds of laundry were washed for Western State School and Hospital. The same month, the Youth Development Center, in its final year, had 8,280 pounds of laundry. (Courtesy of Diane Hickman.)

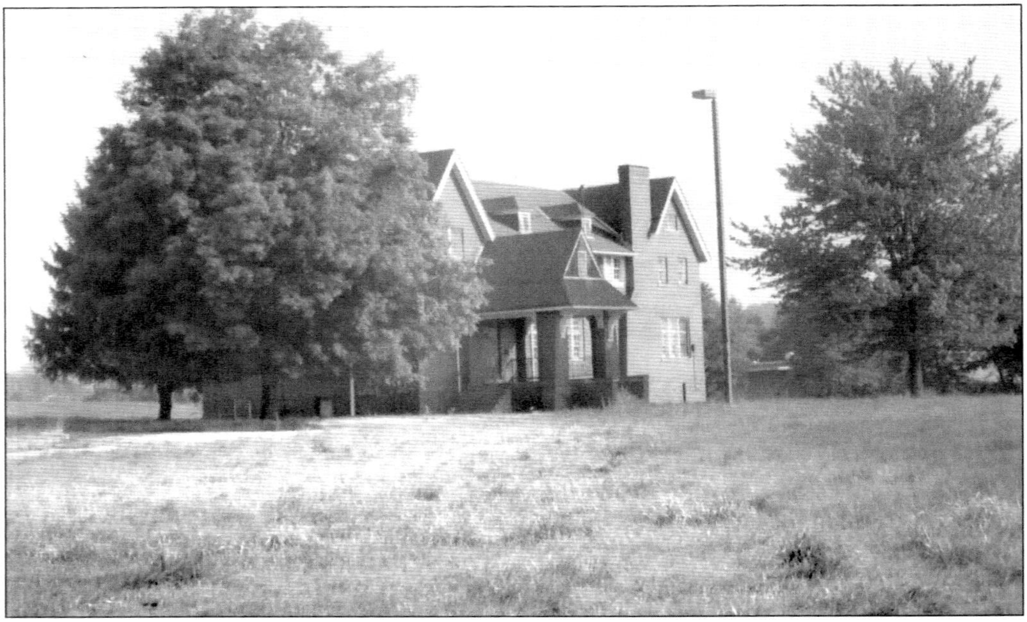

The cottages that were once used by the training school were now reused as out-cottages, which housed the higher-functioning patients. The one-story ward buildings housed the lower-functioning patients. Unlike the three wards, the out-cottages did not have a fenced-in area for patient recreation. Any time a patient from the wards was moved, a staff member had to escort them. (Courtesy of Pennsylvania Historical and Museum Commission.)

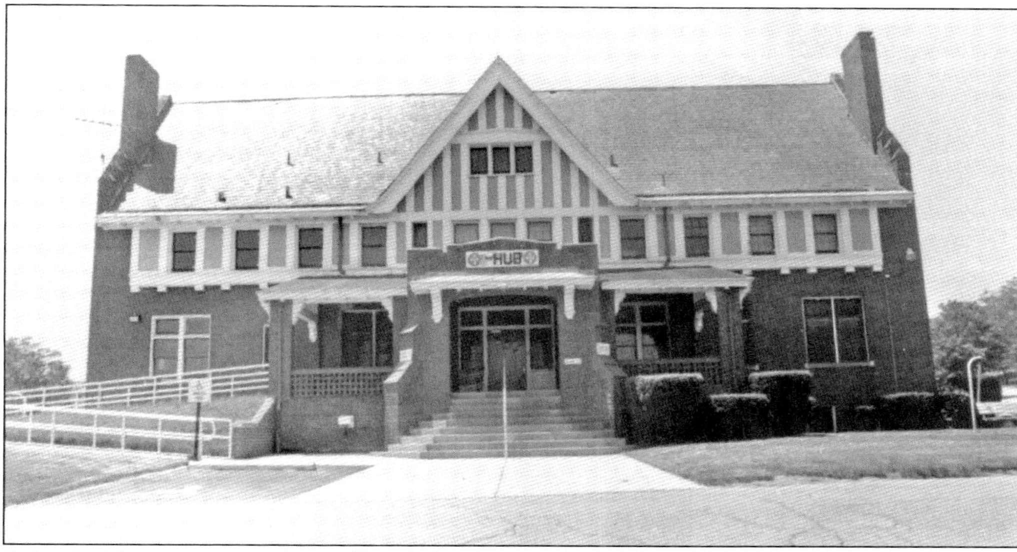

Other buildings were reused as well, including Cottage No. 5, which became known as the Hub and was used for resident training activities. Modifications were made to accommodate handicapped patients, with additional railings and ramps added to each building. (Courtesy of Pennsylvania Historical and Museum Commission.)

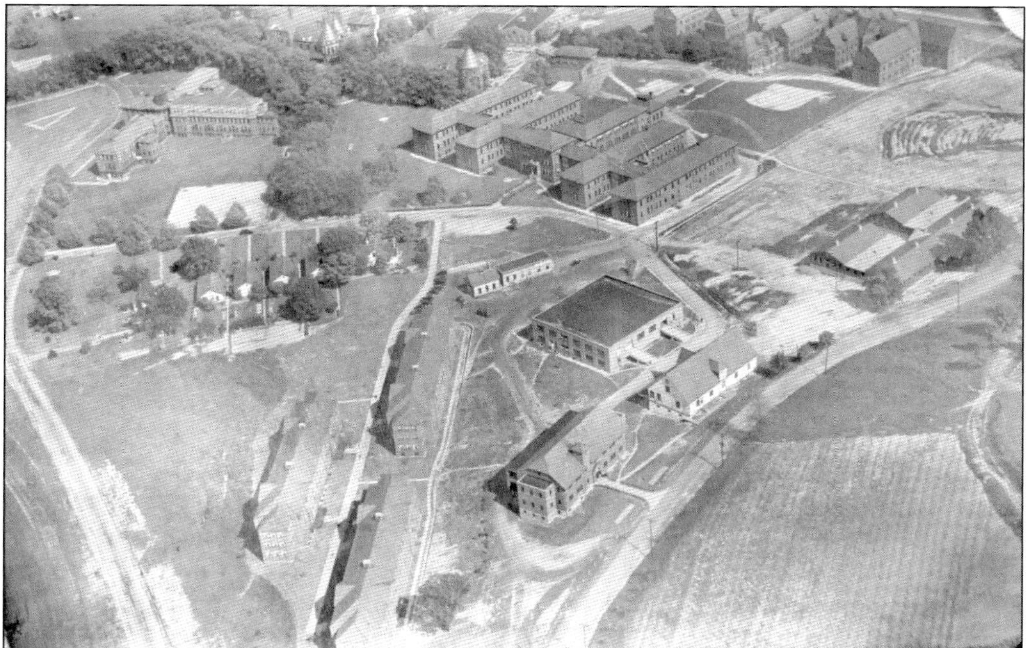

In October 1974, there were 653 residents at Western Center; by October 1976, there were 526. The 20-percent reduction was due to the transfer of the emotionally disturbed children's unit to Mayview State Hospital in Upper Saint Clair. The move helped the staff aid the mentally handicapped. In addition, 40 more staff members were added within two years. Seen here is an undated aerial view of Mayview State Hospital, which announced its closing in 2008 and has since been razed. (Courtesy of Pennsylvania State Archives.)

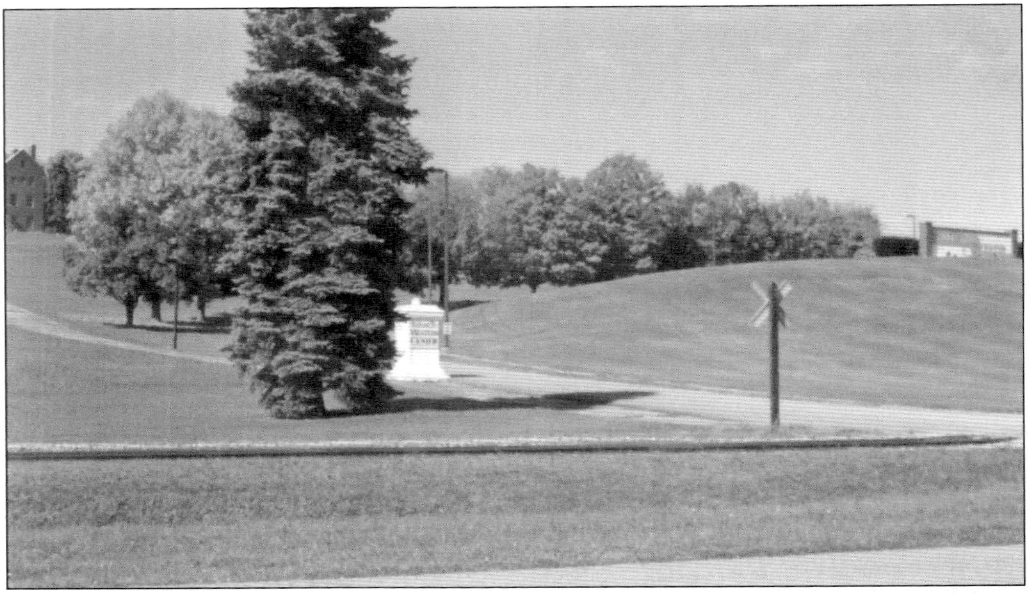

In 1976, the Western State School and Hospital was renamed Western Center. A proposed three-phase plan in 1957 had included a clinic, three wards, and the central kitchen and boiler house that were already complete. In 1972, Gov. Milton Shapp visited the Western State School and Hospital. During his observation, he was asked about the proposed three-phase plan. He replied that methods of care for the mentally handicapped had changed since the proposed plan and that the remaining phases were not necessary. (Courtesy of Diane Hickman.)

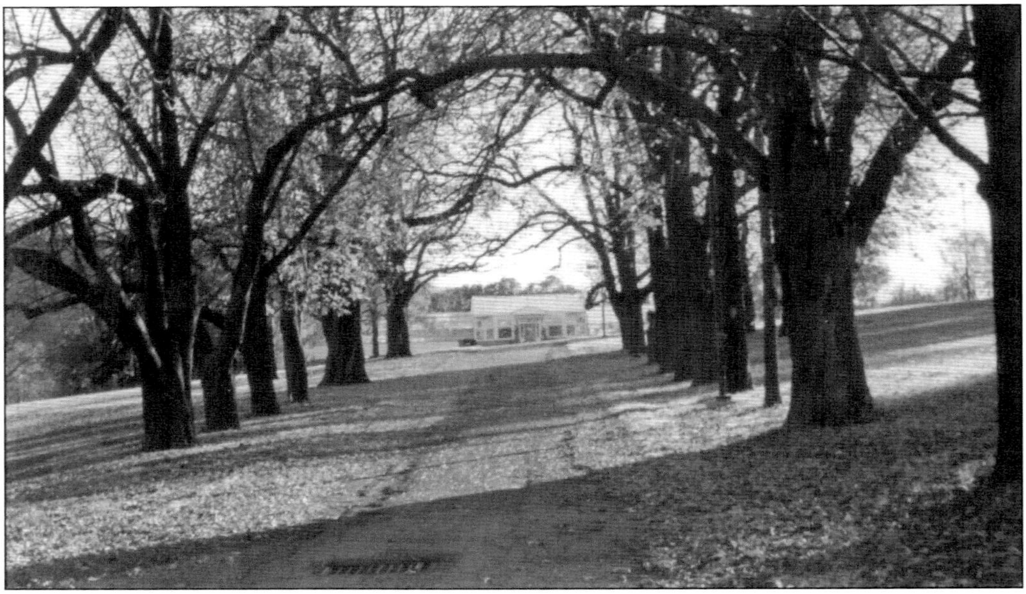

Western Center's reuse of the greenhouses allowed residents to nurture flowers and other plants if they so chose to, and they could then be sold to the public, who were permitted to drive up to the greenhouse and park without any questions. Other patients designed stuffed animals, ceramics, macramé wall hangings, and dolls, some of which were sold by designated nearby outlets. The patients earned a sales commission for their work. (Courtesy of Diane Hickman.)

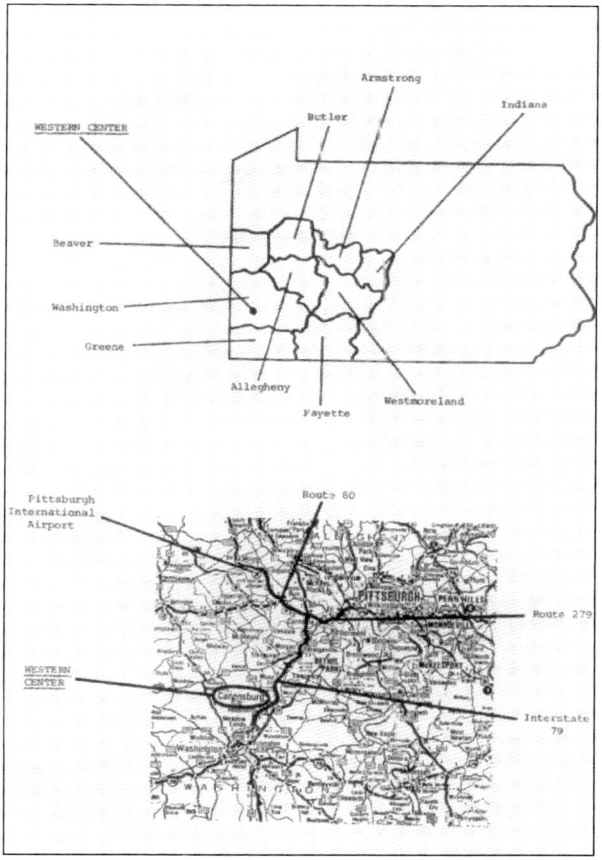

These maps, in a booklet created by the Pennsylvania Department of Public Welfare, shows the counties of southwestern Pennsylvania from which patients were admitted to Western Center. (Courtesy Diane Hickman.)

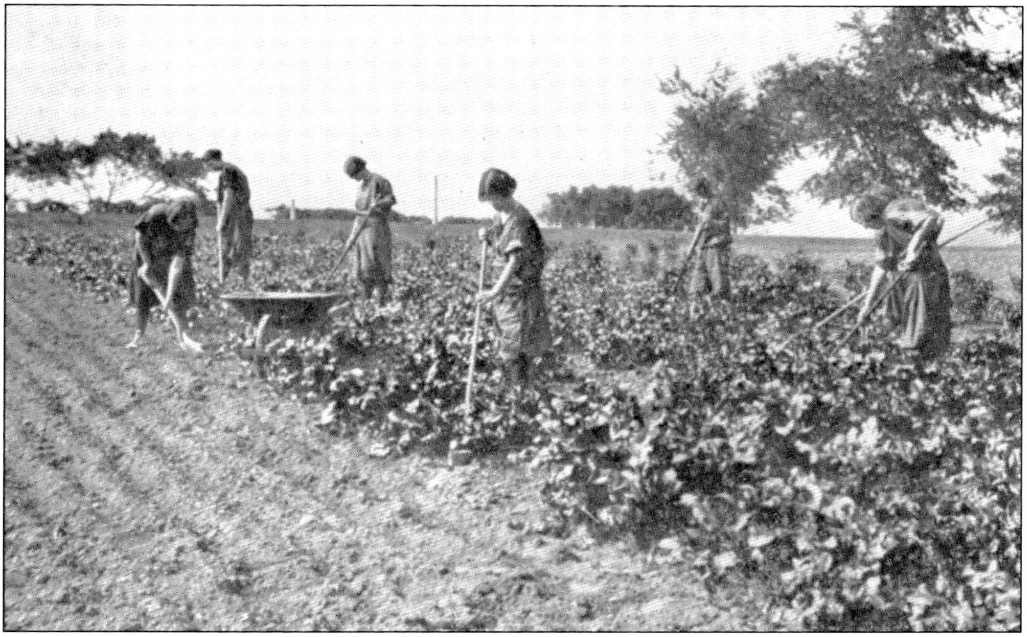

In 1983, the idea arose to redevelop the former farmland, which was now sitting vacant, into an industrial and commercial business park and residential development that would generate revenue for the county and bring more jobs. It did not move forward, however, until May 1987, when Gov. Robert Casey turned the state-owned land over to Washington County. The 589-acre tract was sold to the county at an estimate of $700,000. The Pennsylvania Department of Transportation encouraged development around the same time with its approximately $31 million interchange project connecting to Interstate 79. This was the beginning stages of the Southpointe business park.

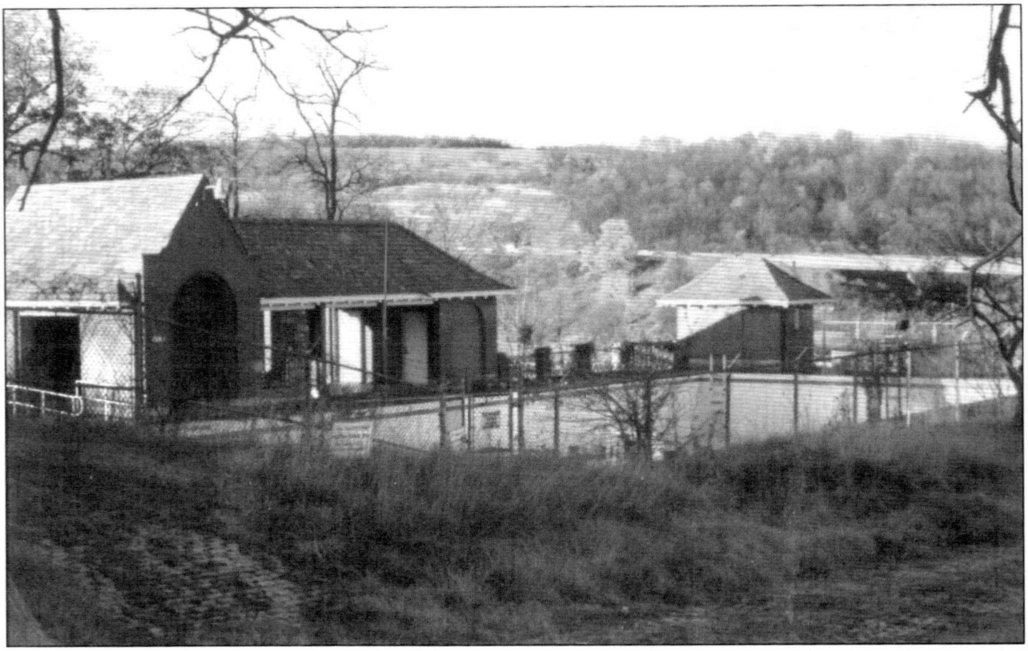

In 1984, the Western Center board of trustees and parents of the estimated 525 residents of the facility advocated for an outdoor pool that could serve the residents of Western Center as well as the public. Linda Wilson, the acting director at the time, responded that the facility already had two pools, one in the gymnasium and another outdoors. The outdoor pool, seen here, was built in 1934. (Courtesy of Diane Hickman.)

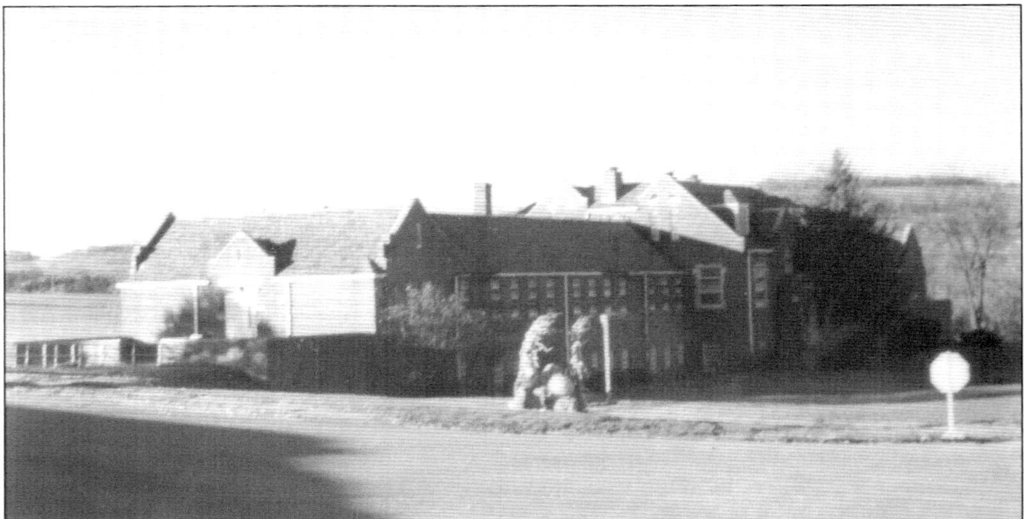

This is a view of the building known as Evergreen, which offered vocational training. In 1990, a program was instituted at Evergreen whereby the public could drop off newspapers there, which were then shredded and baled into 50-pound bales and sold for $1 each. The shredder and baler were purchased for $14,000 with the assistance of the *Observer-Reporter*. The bales were purchased by farmers, who used the shredded paper for horses and cows bedding as well as for mulching. (Courtesy Diane Hickman.)

Four

Closure and Demolition

A contributing factor that may have led to the closing of Western Center was an investigation launched in 1989 after reports of patient abuse, which resulted in the firing of 22 employees. New admissions were banned by the Pennsylvania Department of Public Welfare in April 1989 until conditions improved.

The closure of Western Center was announced in 1998 by Gov. Tom Ridge's administration. It was part of a plan to shift away from large institutional treatment centers, and it would save the state money. The center would close in 1999, allowing families to prepare and find other placement for residents. Most residents of Western Center would be sent to group homes and cared for by community-based programs. Many family members of residents were disturbed by this announcement, and some did not want family members in group homes. Some concerns about group homes were that they did not have doctors and nurses, which some patients needed. Some voiced their opinions through protests and others by letters to the state. In the end, nothing could prevent the decision, and Western Center was closed.

Within a short time of the closure, many developers became interested in the land, including Millcraft, Horizon Properties, and Scalo Case Development, among others. Millcraft had already had great success in helping develop nearby Southpointe. After much planning, a decision was made that was judged to be best for Washington County. The redevelopment of the new area is known as Southpointe II.

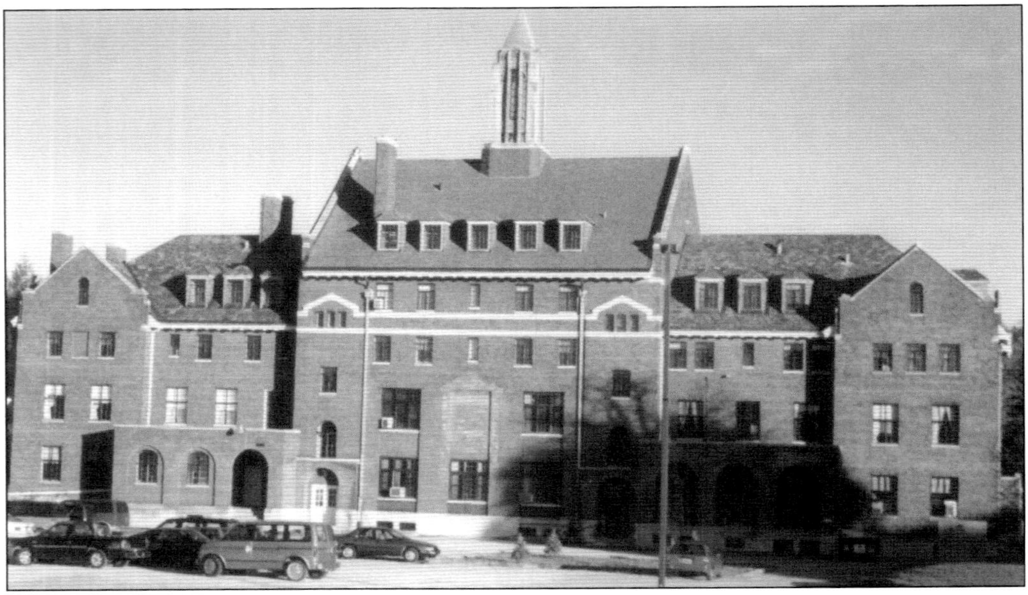

In 1998, it was announced that Western Center would close by the summer of 1999. At the time of the announcement, a total of 380 residents resided there; by the summer of 1999, there were 79 residents. A settlement from a 1992 federal lawsuit prohibited movement of residents to group homes unless the conditions were appropriate. This delayed movement of the patients. Finally, in April 2000, all remaining residents were moved off the grounds. This view of the rear of the administration building in the mid-1990s shows the outline of where the auditorium was once connected to it. The chapel had been razed shortly before the photograph was taken. (Courtesy of Diane Hickman.)

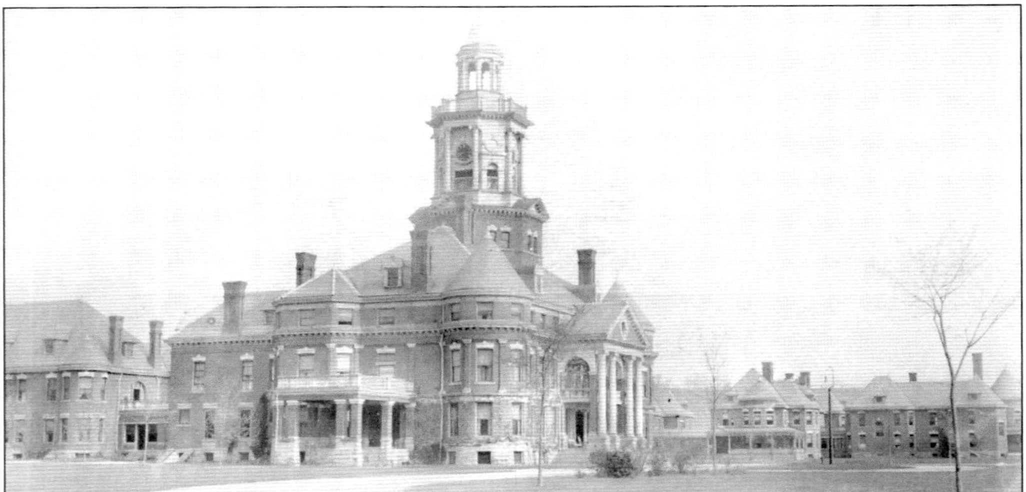

With the closing of Western Center, only seven state-run centers remained for the treatment of the mentally handicapped in the state of Pennsylvania. Polk Center, in Venango County, was one of them. After the announcement of the closure, moving residents to Polk was considered; however, it was denied by the Department of Welfare, even though Polk was functioning below its capacity. Many believed the state's goal was to shut down all state institutions. As of 2013, Polk still operates in northwestern Pennsylvania.

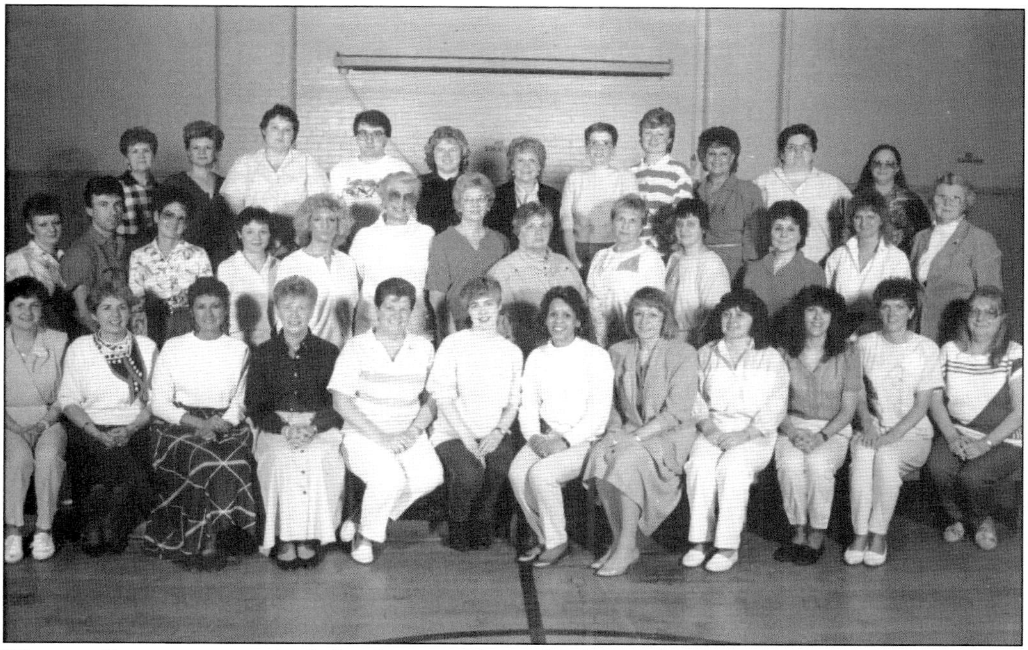

Western Center nurses, who helped treat and care for the residents, posed for this photograph in the gymnasium in the 1980s. The remaining staff members still hold an annual reunion in the summertime at Washington Park in the Stone Pavilion. (Courtesy of Diane Hickman.)

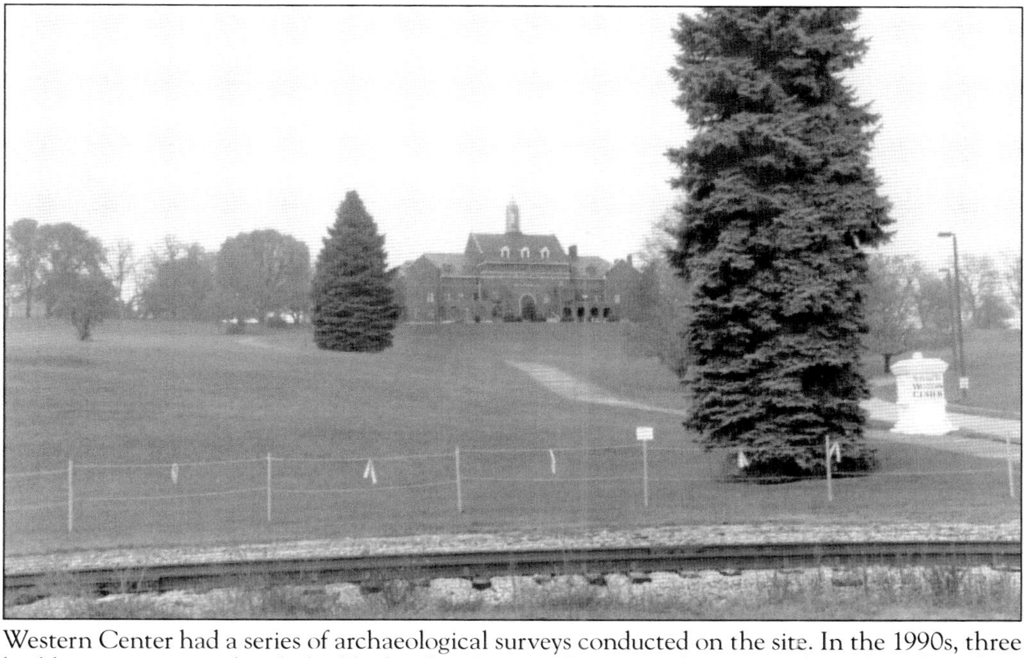

Western Center had a series of archaeological surveys conducted on the site. In the 1990s, three buildings were considered eligible for the National Register of Historic Places based on their significance in juvenile reform: the administration building, Redwood Cottage (Cottage No. 8), and the chapel. Many other buildings were considered of interest as well. (Courtesy of Pennsylvania Historical and Museum Commission.)

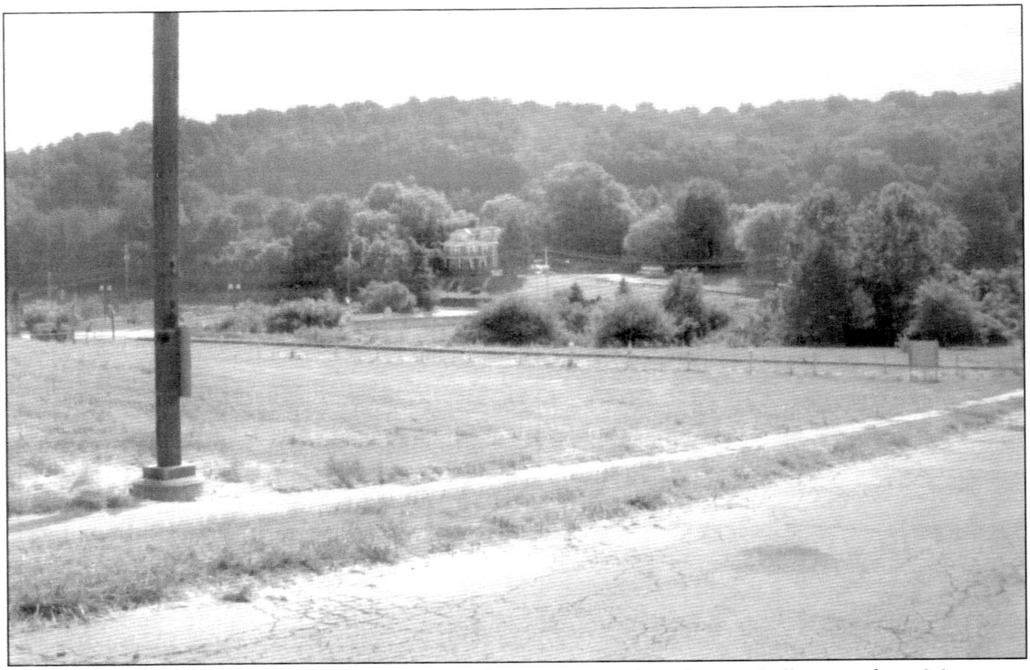

This view from the entry road shows the Charles House, on the adjacent hill across from Morganza Road, which served as a nursing home for many years. As part of the Southpointe II redevelopment plan, it was purchased with the intent of widening Morganza Road. The Charles House was razed before 2010. (Courtesy of Pennsylvania Historical and Museum Commission.)

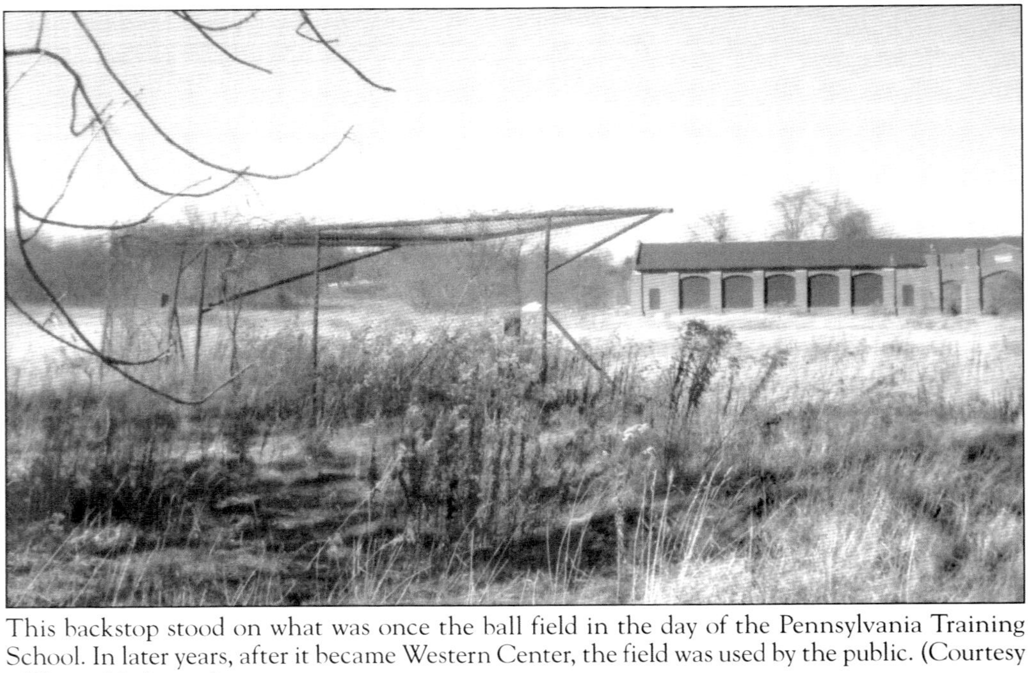

This backstop stood on what was once the ball field in the day of the Pennsylvania Training School. In later years, after it became Western Center, the field was used by the public. (Courtesy of Diane Hickman.)

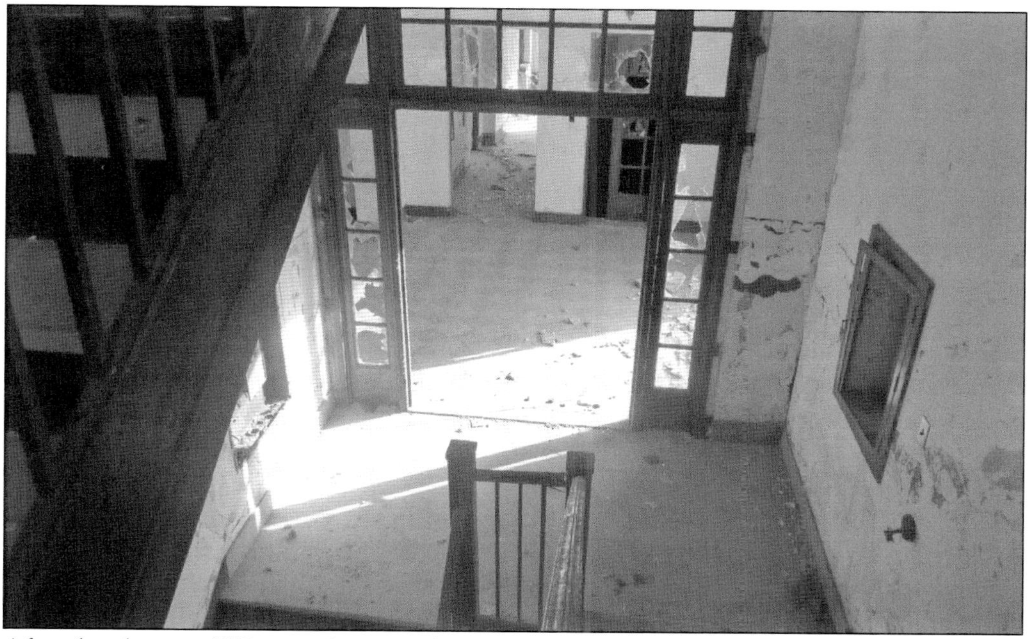

After the closure of Western Center, urban explorers, ghost hunters, and other curious people would trespass in hopes of seeing something of interest. This photograph of the inside of the administration building shows the work of vandals. The building quickly deteriorated after the closure of Western Center. (Courtesy of David Flinchbach.)

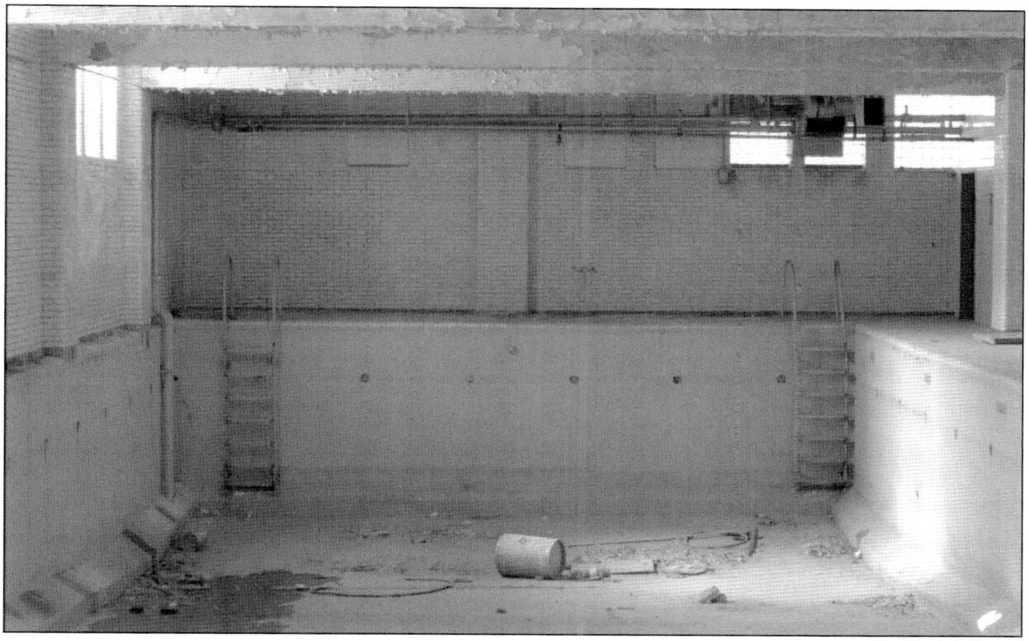

This view of the indoor swimming pool shows cracked and peeling paint covering the ceiling. The pool became nonfunctioning during the years of Western Center when the pool liner began leaking and needed to be replaced. Funding to fix the pool was not placed into the budget, and the pool was closed. (Courtesy of Adam Ryan.)

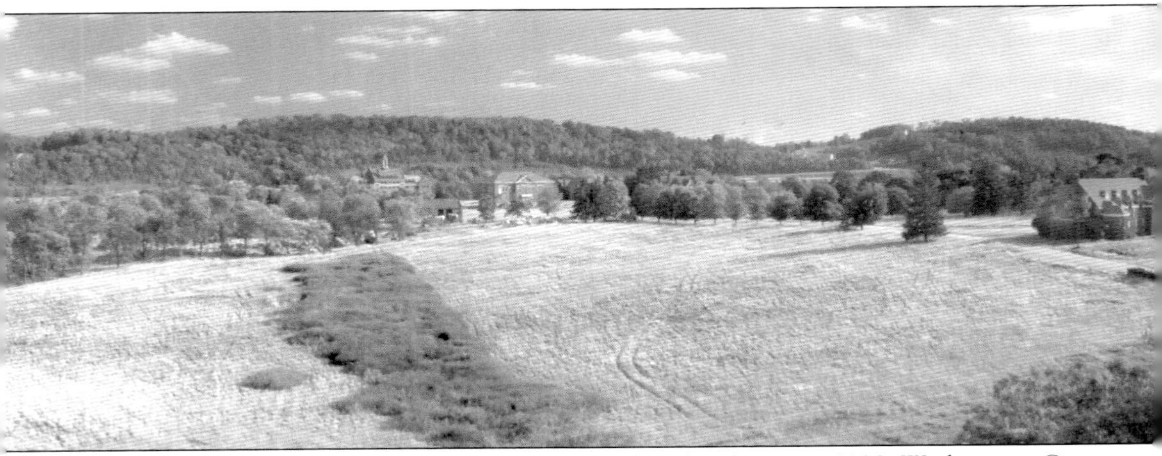

Several developers were interested in the land after the closing in 2000. Washington County offered to purchase 225 acres and to include an additional 80 acres of state-owned property on the other side of Interstate 79 from the state for $1.5 million. As part of the deal, Washington County asked for a 10-year payback period with no interest, with the first payment to be made in 2003. The state appraisal of the land was $9.5 million, and it was seeking interest during the payback period. Gov. Ed Rendell gave authorization in 2003 to the Department of General Services to sell the property and the approximately 37 buildings once used by Western Center to Washington County for $2 million with no payable interests, which they would pay in $200,000 annual increments for 10 years. (Courtesy of Adam Ryan.)

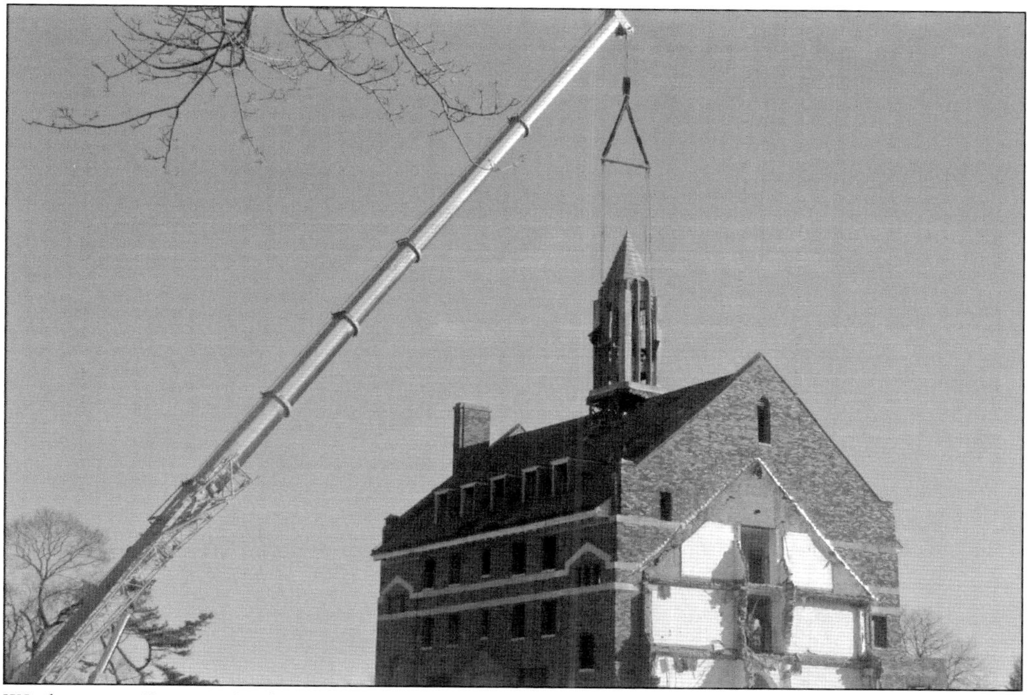

Washington County Authority project manager Bill Sember, public officials, and local developers held a conference at the Southpointe Golf Club in 2004. A proposed site plan presented a design that included shops, houses, a cinema, a hotel, and a two-story department store. Four of the older buildings were included in the plan. Announced in 2006, the future main developers were Horizon Properties and Cullinan Properties. (Courtesy of David Flinchbach.)

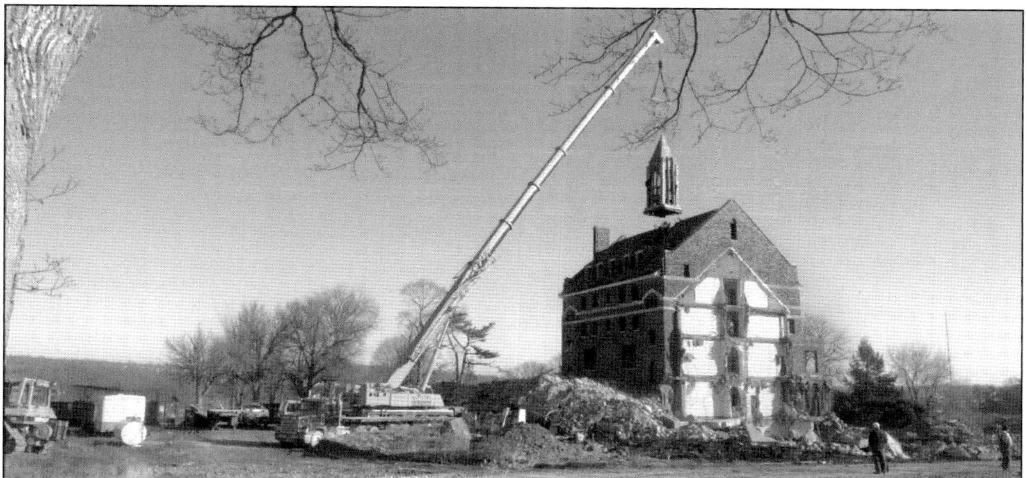

The old administration building was to be reused as a cultural center with an amphitheater nearby. A 55-acre tract along Southpointe Boulevard would allow for commercial expansion. Abutting the Canonsburg border, townhouses and single-family homes would be constructed. The estimated construction cost for the project at the time was $200 million, and it could create an additional 3,000 jobs. A nine-hole golf course was proposed early in the plan but was later removed. (Courtesy of David Flinchbach.)

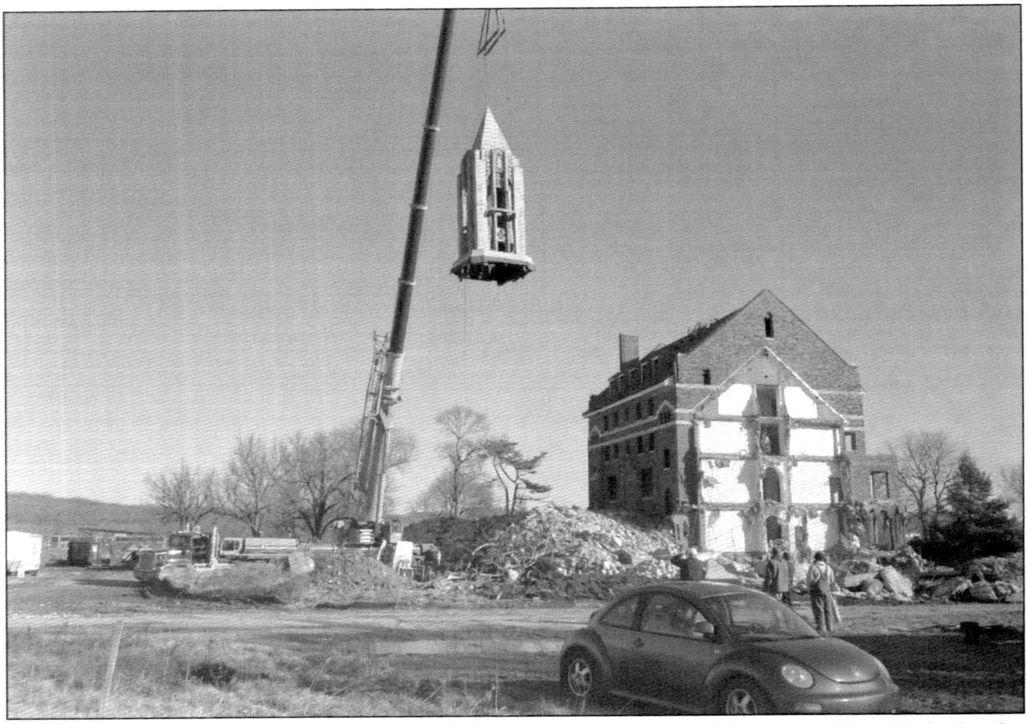

In 2005, a demolition contract was awarded to Titan Wrecking of Kenmore, New York, for the razing of 13 buildings on the site. In 2008, the seven-story Sherwood Towers was razed by Homrich, Inc., of Carleton, Michigan, who had submitted a low bid of $694,000. Homrich dismantled the high-rise and was responsible for the removal of potential environmental hazards within it. (Courtesy of David Flinchbach.)

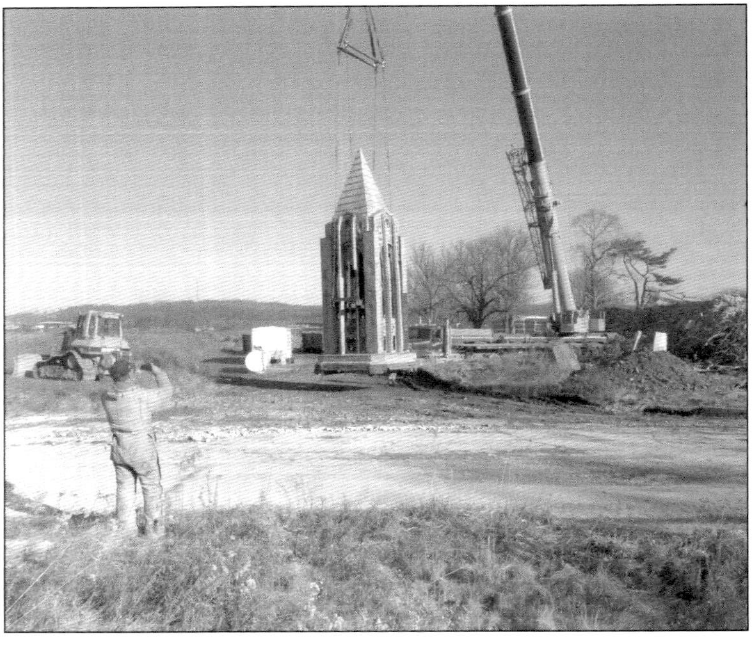

A study conducted in 2007 by Kamball & Associates estimated that it would take at least $10 million to bring the administration building up to building code. The exterior and interior walls were nearly 18 inches thick and made of poured concrete, with no ductwork and heated by steam. The estimated cost of tearing down the structure in 2010 was between $250,000 and $300,000. (Courtesy of David Flinchbach.)

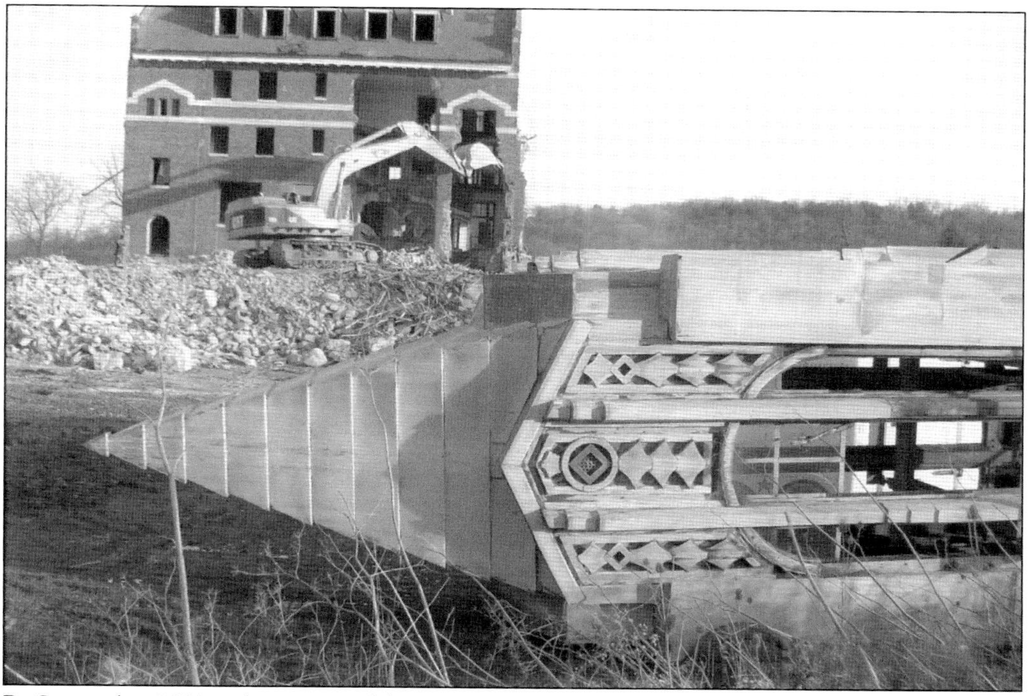

By September 2011, only a group of shop maintenance buildings and the administration building still remained. A proposed plan showing a parking lot in the area of the administration building was presented to the Washington County commissioners and the Cecil Township supervisors. The site was already approved by the commissioners, and Cecil Township was to vote on the plan by the end of September. (Courtesy of Richard Nowe.)

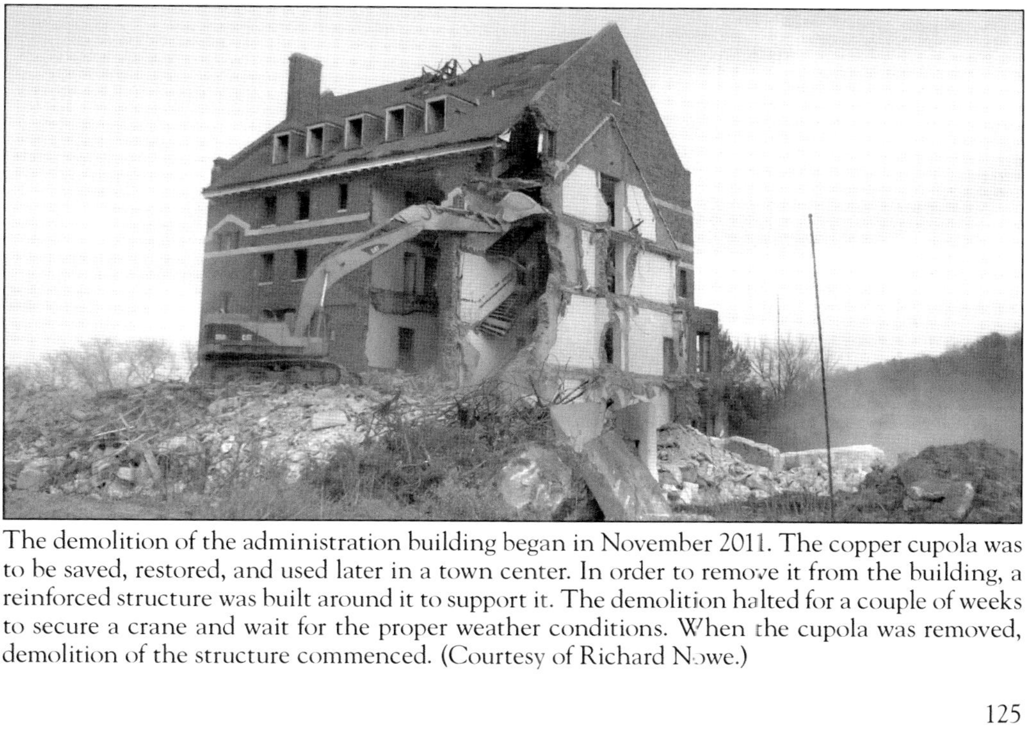

The demolition of the administration building began in November 2011. The copper cupola was to be saved, restored, and used later in a town center. In order to remove it from the building, a reinforced structure was built around it to support it. The demolition halted for a couple of weeks to secure a crane and wait for the proper weather conditions. When the cupola was removed, demolition of the structure commenced. (Courtesy of Richard Nowe.)

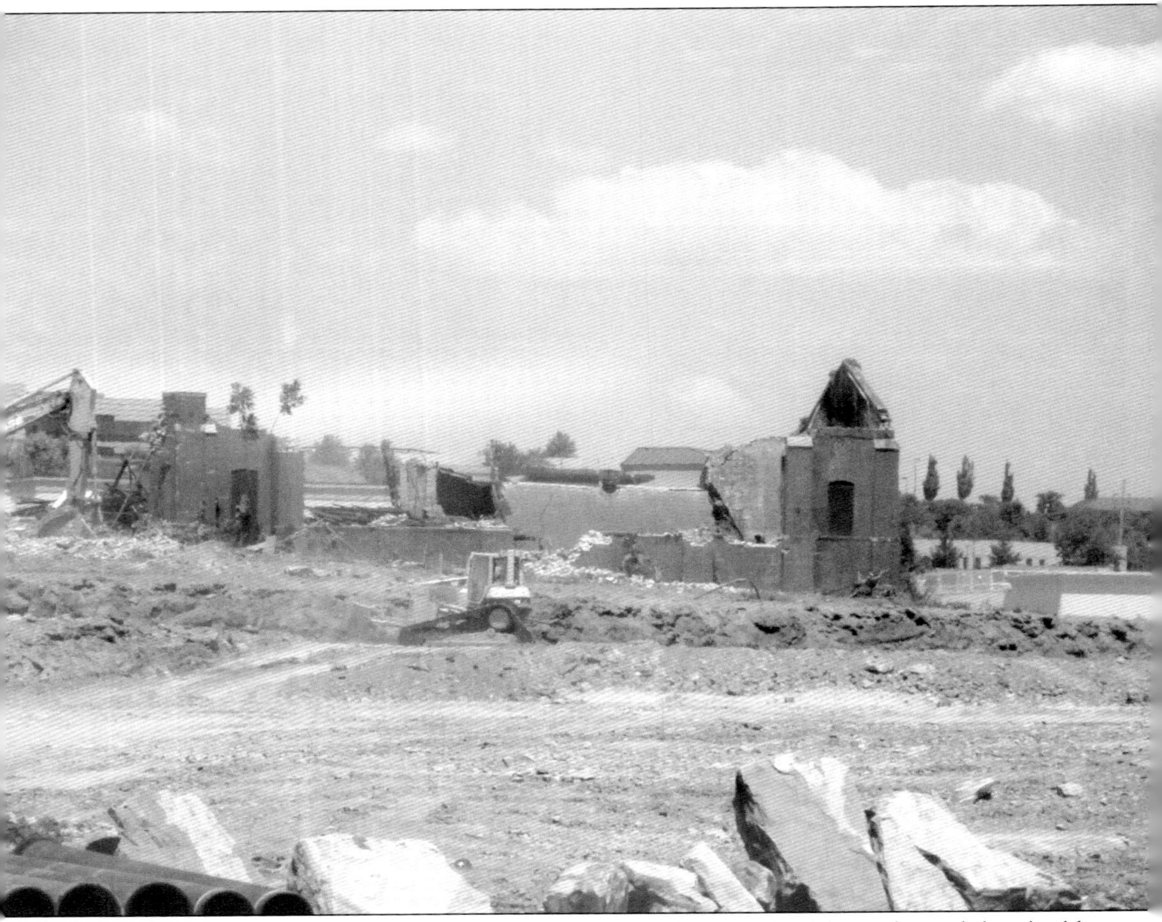

After nearly all the other structures had been demolished, the final few industrial shop buildings of the Pennsylvania Training School met the same fate. In May 2012, the final structures on the grounds were razed.

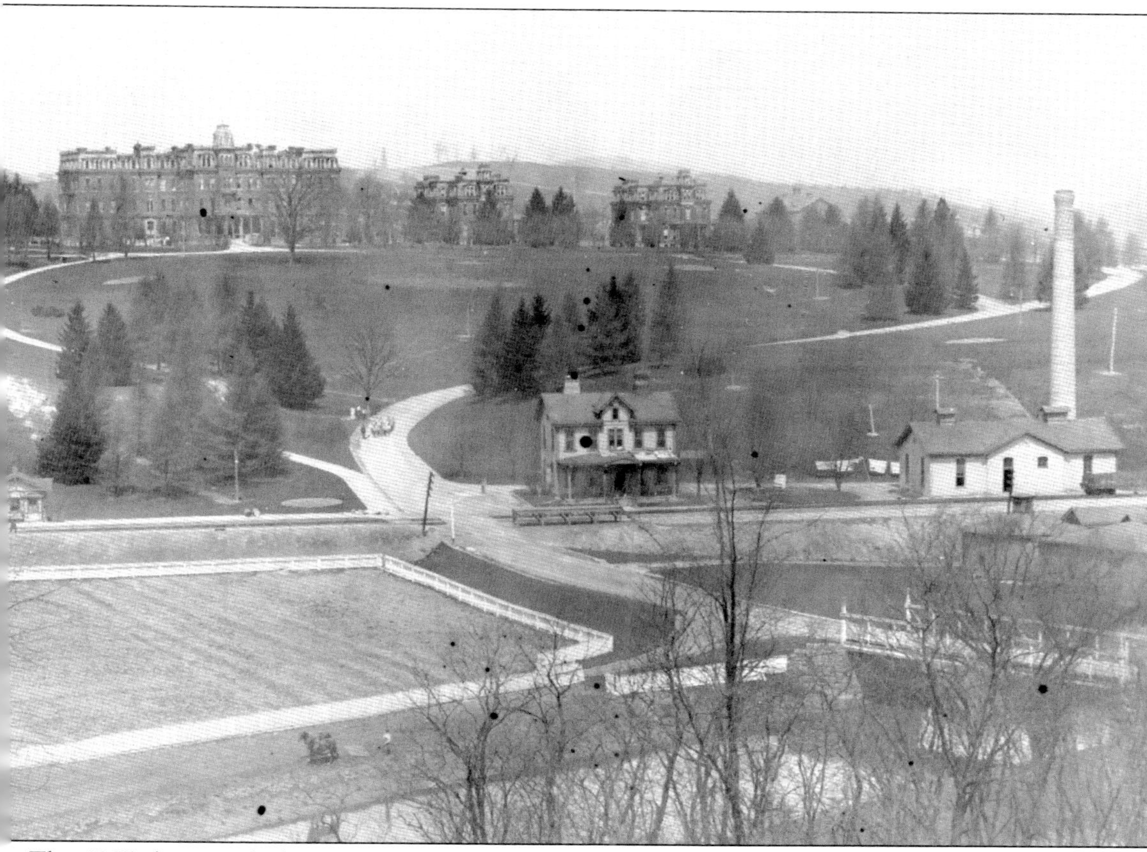

This 1905 photograph shows the institution that changed thousands of lives, most for the better. As of 2013, the concrete entry bridge, cemetery, and the reservoir at the Southpointe Golf Club still remain. Much of the land has changed since the days when the Pennsylvania Reform School opened. These remaining features of the land are the only indications left of Pennsylvania's first state-owned exclusively juvenile reformatory.